tear here

The Complete Idiot's Reference Card

D1254592

Communication Between the Sexes: Life

When Men Talk to Women:

1. Don't hog all the space.
2. Compliment and be sincere.
3. Don't stare.
4. Open up! Say how you feel.
5. Ask for help if needed.
6. Sound enthusiastic.
7. Don't fidget and rock back and forth.
8. Don't tell off-color jokes.
9. Don't give "yep"/"nope" answers.
10. Give positive feedback.

When Women Ta...

1. Be direct. Get to the point.
2. Talk about accomplishments.
3. Don't be defensive.
4. Don't demand he open up.
5. Don't bring up past arguments.
6. Speak up and be heard.
7. Don't whine.
8. Don't criticize.
9. Don't blame or accuse.
10. Don't let negative feelings fester.

Communication Between the Sexes: In the Bedroom

When Men Interact with Women:

1. Be observant to nonverbal cues.
2. Make constant eye contact.
3. Listen closely for subtle nuances.
4. Say "I love you" enthusiastically.
5. Don't make commands; ask for what you want.
6. Use "I wish," or "I'd love it if."
7. Constantly use terms of endearment.
8. Open up! Let go emotionally.
9. Constantly compliment.
10. Cuddle, caress, and hug a lot.

When Women Interact with Men:

1. Verbalize your desires.
2. You can make the first move.
3. Keep continuous eye contact.
4. Give immediate positive feedback.
5. Use tender tones to breed openness.
6. Be a diplomat at all times.
7. Never bring up his intimate secrets.
8. Don't withhold sex as punishment.
9. Let fantasies flow.
10. Be an attentive, caring listener.

alpha
books

Communication Between the Sexes: In the Boardroom

When Men Talk to Women:
1. Look directly at the woman when speaking.
2. Don't interrupt.
3. Provide more verbal feedback.
4. Provide more facial feedback.
5. Don't issue commands or orders.
6. Don't make sexist jokes or comments.
7. Use terms of politeness always, such as "please."
8. Don't use swear words.
9. Control anger and temper.
10. Don't brag about yourself.

When Women Talk to Men:
1. Never cry, no matter what.
2. Don't discuss personal life.
3. Don't use "tag endings," such as "isn't it?"
4. Don't hold grudges.
5. Don't apologize unless you're wrong.
6. Be objective and less emotional.
7. Monitor smiles and head nods.
8. Get to the point.
9. Speak louder with confidence.
10. Take rejection less personally.

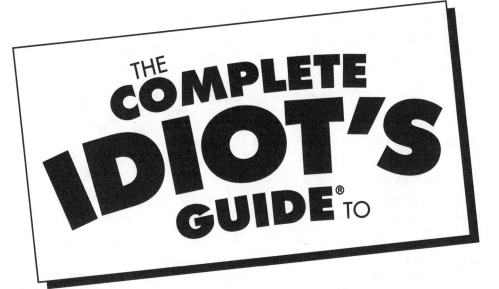

THE COMPLETE IDIOT'S GUIDE® TO

Understanding Men and Women

by Lillian Glass, Ph.D.

alpha books

Macmillan USA, Inc.
201 West 103rd Street
Indianapolis, IN 46290

A Pearson Education Company

Publisher
Marie Butler-Knight

Product Manager
Phil Kitchel

Associate Managing Editor
Cari Luna

Acquisitions Editor
Randy Ladenheim-Gil

Production Editor
Christy Wagner

Copy Editor
Susan Aufheimer

Illustrator
Jody P. Schaeffer

Cover Designers
Mike Freeland
Kevin Spear

Book Designers
Scott Cook and Amy Adams of DesignLab

Indexer
Nadia Ibrahim

Layout/Proofreading
Donna Martin
Gloria Schurick

Contents at a Glance

Part 1: Sorting Out Our Differences   **1**

1 Finding Common Ground in Gender Differences   3
This chapter deals with how essential it is to understand the differences between the sexes and how, although there are some who may be resistant to studying these differences, if we ever want to get along better with the opposite sex, we need to have as much knowledge about one another as possible. It is essential to explore those differences and what we can gain.

2 What Do We Really Know About One Another?   13
Decipher the facts and examine the myths of women's intuition, and learn about some verbal surprises among the sexes, such as who talks more and faster, and why this happens. We'll learn who is the more verbally friendly and funnier gender and what verbal language and communication nuances are indigenous to the specific sexes that can affect their love, business, personal, and family lives.

3 Communication Breakdown, Gender Style   27
This chapter focuses upon the breakdown in communication between men and woman as related to their specific communication styles, body language, facial expressions, language, tones, and actions.

Part 2: Understanding the Great Nature/ Nurture Debate   **37**

4 The Role of Mother Nature   39
The role of biology, brain anatomy and physiology, genetics, and hormones in creating sex differences.

5 The Role of Mother Nurture   47
How differences arise from the different ways boys and girls are raised in terms of cultural expectations and unconscious parental conditioning. We will explore the effects of social conditioning at play, and in the worlds of nursery rhymes, cartoons, bedtime stories, and play toys; verbal reinforcement of sexual stereotypes during childhood development; and avoiding gender-role stereotyping in the future.

6 Nature Meets Nurture   57
   *An examination of how certain differences between the
   sexes are best understood as the result of both nature and
   nurture. We will discuss some of the influences that
   genetics has on environment and how it affects each sex.
   The selection of various professions as a result of the
   interaction between these two forces will be discussed
   along with reading between the lines as to vocal characteristics of the opposite sex.*

Part 3: "Mr. and Ms. Understanding"   65

7 Learning the Language of Gender   67
   *In this chapter we take you through the social develop-
   ment of male and female language from early childhood
   through the crucial teen years. Certain ways of talking
   are indigenous to boys and girls respectively early on in
   their lives, and they remain a part of their verbal reper-
   toire as they have continued to grow. We clearly see differences in what girls talk about and what boys talk
   about early on and how difficult it is to communicate
   with one another when they finally are confronted with
   communicating with one another.*

8 Blue Versus Pink   79
   *In this chapter you will learn the most common mistakes
   that men make when it comes to dealing with women. It
   explains some of the things women do and the reasons
   why they do them. With this added insight, men can
   now help avoid unwanted arguments and ill feelings
   toward women.*

9 Pink Versus Blue   91
   *This chapter deals with misinterpretations women make
   about men that often leave them frustrated and angry.
   You will learn ways to join him or help him with tasks
   and not fight him so that you can get along with one
   another a lot easier.*

10 Learning the Basics of Good Communication
   with the Opposite Sex   101
   *No matter what sex a person is, there are basic rules that
   we all need to obey when it comes to communicating
   with another person. You will learn some of the most
   basic and most important steps that so many of us forget, don't use, or don't know. We will learn how to speak
   up, be heard, listen, say what we mean, and mean what
   we say.*

Part 4: Battleground of the Sexes   **109**

11 Basic Madness: Unmanaged Anger   111
This chapter deals with what happens when anger rears its ugly head and words are said that shouldn't be said. We will learn the root of basic anger between men and women and understand how some relationships between men and women have nothing to do with the battle of the sexes but rather with the battle of individual "toxic" people.

12 Mad About Women   121
This chapter focuses upon the most essential things women do that are annoying to men, such as not getting to the point, asking too many questions, getting too close when the man needs his "space," and insisting on knowing about what he's feeling at all times, to name a few.

13 Mad About Men   133
This chapter focuses upon the most crucial things men do that are extremely annoying to women, such as withholding information, not being generous with words, not doing what they say they will, and trying to solve her problems instead of commiserating with her, among other key issues.

Part 5: The Art of the Turn-On   **141**

14 Playing (and Winning) the Dating Game   143
This chapter discusses how men and women approach the dating game and what is important to each of them in the areas of attraction, love, and romance. It provides tips for how men and women can start off on the right foot in dating and in courtship and shows how understanding these differences and similarities between the sexes can make finding their match a lot easier.

15 Attracting the Opposite Sex   153
You will discover what it is that really *attracts the opposite sex, and using this to your advantage, you will learn to do things that make you more and more appealing to the opposite sex.*

16 Intimate Misunderstandings   161
This chapter deals with effective communication during physically intimate moments and discusses affection between men and women, how to avoid unintentional but bruising messages, and sending the right intimate messages to one another by letting your partner know, in every way, what's on your mind.

17 Top Secrets About Men   171
This chapter gives us insight as to who men really are
and gives us the unbridled truth about what they really
think.

18 Top Secrets About Women   181
This chapter gives you the basic truths about women,
from how they really think to what they think to what
they like to do to what they take seriously. This chapter
provides unique insight into women and debunks many of
the myths surrounding women.

Part 6: Peaceful Co-Existence   191

19 What Men Want and Don't Want from Women   193
This chapter gives us the bottom-line, bold, hard-core
truth about what men most cherish in their relationships
with women—like it or not!

20 What Women Want and Don't Want from Men   207
This life-changing chapter can be the key for every man
to really find out what it takes to please a woman—
gentlemanly behavior and attitudes. Men will learn all
the secrets they ever wanted to know about what it really
takes for a man to make her happy in every way.

21 Men at Work   219
This chapter shows how men approach work and how
they can be more effective in dealing with women so they
won't fall down the corporate ladder by disrespecting their
female counterparts, not to mention avoid potential sex-
ual harassment suits.

22 Women at Work   231
This chapter deals with how women relate in the work-
place and how greater awareness can help them avoid
misunderstandings with men there. It discusses the impor-
tance of respecting a woman for what she does and gives
women some pointers on how to best break through the
glass ceiling so they can be on an equal playing field at
work.

23 Seeking Similarities   243
We see exactly how similar men and women really are in
spite of it all, and exactly what women and men want in
their dealings with others. We see how it all boils down to
respect and love that we are after, and that we all share
insecurities and have human ups and downs, regardless of
our sex.

24 Men and Women in the Millennium   253

This chapter will take a look into the future possibilities for communication between men and women. It will explore such issues as ways to further assure that communication between the sexes is always possible, changing issues in the workplace and on the intimate front as we approach new heights in dealing with one another. It discusses the future in terms of what science, research, psychology, and computer technology can offer us to enhance our relationships with the opposite sex so that we can once and for all live in greater peace and harmony.

Appendixes

A To Order *Dr. Lillian Glass'* Products   265

B References and Further Reading   271

Index   277

Contents

Part 1: Sorting Out Our Differences   **1**

**1 Finding Common Ground in
Gender Differences**   **3**

Resistance to Difference 4
Knowledge Is Power..5
Nature Versus Nurture: Part I 6
    The Math Equation 6
    The Language of Gender..7
The Benefits of Better Understanding................................8
Lesson #1: Listen, Listen, Listen 9

2 What Do We Really Know About One Another?   **13**

How Much Do *You* Assume: Dr. Glass' Sex Talk Quiz..........14
The Truth About "Intuition" 16
The Truth About Talk 16
    Men Are the Talkers 17
    Fast-Talking Women 17
    And What's Important to You?..17
The Friendlier Gender 18
    Praising Women...18
    Ahem: Men Interruptus! 18
    Demanding Men and Tentative Women 19
Different Strokes for Different Genders 20
    Where's That Funny Bone? 20
    Talking in the Dark 20
Men Don't Ask for Help! 21
It's Tough Being a Girl..21
    Undermining Self-Talk 21
    Straighten Up and Fly Right! 22
    Attention to Detail: A Woman's Prerogative 22
Gender Communication: Touch Versus Eye Contact..........22
Emotional Equality 23
    Women Get Personal!...23
    Women Bring Up the Topics! 23
Communication Family Style 24
    Confronting Problems...24

3 Communication Breakdown, Gender Style **27**

The Body Language of Dominance 28
  Body Space 29
  Hand Me This! 30
Face It! 30
Male Versus Female Conversational Tones 32
How We Act 33
The Power Is Yours 35

**Part 2: Understanding the Great Nature/
Nurture Debate** **37**

4 The Role of Mother Nature **39**

The Human Brain: Male and Female 40
  The World of the Brain 40
  Gender Pathways 40
XX and XY: Genetics 101 41
The Role of Hormones..42
There's Only One Brain! 43
  Male Brain Development 43
  Female Brain Development...44
Baby Doll Versus Keep on Truckin' 45

5 The Role of Mother Nurture **47**

Cultural Sex-Pectations 48
Boys Will Be Boys 49
The Crimes of Nursery Rhymes.......................................50
  Little Miss Muffet, Get Off Your Tuffet 50
  Bif! Boom! Bad Cartoons!..52
  Bedtime Brainwashing 52
Toys Are *Not* Us!...53
She's Pretty as a Picture! 53
Talkin' Just Like Her Mom...54
Improving Gender Role Models 54

6 Nature Meets Nurture **57**

The Root of the Problem 57
Aggression in Boys...58
Directions, Please! 60

Details, Details, Details 60
The Gender of Professions......................................61
The Voice of Gender 62
   Reading Between the Lines! 62
   Nods of Approval 63

Part 3: "Mr. and Ms. Understanding"   65

7   Learning the Language of Gender   67

Socialization: Male and Female............................68
Boy Style 70
   The Gross-Out 71
   The Thrill of the Curse Word 72
The Female Side of the Equation 73
   Talk, Talk, Talk 73
   Spilling the Beans...74
   Keeping Secrets 74
The Teen Years 75
   Inter-Gender Speak 75
   Boys and Compliments 76
   Making New Friends 76
Mirror, Mirror on the Wall 77

8   Blue Versus Pink   79

Gaining Emotional Equality 80
   Tapping into Your Feelings 81
   Stop the Blame Game.......................................82
Resist the Instinct to Help! 83
Her Need for Your Approval 84
   Don't Fix Her Up 84
   The Power of a Compliment...............................84
Forgive and Forget? 85
The Long, Long Female Memory 86
Cease Control 87
The Need for Closeness 88
   It's Not About Nagging....................................89
   R-E-S-P-E-C-T 89

9 Pink Versus Blue   **91**

He Isn't (Necessarily) a Jerk! 91
Accept His Need to Boast 92
Humor Him 92
Taking Up Space..93
Resist the Desire to Nurture! 94
Another Word for Control Is ...? 95
"I Want to Do It Myself!" 95
Bridging the Gap 96
I Just Want to Be Loved 97
Don't Fight Him, Join Him! 97
The Space Race...97
Actions Speak Louder … 99

**10 Learning the Basics of Good Communication
with the Opposite Sex**   **101**

Change Is Good...102
Why Should I Change? 102
Finding Common Ground 102
Mix and Match Interests..104
Don't Hog the Dialogue 104
Look and Listen and Stop Missin' 105
Speak Up! Be Heard 106

Part 4: Battleground of the Sexes   **109**

11 Basic Madness: Unmanaged Anger   **111**

Is Your Relationship Toxic? 112
Bursting Out of the Cage..113
Words That Hurt Never Heal..114
The Source of the Toxins..116
That Old Green-Eyed Monster 116
Unconstructive Criticism 118
The Groucho Marx Syndrome 118
Understanding Toxic Relationships 119
Healing Toxic Relationships 119

12 Mad About Women 121

What's Wrong? Nothing! No, Something! 122
Accuse Me! 123
What Are You, My Keeper? 124
The Caveman Cometh 126
Keep the Change! 127
No Competition Allowed Here! 127
Get to the Point Already! 129
Tell Me You Didn't Say That! 129
Treading on Sacred Ground 130
He Just Told *You* He Loved You! 130

13 Mad About Men 133

Is That It? N-I-C-E? 133
Feelings Are a Girl's Best Friend 134
Listen and Enjoy 135
Be a Man of Your Word 136
Grow Accustomed to Her Face 137
Empathize, Don't Solve! 138
No Orders in This Drill! 138
Stop with the Jokes Already! 139

Part 5: The Art of the Turn-On 141

14 Playing (and Winning) the Dating Game 143

Compassion Leads to Passion 144
Finding a Match Made in Heaven 145
In the Eye of the Beholder 146
Men and Their Icons 146
Women: More Forgiving 147
Accent the Positive: Strategies of Attraction 148
The Sound of Music 148
Confident and Sexy! 148
Smiling Faces Go Places 149
Warmth Is the Key 149
That Very Important Next Step 150
The Truth Will Out 150
Be Interested, Not Interesting 151
Flags and Warnings 151
Be a Friend First 152

15 Attracting the Opposite Sex 153

Who's Type Are You, Anyway? 153
What Attracts You the Most? 155
Confidence: The Key to Sexual Attractiveness 156
  Getting Some Confidence and Charisma *157*
The Touch of Attraction 158
  Shake It Up, Baby! *158*
  That First Touch *158*
Translating Body Language 159

16 Intimate Misunderstandings 161

Sexy Differences..162
Styles of Affection 162
  Cuddling Women *162*
  Teasing Leads to Hurt Feelings *163*
  Kissing and Making Up *163*
Speak Up and Speak Out 164
  No Mind Reading Allowed!..*165*
  The Intimacy Questionnaire *165*
Learning the Right Touch 167
Not Tonight, Dear 168

17 Top Secrets About Men 171

Men Are Not (Necessarily) "Commitaphobic" 171
Men Fear Rejection 172
Men Want to Be the Biggest and the Best 173
  Men Like to Avoid Confrontation *173*
  Men Hate to Be Criticized..*174*
  All Men Are Repairmen *174*
Men Like Women with Verve!..175
Men Prefer the "Natural Look" 175
Men Hate Being Changed 175
Men Like to Be Gross and Irreverent 176
Men Lie for Good Reasons, Too 176
Men Don't Want to Be Put on the Spot 177
Men Have a Push-and-Pull Syndrome 178
Men Avoid Toxic Women 178

18 Top Secrets About Women   181

Women Think Nonlinearly 181
Women Change Their Minds Easily 182
Women Appreciate Men Who Cry 183
Women Love to Shop 183
Women Feel Guilt About Anger 184
Women Need Constant Reassurance 185
Women Are Really Little Girls..................................185
Women Are Ambitious 186
Women Start the Arguments......................................186
Women Take Flirtation Seriously 187
Women Are Better Drivers..188
Women Have Better Memories 188

Part 6: Peaceful Co-Existence   191

19 What Men Want and Don't Want from Women   193

Looks Count 193
Men Want to Be King 194
   Men Want Praise *194*
   Men Want to Shine *194*
A Lady at Table, a Mistress in Bed.........................195
Eat, Eat, Eat!...195
No Punishment, Please 196
Get to the Point...197
Leave Feelings Aside 197
   Lighten Up *197*
   Leave Him Be..*198*
Time Out 198
Okay Anger 199
Blending In 199
The Trust Quotient 200
Silence Is Golden 201
Confidence Is Key 202
Hold Back on the Doting 203
Change Him Not! 204

20 What Women Want and Don't Want from Men   207

Be a Gentleman 207
Stop Kidding Around...208
Help Them Eat Less 209
Treat Them Like Queens 209
Women Expect Presents 210
Understanding Biological Time...212
Romance Is Queen...213
Friends, Just Friends..214
Commit, Commit, Commit 214
Widening the Circle 215
Feeling Sexy 216
TLC for PMS..216
Help Out! 216
Courtesy, Please 217

21 Men at Work   219

Avoiding Sexual Harassment Suits 219
  Falling Down the Corporate Ladder 220
  Sexual Harassment: A Quiz 221
Bringing Home the Bacon...222
  Lose the Attitude 222
  Politeness Is Potent! 223
Men and the Woman Boss 224
Office Flirts Hurt 225
  Keep Your Hands to Yourself..225
  Stop with the Jokes Already! 226
Let Her Speak! 226
Making Eye Contact 227
The Art of Constructive Criticism.......................................228

22 Women at Work   231

The Bottom Line: Money Matters..231
  Monkey See, Monkey Do! 232
  She's Not the "B" Word! 232
Bringing in Something Unique...234
Breaking Through the Glass Ceiling 234
She's *Not* One of the Guys...235

Keep Your Personal Life Close and Personal 236
You Don't Have to Answer *237*
Hold No Grudges *238*
No Crying Games *239*
Speak Up! 239
Where's the Mouse? *239*
Spit It Out Already! *240*
De-Personalizing Rejection 240

23 Seeking Similarities   243

We All Carry Baggage 243
We All Want to Feel Like Number One 244
No One Likes Secrets Revealed 244
Nobody Likes a Gold Digger 245
Love Us Just the Way We Are 246
What You See Is *What You Get!* *247*
Slow Down! 248
We're All Afraid of Commitment 248
We All Want That Pedestal 249
We All Hate Personal Competition 249
Equal Aggression *250*
Green with Jealousy *250*
Men and Women Appreciate Good Grooming...................250
No Outside Interference 251
Cat Got Your Tongue? 251
Very Human Cycles 251

24 Men and Women in the Millennium   253

Communication Now Is Key...253
Equal Pay Is Here to Stay...254
An Open Job Market..*254*
Sex Role Changes *255*
A Woman's Touch and a Man's Touch 255
Exploring Neurological Nuances.......................................256
Life-Saving Differences 256
Knowledge Equals Power of the Sexes 257
Keeping Some Territory Sacred *257*
Perhaps We'll Be More Tolerant *258*
Are You Really Compatible?..*258*

Cyber Romance 260
  Virtual Relationships *260*
  Virtual Therapy *261*
Free-Flowing Talk...262
  Better Daddies *262*
  Creating a Hybrid *262*
The Ideal Balanced Human 263
Becoming True Partners...263

Appendixes

A To Order *Dr. Lillian Glass'* Products   **265**

B References and Further Reading   **271**

Index   **277**

Foreword

Men and women have been misunderstanding each other (and themselves) since the second week of creation. In week one, God created Adam in his image. In week two, Adam's spare-rib sidekick Eve arrived (Adam's rib is quite a step down from God's facsimile), and things seemed to be going fairly well in Eden (like a giant Club Med with all the amenities but even better because everyone was naked!) for a day or two until the snake came and upset the proverbial apple cart. The snake took advantage of Eve's trusting nature and convinced her to eat from the Tree of Knowledge; Adam didn't resist Eve's invitation to join him. And he didn't resist insisting that she made him do it when God swooped down and expelled them from paradise, condemned to onerous lives of work and childcare, respectively. There's been some lingering discord between men and women ever since ...

Most idiot's guides are really just that: written by idiots for idiots about idiotic things; and there's nothing more dangerous than an idiot guide by a charismatic guru with a slick vocabulary and strong entrepreneurial spirit unencumbered by expert knowledge and genuine concern for his or her readers. When psychoanalyst Karen Horney published *Self-Analysis* (1942; the first "self-help" book and still the best in this genre), she was painfully aware that offering simple-minded solutions to complex problems based on inadequate understanding of the relevant issues leaves people disillusioned, demoralized, and disinclined to make serious subsequent efforts toward genuine improvement.

But I am delighted to report (and I suspect Karen Horney would be, too) that this book is different. Dr. Lillian Glass is no idiot: She writes with (com)passion and conviction infused with intelligence informed by good scholarship. The material presented in *The Complete Idiot's Guide to Understanding Men and Women* is current and accurate. It compares favorably with the information on these matters in the excellent text I use in my introductory psychology course at Skidmore, published in 1999 by a professor at Harvard—a decent school I'm told! And *The Complete Idiot's Guide to Understanding Men and Women* is most assuredly not written for idiots. Dr. Glass poses good questions and offers thoughtful answers and sincere advice based on our best current understanding of the fundamental similarities and differences between boys and girls and women and men.

Reading this book reminded me that pervasive misunderstandings between men and women result from gender differences that can only be understood as a complex mosaic of biological imperatives, social constructions, and individual choices. It will take hard work to recognize and accept the biological imperatives; and to identify and alter the social constructions that undermine our individual choices and hence threaten men's and women's most basic commonality: our humanity.

So let's go back to Eden (metaphorically speaking) and get it right this time around. In the original Genesis story (the one above is from Chapter 2), men and women are both created simultaneously in God's image; different of course, but equally divine.

Let's start there, and then each choose our own fruit to consume from the Tree of Knowledge: It's not a sin anymore, and we don't need reptiles to tell us what to eat. This book is a fine apple! Bon appétit!

Sheldon Solomon, Ph.D., Professor of Psychology at Skidmore College

Sheldon Solomon, Ph.D., has been Professor of Psychology at Skidmore College since 1980 and was honored by his faculty colleagues as the 1998 Edwin Mosley Lecturer. As an experimental social psychologist, his interests include the nature of self-consciousness and social psychology. His work exploring the effects of the fear of death on all aspects of individual and social behavior has been supported by the National Science Foundation and reported in *The New York Times,* the *Herald Tribune, The Boston Globe, Psychology Today,* and *Self* magazine. He is coauthor of the forthcoming book *Self-Esteem and Meaning* (APA Books).

Introduction

The divorce rate remains more than 50 percent across the country. Sexual harassment issues continue to plague the workplace. The content of talk shows, bookstore shelves, and magazine pages are chock full of men and women crying out for help and understanding from one another. And clearly you're among them since you've picked up this book.

I'm here to help. With *The Complete Idiot's Guide to Understanding Men and Women,* I first outline the issues that plague relationships between the genders—issues of communication, of sexuality, of power and equality, of passion and gentleness; issues that arise primarily because of our very different biological make-ups and societal influences. Then I show you how to better understand those differences and break them down so that true communication—in the bedroom, in the boardroom, and everywhere in between—can finally take place.

How This Book Is Organized

I've organized the book into six relatively equal parts that will take you through the process of developing healthy and fulfilling relationships with the opposite sex. With the knowledge you derive from this book—and from what you learn as you begin to really talk to and evaluate members of the opposite sex—you'll be better able to form lasting, meaningful relationships. Let's start from the beginning.

Part 1, "Sorting Out Our Differences." Before you can solve a problem, you've got to define it, and that's what I do in this part. I'll outline the differences between men and women, especially when it comes to communication issues. You'll even get to take a quiz to find out what you really know about the opposite sex.

Part 2, "Understanding the Great Nature/Nurture Debate." There's no doubt about it: Men look at the world differently and certainly talk about it differently than do women, and vice versa. In Part 2, I discuss the various scientific and sociological theories that explain these differences. I'll also explain some of the ways scientists think we develop our distinct, gender-related communication skills.

Part 3, "'Mr. and Ms. Understanding.'" In Part 3, I outline for you some of the most common ways that men and women typically misunderstand each other. What creates the wrong impression? Why is your partner angry or distant? How can you bridge the communication gap without losing your sense of self or self-respect?

Part 4, "Battleground of the Sexes." Without question, anger is the most destructive emotion known to humankind. In Part 4, we'll explore what ticks women off about men and vice versa. We'll learn how men and women can better express their anger and frustration to avoid setting up a cycle of resentment, despair, and more anger toward one another. You'll learn the skills needed to avoid hurting each other and getting hurt yourself. You'll see in black and white what *not* to do if you want to keep peace and harmony with the opposite sex.

Part 5, "The Art of the Turn-On." Ah, sex. Where would a book about men and women be without it? And where is communication more important than within an intimate, sexual relationship. But—as you've probably figured out for yourself— a good sexual relationship takes a lot of love, a lot of work, and very open lines of communication. In Part 5, I'll show you what men want from women and what women truly desire from men.

Part 6, "Peaceful Co-Existence." Never mind the bedroom, what about the board-room, you ask? Well, it seems as if getting along as equal partners and professionals in the workplace has never been more fraught with communication challenges than it is today. In Part 6, you'll learn the best strategies for working together as professionals without falling victim to sexual harassment pitfalls and unhealthy competition. Finally, we will take a futuristic hop into the next century as we explore all the possibilities that will be available to men and women in the new millennium.

Extras

In addition to the main text, you'll also find some tips, warnings, definitions, and extra tidbits of information scattered throughout the book. Here's what to look for:

He Says, She Says

These sidebars provide you with facts, study results, and other fascinating tidbits of information about how men and women behave and communicate—together and separately.

What I Mean Is ...

These little boxes offer you clear and concise definitions of words and concepts related to the differences between men and women.

Communication Breakdown!

These "red flags" are designed to protect you from making some common communication mistakes, and thus creating an even wider gap between you and the opposite sex.

Bridging the Gap

These tips offer you some new, more constructive ways to communicate with one another and to learn from each other so that healing, growing, and true nurturing is possible.

While it's true that men and women have very different styles of communicating, and often very different ideas about what's important to communicate, in the end we all have the same goal: to meet each other half-way—for comfort, for companionship, for love, for respect—in a world that would otherwise be too cold and lonely. Read on for advice on how to bridge your communication gaps.

Acknowledgements

This book is dedicated to Manny M. Glass, my dearest friend and late brother—what a gem of a human being—what an inspiration—what a loss! Manny, you are always with me and will always be part of me and part of the lives of the many people whose lives you touched! I adored you as did everyone else whose life you so deeply touched! Many of your words resonate throughout the pages of this book. May you live on in our hearts forever!

To my late father Abraham Glass for watching over me and giving me the strength to deal with all that I have to endure during these most trying moments.

I also wish to thank the following people who made this book possible:

To my lovely mother Rosalie Glass for her love and support and constant encouragement throughout this project, especially during the most difficult of moments. It was her strength and caring that allowed me to focus and complete this Herculean task.

To Jane Dystel, my terrific agent, for her high standards of professionalism in handling all of my literary business affairs and for her keen guidance of the literary aspects of my career.

To Dr. H. Harlan Bloomer, Professor Emeritus of the University of Michigan, for his wonderful education into the world of gender differences and for telling me early on, while I was a student, that I had what it took to make it in the world.

To Dustin Hoffman, the most brilliant performer of all time. I am grateful for the opportunity to have been a part of the process of helping him transform himself into his brilliant Academy Award–winning portrayal of a woman in the movie *Tootsie*.

To the Hollywood community for embracing me throughout the years and, among other things, for calling upon me to help whenever a role called for an actor to undergo a cosmetic gender change.

To members of the trans-gender community who have been some of my best teachers. They have given me so much more insight into the differences between men and women as they unabashedly shared with me their most intimate thoughts and feelings.

To all my wonderful clients who have allowed me to contribute to their lives as much as they have contributed to mine.

To all of the organizations I have spoken to on the topic of gender differences, and in particular, the Minnesota Bar Association, Indiana Bar Association, Rhode Island Bar Association, St. Louis Bar Association, Kansas City Bar Association, Bar Association of New Mexico, American Association of Continuing Legal Education, Washington Trial Lawyers Association, Kentucky Bar Association, Maricopa County Bar Association, King Country Bar Association, San Diego Bar Association, Virginia Bar Association, Women in Federal Law Enforcement, National Black MBA, Minnesota Hospital Association, HIMA, Virginia Realty Association, Country Club of the South, Infinity, Coca Cola, IBM, and others I have spoken to which are too numerous to mention.

To the readers of *He Says, She Says: Closing the Communication Gap Between the Sexes* who have written me lovely notes and letters expressing how the book has enhanced their lives with the opposite sex. Your positive feedback and heartfelt words have continued to motivate me and are what give my life true meaning. Hopefully this book, *The Complete Idiot's Guide to Understanding Men and Women,* will give you even more insight and can enhance your relationships to an even greater extent.

And finally to Tom Brennan, Susan Kaplan, Laura Kovach, Ann Convery, and Kevin Thranow and Anthony Mora of Anthony Mora Communications.

Trademarks

All terms mentioned in this book that are known to be or are suspected of being trademarks or service marks have been appropriately capitalized. Alpha Books and Macmillan USA, Inc. cannot attest to the accuracy of this information. Use of a term in this book should not be regarded as affecting the validity of any trademark or service mark.

Part 1
Sorting Out Our Differences

Welcome to the wonderful—and confusing—world of men, women, and communication. As you've no doubt already figured out, it isn't always easy to understand your mates, colleagues, or even siblings of the opposite sex. Nor is it easy to be understood by them, even when you try and try to make your feelings and thoughts clear.

Don't give up yet! In the chapters that follow, I'll outline for you what we know about the basic communication differences—I'll even give you a little quiz to see what kinds of false assumptions you're making about the communication between men and women. And then we'll start to map out some strategies that will slowly but surely bring greater understanding between the sexes.

Well, we're both human, right?

Chapter 1

Finding Common Ground in Gender Differences

In This Chapter

➤ Men and women are different—and that's a good thing!

➤ Accepting differences

➤ How boys and girls learn differently

➤ Learning to listen—really listen

Chances are you've picked up this book for several reasons. Perhaps you're just starting out in a brand-new relationship and want to make sure you get it right this time. Or you've just broken up with someone and are trying to figure out what went wrong so you won't make the same mistake again. It could be that you're in the middle of a loving relationship that you want to keep on track by learning to understand one another better. Or maybe it's communication in the workplace that's got you confused: You're a man with a woman for a boss, or a woman fighting for equity in a world that still seems "man-made."

Well, you're not alone. Despite all the attention paid in recent years to closing the gender gap—in the workplace, in the bedroom, and on the dating scene—we've still got a long way to go. There's still a lot men don't understand about women and vice versa. Men and women are different, partly because of biology, partly because of the way we're brought up, and partly as a result of continuing societal pressures on us all as adults. Thus, men and women continue to look at the world just a little differently, feel emotions in their own ways, and communicate what they see and feel in very, very different ways.

In this chapter, we'll discuss how important it is to recognize and accept—even revel in—those differences. Once we can do that, we'll be on our way to finding some common ground and understanding. Only then can we hope to build strong, healthy, and lasting relationships.

Resistance to Difference

Right up front—before we can talk about the differences between men and women—it's important to note that accepting that tangible differences exist between genders has been a bit of a touchy issue among women over the past several decades.

That's because many women have been struggling for that intangible idea of "equality"—in the workplace, in the home, and in the bedroom. And for many, admitting "difference" in anything but the most basic biological terms actually meant admitting "weakness."

Before you go laying blame for the current communication gap at the feet of feminists, it might help to take a look at what life was like before their groundbreaking efforts. Remember the kids on the *Brady Bunch?* (And if you were too young—or not yet born—when the show first aired, you can catch them on *Nick at Night* today!) It was big news—worthy of an entire episode—when Marcia turned out to be a better driver than her brother Greg.

He Says, She Says

The differences between individual men and women involve far more than gender. Indeed, each person enters every relationship in his or her life with a unique "world view." This world view is based on his or her earlier life experience, prior relationships with members of both genders, and individual personality and temperament. It is rare—if not impossible—for two people (no matter their gender) to share identical world views. But, in order for true communication to occur and honest relationships to continue, we must try to understand the way the world looks from the other person's perspective, and then hear the words he or she speaks from that—and not our own—point of view.

Among the women who lived through the 1960s and 1970s when feminism came into being, many fought hard against the prejudice that such a connection engendered, whereby sex differences meant being "inferior" or not as good as or as qualified as the opposite sex. Much has changed today for women, and especially for young girls, as a result of many of the vocal efforts brought forth by our foremothers. Today, women can captain a space shuttle, sit on the Supreme Court, and become wealthy executives in the entertainment industry. Some can do this and still run entire households and nurture their children.

So now there's no reason why we can't look at the very real differences between men and women in an open and objective way. Only by doing so can we reach across the gaps that so clearly exist between us.

Knowledge Is Power

If we as a society are going to thrive as we enter the next century—and not simply repeat the mistakes we've made in the past—we'd better translate what have become almost foreign languages between genders. Only then will we really be able to hear each other, heal each other, and grow together.

As we'll discuss throughout this book, men and women develop very different communication skills, and the sooner we understand and accept that fact, the better able we'll be to meet problems and challenges that spring up between us. In the many seminars I've given to legal groups across the country on gender difference in negotiation, I've always reinforced one essential point: These differences can become the ties that bind us and are instrumental in our communication with one another.

Now that's not to say that individuals of both genders need certain gender-specific skills in

Bridging the Gap

Take the time to learn about the differences between men and women, and you'll start to improve your inter-gender relationships almost immediately. Once you have a deeper understanding of the issues and styles that separate you, you can learn to speak to your partners, friends, and coworkers without risking miscommunication and unnecessary petty misunderstandings.

order to get their points across. You'll need to learn to articulate your thoughts in an understandable way (and not simply expect your partner or colleague to guess what you're thinking). Even more important, both men and women first need to identify what they're feeling and what they want from whatever relationship they're in. Putting aside the old fable of the tortoise and the hare, we don't really expect two members of different species to compete on completely equal grounds. And when it comes to communication skills and strategies—to say nothing of physical strength or biological imperatives—men and women are very different even though they are members of the same species.

Although, as we'll see throughout this book, women often tend to be better at communicating certain types of issues and feelings, each gender brings something special and valuable to the communication/relationship table. Both genders are capable and competent, even though they may approach things from quite different perspectives. The sooner we understand, accept, and embrace this concept, the sooner we can let go of the instinct to compete, dominate, and win!

Communication Breakdown!

Stop making snap judgments about members of the opposite sex based solely on their gender. Really listen to their words and observe their behavior before assuming you understand where they're coming from.

That said, shall we take a look at some of the fascinating variations in the ways men and women learn, think, and communicate? Let's first look at the way we learn as children.

Nature Versus Nurture: Part I

Once we've accepted the fact that women and men are different in almost every way, the fascinating next step is to find out why we're so different. In Part 2, "Understanding the Great Nature/Nurture Debate," we explore this subject in some depth; for now, it's enough to say that each individual becomes the adult he or she is through a splendid cooperation of their natural, inborn characteristics and societal influences.

The Math Equation

Here's an example of how that interplay works. You've probably heard about the studies showing that boys are better at math than girls. Indeed, national test scores consistently show that girls score lower than boys on standardized math tests. But what does that really tell us?

First, it indicates that there could be biological reasons why boys are better at math. And, in fact, there is some truth to that: Boys' brains are organized in such a way that it's easier for them to see patterns and connect abstract relationships—just the skills you need to do math.

In addition, and probably just as important, it appears that boys learn math better than girls do because of the way math is taught. Girls, it seems, learn best by working out problems verbally and within a group dynamic. But as anyone who's taken a math class knows, that's not the way any of us are taught to add, subtract, or multiply. Instead, we're taught to work on our own and to compete for the right answer.

In an attempt to see if girls' grades improved when teaching methods favored the way girls learned, a school conducted a groundbreaking study. What they found was that girls' math scores improved considerably when cooperation, group dynamics, and verbal coaching became part of the teaching strategy.

The Language of Gender

And it works in reverse, too. For instance, in general, most boys develop language and reading skills at a slower rate than most girls do, at least until they reach a certain age. Again, part of the explanation has to do with the anatomy and physiology of the brain. In girls and women, brain functions related to the mechanics of language, such as grammar, spelling, and speech production, are more focused and concentrated in one part of the anatomy of the brain—thereby making them more efficient in these skills—than are those in boys.

Unfortunately, few teachers have been aware that this very real physiological difference was at the root of their male students' challenges when it came to learning to read. Instead of taking the time to help the boys along, they too often reprimanded or belittled them in front of their peers for not keeping up during their most vulnerable development stages. This attitude not only slows boys down, but creates emotional barriers to learning—and to language skills in general—that could be avoided.

He Says, She Says

As you'll see in Part 2, sex hormones—testosterone in men and estrogen and progesterone in women—influence the way men's and women's brains work throughout their life spans. In the womb and during infancy, sex hormones influence brain development, and in the elderly they affect memory. Some scientists believe that the presence of sex hormones may influence various neurological disorders that are more prevalent in one sex than the other.

Unfortunately, in my practice, I've seen what happens to young boys and girls who've been belittled at school after they've grown up. So many men, who are now CEOs of companies and prominent individuals, recount the same story for me time after time: A teacher humiliated them in front of their classmates, their classmates laughed, and now, today, they have trouble getting up and speaking in front of their coworkers and colleagues.

This is just one example of how understanding the differences between boys and girls can help foster the development of more secure, self-confident men and women, which in turn will foster better communication and healthier relationships.

But that's only the beginning. Men and women not only learn math and language at different rates and in different ways as children, but we grow up speaking almost completely different languages that require interpretation and finesse for true understanding to take place. And too often, when we're all grown up, we find out we never learned the skills to do just that.

Communication Breakdown!

Don't buy into the myth that only girls or women are shy with members of the opposite sex. Both sexes find it hard to take risks and reach out. Compassion and understanding go a long way with both sexes.

The Benefits of Better Understanding

Understanding how very differently men and women communicate with one another can go a long way in fostering healthier, sexier (when appropriate), more professional (when appropriate), and more satisfying relationships between men and women. Let's take a look at just a few of the ways better understanding can bridge the gender gap:

➤ **Fewer "toxic" relationships.** Bitterness and disappointment that come from constantly misunderstanding and misinterpreting are the fastest ways to both personal failure and relationship destruction.

➤ **Better and more emotionally satisfying sex.** Throughout my years as a therapist, I've had the honor of working through some pretty intimate issues with my clients. And even though it may sound like a cliché, it's very certainly true: The secret to having good sex is having great communication—the kind of communication that can come only through understanding the other person's perspective. In addition, knowing what you need and how to ask for what you need is crucial. We'll talk more about sexual issues in Part 5, "The Art of the Turn-On," but for now it's important to recognize that our different communication styles could also affect what happens in bed. Even the words a man might use to describe his needs could turn his partner off, without him ever realizing what's happened.

➤ **Fewer extramarital affairs.** Without question, the number-one reason that men and women have affairs is *not* sex but communication. Believe it or not, most couples who cheat admit that what they're looking for is not sexual but verbal intimacy. They're looking for someone who truly listens to what they say about how they feel. If men and women can learn to give that attention and understanding to their mates, then it's likely there'll be far fewer straying mates of both sexes.

➤ **Less anger.** Developing a deeper understanding of the opposite sex will allow you
to enjoy, rather than resent, the differences
between you, which results in a lot less
anger. Believe it or not, the next time your
mate or coworker does a "guy thing" or a
"woman thing," you may have already
learned to smile and laugh rather than ruffle
your feathers and fan the flame.

Now all of this isn't to say that it's okay to be
insensitive or as bitchy or macho as possible. In
fact, that kind of behavior leads not only to poor
romantic relationships, but also often to legally
actionable professional ones. Think of how many
fewer *sexual harassment* suits would be filed if
men learned not to make crude jokes or unwel-
come advances. And think of how many power
struggles and office coups could be avoided if
women bosses learned to be more sensitive—and
less defensive—about the impact their leadership
has on office hierarchy and structure. Indeed,
communication between the sexes is very much
a two-way street, and it takes a lot of finesse to
travel down it.

Lesson #1: Listen, Listen, Listen

It may sound silly to spell it out, but in order to
really hear what another person is saying, you
actually have to really listen to that person's
words and pay attention to his or her gestures.
And that means you have to stop assuming you
know exactly what someone is going to say or exactly what someone means to say
without having heard the person all the way through. When you think about it, how
many of your past arguments with a member of the opposite sex have occurred
because you're too busy thinking you know *just* what's on his or her mind instead of
listening to what's actually being said?

Men and women tend to be pretty equal offenders when it comes to this behavior.
Instead of listening or even watching for physical clues as to the true feelings of our
mates or friends, we all too often lash out and accuse the person of doing something
or feeling something that hasn't even occurred to him or her. As you yourself may

Bridging the Gap

Your first step in breaking
through to the other side of the
gender gap is to stop playing
mind games. Figure out what you
want, then learn to ask for it in a
way that is clear, concise, and to
the point.

What I Mean Is ...

Sexual harassment is a legal
term referring to unwanted sexual attention, usually within the
workplace and between workers
of unequal status, that interferes
with or undermines the ability to
perform one's job with confidence.

9

Communication Breakdown!

Stop using sarcasm to communicate. Many people—especially men, who learn the fine art of belittlement as a survival tactic early on—use sarcasm as an everyday language. Unfortunately, not everyone finds that kind of humor very funny, especially women. Learn to express yourself in more direct and less hurtful ways.

have experienced, this is a losing proposition. The more you tell someone what he or she is thinking, the more anger you engender and the more distance forms between you.

As I mentioned in the introduction to this book, the national divorce rate is well over 50 percent and, in some parts of the country, approaches a shocking 70 percent. And—not to paint a pessimistic picture—it's hard not to wonder just how happy those other 30 or 45 percent of couples who stay married really are. Without question, the better we learn to communicate, the greater our chances for having long-term, happy, and healthy marriages.

As you embark on your journey to better communication, however, it's important to listen not only to your partner—which will take *a lot* of practice—but also to yourself and to the way your words sound to the people you say them to. Here are a few examples of the ways we miscommunicate and misinterpret because we don't take the time to listen to the words we say from the other person's perspective:

He says:	[Trying to be helpful] "You should never do it that way."
She hears:	[Feeling small and unappreciated] "He's putting me down and being critical and judgmental."
He says:	[Hoping to encourage and comfort] "Don't sweat the small stuff."
She hears:	[Feeling resentful and diminished] "How condescending!"
He says:	[Wanting simply to vent] "I think John's trying to move in on my territory."
She replies:	[Attempting to be empathetic] "I know what you mean. When I worked at XY Company, the same thing happened to me."
He hears:	[Feeling frustrated] "She's trying to compete with me."

As you can see, the gender communication landscape is fraught with challenges. Fortunately, that's why I'm here—to help you navigate through these roadblocks and establish healthier, stronger inter-gender relationships.

In the next chapter, I'll define and explore the gender differences in communication strategies and tendencies in some depth. I'll even help you see what kinds of assumptions you've been making about the member of the opposite sex in your own life.

The Least You Need to Know

➤ While it's important not to exaggerate the differences between women and men, the differences are real.

➤ By being aware of sex differences, we might be able to set up classrooms so that our children learn more effectively.

➤ A lot of the anger each gender feels toward the other would evaporate if each could truly understand in an informed way what the other means, instead of guessing and assuming.

➤ What women think of as "sharing" and being empathetic can be heard by men as competition and one-upmanship.

Chapter 2

What Do We Really Know About One Another?

In This Chapter

➤ The Sex Talk Quiz

➤ Being attentive to sex differences

➤ Commands and requests

➤ Long-talking men and fast-talking women

➤ Women who stay on topic

Now that we've taken a look at some of the most obvious differences in communication styles between men and women, it's time we examine how much we actually know about the opposite sex—not the stereotypes we learned as children, not the characteristics we assume exist based on our past experiences with individuals, but the fundamental truths about the ways genders—in general—view the world and each other.

If we don't take the time to see the world from the other side of the gender gap, it's all too easy to develop persistent misconceptions that can be harmful to the communication process. In order to build understanding and move forward into more positive inter-gender relationships, you need to develop a greater understanding. Reading this chapter can be one step in the right direction.

How Much Do *You* Assume: Dr. Glass' Sex Talk Quiz

I've devised this Sex Talk Quiz you can take to see how much you really know about the opposite sex. I derived the questions from several scientific studies and public opinion polls, including a few from the illustrious Gallop and Roper polling organization. The quiz first appeared in my book *He Says, She Says: Closing the Communication Gap Between the Sexes* (Putnam, 1992). In the years since it first appeared, it's become extremely popular and has been translated into many languages and used in textbooks and conferences on gender differences conducted by myself and other experts in the field.

Dr. Glass' Sex Talk Quiz

	True	False
1. Women are more intuitive than men. They seem to have a sixth sense, typically termed "women's intuition."	❏	❏
2. At business meetings, coworkers are more likely to listen to men than they are to women.	❏	❏
3. Women are the "talkers." They talk much more than men in group conversations.	❏	❏
4. Men are the "fast" talkers. They talk much more quickly than women.	❏	❏
5. Men are more outwardly open than women. They use more eye contact and exhibit more friendliness when first meeting someone.	❏	❏
6. Women are more complimentary and offer more praise than men.	❏	❏
7. Men will interrupt more and will answer a question even when it is not addressed to them.	❏	❏
8. Women give more orders and are more demanding in the way they communicate.	❏	❏
9. In general, men and women laugh at the same things.	❏	❏
10. When making love, both men and women want the same things from their partners.	❏	❏
11. Men ask for assistance less often than women do.	❏	❏
12. Men are harder on themselves and blame themselves more often than women do.	❏	❏
13. Through their body language, women make themselves less confrontational than men.	❏	❏
14. Men explain things in greater detail than women do when describing an incident.	❏	❏

	True	False
15. Women tend to touch others more often than men.	❑	❑
16. Men appear to be more attentive than women when they are listening.	❑	❑
17. Women and men are equally emotional when they speak.	❑	❑
18. Men are more likely to discuss personal issues.	❑	❑
19. Men bring up more topics of conversation than women do.	❑	❑
20. Today we tend to raise our male children the same way we raise our female children.	❑	❑
21. Women tend to confront problems more directly than men and are likely to bring up the problem first.	❑	❑
22. Men are livelier speakers than women and use more body language and facial animation.	❑	❑
23. Men ask more questions than women do.	❑	❑
24. In general, men and women enjoy talking about similar things.	❑	❑
25. When it comes to asking whether a partner has had an AIDS test or discussing safe sex, a woman will likely bring up the topic before a man does.	❑	❑

Now check your answers with the following answer key. Add up how many you got right.

1. F	6. T	11. T	16. F	21. T
2. T	7. T	12. F	17. T	22. F
3. F	8. F	13. T	18. F	23. F
4. F	9. F	14. F	19. F	24. F
5. F	10. F	15. F	20. F	25. T

If you did not answer all the questions correctly, don't be discouraged. Most people don't. Too often people carry with them stereotypes and misconceptions—perhaps based on their past experiences with the opposite sex. This is a good eye-opener to allow you to become more aware of how members of the opposite sex present themselves.

If, on the other hand, you got all the answers correct, keep reading anyway. You may learn even more about the ways members of the opposite sex tend to think, feel, and behave.

Let's explore and discuss some of the most common misconceptions we have about each other.

The Truth About "Intuition"

According to scientific studies, there's no truth to the myth that women are more intuitive than men. However, research shows that women tend to pay greater attention to detail. For instance, according to world-renowned anthropologist Ashley Montagu, women have a greater sensitivity to and acuity for color discrimination than men do. Linguist Robin Lakoff, in her classic book *Language and Women's Place* (Harper Colophon, 1975), confirms this claim and states that women tend to use finer descriptions of colors.

Communication Breakdown!

Don't jump to conclusions—based on bad experiences you've had in the past—about the behavior or language used by a member of the opposite sex. Be sure to educate yourself so that you can make more careful observations and correctly assess what's really going on with the opposite sex.

For example, women will use words like "lemon," "persimmon," and "ebony" to describe certain colors, while men will probably just say "yellow," "orange," or "black." Now that may be partly because women buy cosmetics, linens, and clothing labeled by manufacturers eager to be clever, but it's also clear that they see more subtle shadings than their male counterparts see.

This fine attention to detail makes women appear to be more intuitive because they often notice characteristics men might miss, such as a person's body language, facial expressions, and vocal tones.

You can see this sensitivity even in early childhood. Certain studies show that baby girls seem to be more aware of parents' and others' facial expressions than are baby boys, a tendency frequently carried over into adulthood. Such an ability may explain why women can often perceive a person's mood and present emotional state better than men. As a result of their conditioning, women have also been found to have a greater acuity and sensitivity to "nonverbal communication" than men, which also makes them appear to be more intuitive.

The Truth About Talk

Even today, as we head rapidly into the twenty-first century, there exists a startling communications gender gap: No matter their position, age, or level of knowledge, men command more attention when they speak than women do. In their study, "Sex Differences in Listening Comprehension," researchers Kenneth Gruber and Jacqueline Gaehelein found that both men and women audiences tended to listen more attentively to male speakers than to female speakers. Audiences also tended to remember more information from the presentations given by male speakers than from those given by female speakers, even when the presentations were identical. Another study showed that audiences at a conference were quieter and less distracted when listening to a male than they were when listening to a female speaker.

Before we get upset about the political and social unfairness of such a tendency, there could be a simple biological reason—at least in part. Because of their physiology (larger, wider vocal cords), men tend to speak in lower tones and pitches, which oftentimes tend to be easier on the ears. A high-pitched voice, on the other hand, can turn the audience off and prevent people from actually hearing the information presented.

Men Are the Talkers

Contrary to popular myth, men talk more than do women, especially when it comes to showing off their expertise or giving their opinions when asked. Studies, like the one performed in 1974 by linguist Lynette Hirshman, show that men far out-talk women under these circumstances. In fact, men tend to give more, lengthier, and more involved answers than necessary for the questions they are asked. When asked to describe a painting, for instance, men spoke an average of 13 minutes, while their female counterparts spoke an average of only three minutes. In addition, several studies—from a study by Fred Strodtbeck in 1951, to a study by Marjorie Swacker in 1975—all confirm that women speak less than men do when participating in mixed-sex conversations.

Fast-Talking Women

Several studies show that women talk at a more rapid rate than men do, perhaps because they're so used to being interrupted by men (see the following section "Ahem: Men Interruptus!") that they feel they must hurry to express their ideas! The good news, however, is that their talking fast doesn't make them unintelligible. In fact, one study showed that women articulated or pronounced their words more precisely than did men.

And What's Important to You?

As I mentioned earlier, men and women talk about different things. Women's top topics concern relationships, appearance, clothes, personalities, the actions of others, relationships at work, and emotionally charged issues that have a personal component. Men, on the other hand, enjoy talking about themselves, their achievements, sports, what they did at work, where they went, news events, mechanical gadgets, technology, vehicles, and music. If we are more aware of what the other sex is more apt to speak about, we can accommodate them and better relate to them and address their needs. This compromise and speaking in terms of the other sex adds to more of a unity in the communication between the sexes.

The Friendlier Gender

When it comes to interpersonal communication, studies show that women maintain more eye contact and offer more facial pleasantries. Body language expert Dr. Albert Mehrabian's study showed that, while participating in positive interactions, women made more eye contact during their conversations than men did. Perhaps men felt more uncomfortable doing so. Women also tend to smile more and nod their heads in a show of attention and approval when first meeting a new acquaintance, according to linguist Dr. Nancy Henley.

He Says, She Says

Smiling seems to be more prevalent among women than men. One study showed that women smiled 93 percent of the time when meeting new people. If the person she met was male, she received a smile in return only 67 percent of the time. But if she was meeting a woman, she got a smile right back about 97 percent of the time.

Praising Women

Women tend to be more open in their praise and give more head nods of approval than men. They also use more complimentary terms throughout their speech patterns and vocabulary usage. Linguist Robin Lakoff discovered that women tend to interject more "um-hums" in order to indicate approval when listening to both men and other women.

Ahem: Men Interruptus!

When men and women speak together, men interrupt much more than women do. In fact, a classic study at the University of California shows that men made 75 to 93 percent of all inter-gender interruptions. Another study showed that a woman interrupted a man in just one out of 11 conversations, but the man interrupted the woman in all 10 of the others. In addition, it seems that—once so rudely interrupted—women become increasingly quiet and pause more than usual during the rest of the conversation.

This same apparent meekness was not the case when the man was interrupted. Dr. Donald Zimmerman and Dr. Candace West, who conducted the study, surmised that men tend to interrupt more as a means of establishing dominance and, judging by the women's response, are successful in doing so. Such male "conversational dominance" was confirmed by researcher Judy Kester, who discovered that men are more likely to answer questions even when the questions are not addressed to them, which in actuality, may be another way of interrupting.

As you might imagine, this communication pattern between men and women can lead to a self-perpetuating cycle of resentment among women and assumptions of power and superiority among men. Indeed, as you'll see next, women end up speaking in more conditional terms than the absolute terms in which men speak.

Demanding Men and Tentative Women

Men use more command terms or imperatives (such as "get me a beer") than women do, which often makes men seem to be aggressive and demanding to those they speak to.

Women, on the other hand, tend to couch their commands with terms of politeness or terms of endearment, such as, "Honey, can you please get me a beer?" or "Please get me a beer." Linguist Dr. Mary Ritchie Key, a well-known expert in the speech patterns of women, found that on the whole women tend to be more tentative when they talk.

Another researcher, Dr. Robin Lakoff, confirmed this finding, discovering that women tended to use more *tag endings*, questions added to the end of what could—and often should—be declarative sentences. "This salad is delicious, isn't it?" is a perfect example of this kind of qualification. Instead of making her opinion clear and unambiguous with "I love this salad" or "This salad is delicious," the female speaker will qualify it with a question. Such a tendency adds to the persistent image of women being less sure of themselves in conversations.

What I Mean Is ...

A **tag ending** is a question attached to what would otherwise be a declarative statement. Women tend to use tag endings more than men, saying, "It's really nice outside, isn't it?" instead of saying what they really mean, which is, "It's really nice outside."

Different Strokes for Different Genders

Women and men also have very different senses of humor and ways of communicating in intimate situations. Let's take a look.

Where's That Funny Bone?

According to most researchers, another difference between men and women may be in the location and function of their funny bone! Indeed, while women are more likely to tell jokes in a smaller, single-sex group, men tend to be the complete opposite, telling jokes in larger, mixed-sex groups. Women tell jokes less frequently than men do, and their humor tends to be focused more on word plays and puns than men's jokes are. Indeed, studies show that, on average, men's humor tends to be more aggressive, abrasive, and sarcastic than women's humor, perhaps because men use humor as a way of bonding with one another. Men will often joke with complete strangers in order to try to establish camaraderie, whereas women will use compliments to form this initial bond.

Although gender differences in the expression of humor may not seem like such a big deal, courtrooms are filled with cases involving sexual harassment based upon what is perceived to be humorous and what is not. Clearly, men need to be more sensitive in their use of humor, and women should realize that—as offensive as they may be—the jokes and ribbing they receive in the "man's world" may not necessarily be meant as personal affronts.

What I Mean Is ...

Terms of endearment are words like "darling," "sweetheart," "baby," "love," "darling," and "gorgeous." Uttered in loving tones, these words help to form a deeper, sweeter connection between two love partners, especially during moments of intimacy.

Talking in the Dark

When it comes to talking during sex, our communication styles are also quite different. Generally speaking, men often want to hear about their own physical prowess during the sex act—how well they're able to satisfy their partners—while women usually want to hear that they are loved, that they are beautiful, and that they are desirable.

In a survey I conducted, I found that only 30 percent of the men and women surveyed were pleased with what they heard from the opposite sex while making love. In general, fewer women were satisfied by what their partners said to them in bed. The majority of women in the survey expressed how important it was to them for their mates to be generous with *terms of endearment* and compliments during lovemaking.

Needless to say, this difference in the way men and women communicate in bed often leads to hurt feelings, unmet expectations, and even sexual dysfunction. Learning new strategies for communicating your sexual needs—which you'll have the opportunity to do later in the book—may open a whole new world of intimacy for you.

Men Don't Ask for Help!

You've been there before ... we all have. A man will simply not ask for directions even when he finds himself in the middle of nowhere almost out of gas on a moonless night. In her book *You Just Don't Understand* (Morrow, 1995), linguist Deborah Tannen confirmed that women are the ones who'll ask for directions, not their mates—no matter who's driving or who got them lost in the first place. Tannen suggests the reason for this annoying tendency is that women consider themselves to be "takers" of information, while men see themselves as the "givers" of information and the experts on all kinds of subjects and matters.

In addition to this psycholinguistic analysis, there could be another more biological explanation. As we'll see in Chapter 4, "The Role of Mother Nature," men perceive space and distance differently than women do and they may, in essence, not feel as though they are lost.

It's Tough Being a Girl

Sometimes it seems as if women are their own worst enemies. Indeed, they tend to judge themselves more harshly and carry themselves with less confidence than men do.

Undermining Self-Talk

Ask most women if they are happy with what they see when they look in the mirror, and you'll hear a resounding *"No!"* According to literally hundreds of surveys and interviews conducted by psychotherapists and journalists, women not only tend to be more self-deprecating about their looks and their accomplishments, they also tend to blame themselves, even for things for which they couldn't possibly be held responsible. Tannen's findings refer to this self-criticism, willingness to please, and attempts to make sure that "things are fine." These findings confirm that women tend to use more apologetic phrases, such as "I'm sorry," "I didn't mean to," or "Excuse me," than men do.

If a women is self-deprecating she does not exude the self-confidence necessary to have a healthy and substantial relationship with a man. It has a detrimental effect upon the relationship whereby the women gives away a lot of her power. Even though the woman may in essence be a powerful woman, she may be giving a false impression of who she really is. Her self-deprecatory behavior may reflect someone who is weak and meek. When she is treated as such she may harbor inner resentment for being treated in a manner that doesn't reflect who she really is. This is very confusing to a man and adds additional conflict to the relationship. Therefore, it is essential for the woman to never put herself down in any way and limit disparaging remarks about herself.

Straighten Up and Fly Right!

Researchers Ray Birdwhistell, Albert Mehrabian, and Marguerite Pierce found that women tend to physically inhibit themselves by crossing their legs at the ankles or knees or by keeping their elbows to their sides, thereby making themselves seem less confrontational to men. Linguists interpret this female body language or body posturing as tending to reflect less power or status. This means that in many cases women may not be presenting themselves with the body and head posture and facial expressions that reflect self-confidence. This may result in an initial lack of respect as compared with men who exhibit a more powerful physical stance.

Bridging the Gap

Be sure to pay attention to body cues and their many meanings. If a man sees a woman nodding when he talks, he may assume that everything he's said is agreed to—she's nodded "yes." But in fact, she may simply be giving support and encouragement, showing that she is paying attention and giving his words a fair hearing.

Attention to Detail: A Woman's Prerogative

As you'll see in Chapter 4, school-aged girls answer quite differently from school-aged boys when asked to describe their days at school. Little girls explode with lots of details, often providing more information than you need or want. Unfortunately, when they grow up, they continue to do just that. Later in the book, we'll discuss how women can sidetrack conversation by going overboard on details and how much this tendency disturbs men.

Gender Communication: Touch Versus Eye Contact

Studies show that men touch other men more (with backslapping and handshaking), especially during participation in sports. Men also touch women more than women touch men, often while men are performing "gentlemanly" duties such as helping women in and out of cars, assisting them with jackets and coats, and leading them through doors. Nancy Henley's research substantiates these findings. She found that in a variety of outdoor settings, men touched women four times as often as women touched men. It's important to note that, in most cases, a woman shouldn't interpret these touches as sexual overtures, especially if a man puts his hands on her back, arms, or shoulders.

Although they may not touch each other or men as often, women appear to be more attentive than men, exhibiting greater eye contact and expressing approval. Sally McConnell-Ginetts's research at Cornell University showed that women were more inclined to say "um-hum" than men when listening to another person. They did so not necessarily in agreement, but more as a way of monitoring the flow of conversation, as well as making the other person feel more comfortable and continue speaking.

Emotional Equality

According to studies performed by Paul Ekman at the University of California, San Francisco, men and women are equally emotional when they speak, but they express their emotions differently. This difference in style, however, leads to the impression that women are more emotional than men in their speech. The main reason is that women typically use five tones when they speak, while men use approximately three tones, which makes men's speech sound more dramatic.

Several studies have shown that women are livelier and more animated speakers than men because they use more eye contact, have more body movement, intonation, varied pitch range, and emotionally laden words and phrases. According to linguists, women also appear to sound more emotional because they pepper their speech with more psychological state verbs, such as "I wish," "I feel," and "I hope." When women express negative emotions, they have a greater tendency to become quiet, have a shaky voice quality, or let out tears. Men increase their vocal intensity by yelling or using swear words more often than women do.

Women Get Personal!

Women tend to bring up more personal topics than men do, discussing people and relationships, children, self-improvement, and how certain experiences affected them. Men, on the other hand, are more outer-directed, tending to originate discussions about events, news, sports-related issues, and topics related to more concrete physical tasks. So both men and women need to keep this in mind when speaking with one another, so they can address one another's needs and become more aware of what the other gender is saying and what they mean.

Women Bring Up the Topics!

A study at Queens College by Pam Fishman found that 60 percent of the topics brought up in conversation were brought up by women. Perhaps the reason women introduced topics more often than men did relates to the fact that men tend to interrupt more, thus forcing the conversation to change continually. As discussed, men usually interrupt as a way of controlling the topics that the women organized. Men need to be highly conscious of this and continue to address the topic of conversation the women bring up, out of respect. When a man wants to change the topic he needs to alert the woman he is doing so via a verbal cue and then segue to the next topic.

Just as they bring up more topics throughout a conversation, women ask more questions to facilitate a conversation. They will usually ask questions to keep the conversation going and to make men feel more comfortable and at ease while talking to them.

Communication Family Style

Although there are many socially enlightened and aware parents, there is still the widespread tendency to raise boy and girl children with the same sexual stereotypes with which their parents were raised—even if it's only on a subconscious level. As we'll see further in Chapter 5, "The Role of Mother Nurture," university studies show that even today, mothers tend to be more verbal with their daughters than they are with their sons. Studies also show that boys are still handled more roughly physically, treated more robustly, and spoken to in a louder voice than girls are.

As you might imagine, by raising our children in this way, we're only creating another generation (after generation, after generation ...) of men and women with the same communication, social, and sexual challenges to overcome as we see in the bedrooms and boardrooms today.

Confronting Problems

Even though men tend to be more direct in the statements they make, women bring up problem subjects before men do. In a survey I conducted for my book *He Says, She Says,* 70 percent of the women compared to 30 percent of the men were the first to bring up a problem. When women do bring up problems, however, they still manage to present them more indirectly and more politely, as Deborah Tannen relates, based on her studies.

Perhaps the implications here are that women tend to be perceived by many men as the caretakers of situations. An interesting aspect of the survey was that women tended to bring up the topics of safe sex, sexually transmitted diseases, and birth control, once again giving credence to the notion of women being expected to be the caretakers.

I hope this chapter has raised for you some of the enduring challenges and issues faced by men and women—challenges and issues often caused by the differences in the ways we communicate. The good news is that by gaining a deeper understanding and acceptance of these differences we can learn to communicate with each other in a more helpful and supportive way. In the next chapter, I'll delve even deeper into the communication patterns of men and women.

The Least You Need to Know

➤ Many of us carry around lots of mistaken beliefs about the sexes.

➤ Men typically speak with commands, women with requests.

➤ Men tend to talk more than women do, but women speak more rapidly and articulately.

➤ Women introduce more topics than men do, but men are more likely to change the topic and interrupt than are women.

➤ Learning about the differences in our communication styles and accepting them can help lay the groundwork for deepening our relationships.

Chapter 3

Communication Breakdown, Gender Style

In This Chapter

➤ Dismissive body language among the sexes

➤ Personal space among men and women

➤ What do those facial gestures really mean?

➤ Speaking tones for men and women

In the previous chapter you probably discovered some of the prejudices and assumptions you hold about the opposite sex. Maybe you assumed that women are the chatterboxes who interrupt constantly, or that men are the ones who loathe to touch other people (men or women). Now that you know the opposite is true, you can go from there with the understanding that communication between the genders is more complicated than you may have assumed.

In this chapter we'll explore gender differences in more depth. By examining our very different styles of communication on every front—verbal, physical, emotional, behavioral, and psychological—you'll be able to better understand what messages members of the opposite sex are sending to you when you interact. By doing so—and then applying what you know to every area of your life—you'll find yourself able to form and foster more productive relationships with people of the opposite sex socially, professionally, and intimately.

Let's get started by looking at one of the most fascinating and still little-understood science of body language. Then I'll talk more about differences in the use and style of language in conversation.

The Body Language of Dominance

It has been said that the body communicates emotions, feelings, and even thoughts just as well as speech does, maybe even better. However, people on the receiving end of these physical signals can just as easily misinterpret them as they can misunderstand the spoken word. Let's take a look.

The situation depicted in the following figure shows how easy it is to misinterpret body language. A male executive is interviewing a female prospective employee we'll call Delia. He sits with his feet on his desk and his chair tilted back, frequently looking off to the side as he questions her through a clenched jaw. He furrows his brow, fidgets, and fails to provide much verbal feedback or encouragement such as head nods or "um-hmms." After the interview, based on the man's demeanor more than anything he said, Delia feels sure she won't get the job. She leaves the office almost in tears of frustration, having no idea why the man apparently dislikes her.

Wouldn't you know it, though? Delia receives a call from the executive several hours later offering her the job after all. Despite his body language—which Delia took personally and assumed meant he felt negatively about her—the man had assessed her professional criteria in a positive way. Delia might have avoided feeling despondent had she understood that her prospective boss's body language wasn't a sign of hostility or disapproval—it was just male behavior.

Needless to say, it isn't just men who miscommunicate their inner thoughts and feelings with confusing body language. Take this example of a salesman who meets with a female purchasing agent: Bobby, the salesman, is thrilled when the agent nods and smiles often during their meeting. What he didn't realize at first, but later found out when she didn't place an order, was that these signals were merely her way of letting him know she was listening to him.

As you can see from just these two examples, learning to better read body language can help prevent you from making all kinds of mistakes in interpretation. In the following sections I'll show you how to spot the cues ahead of time and avoid winding up with hurt feelings or worse.

Body Space

In many ways, men situate themselves within a room and within a conversation in order to establish dominance and control. First, men take up much more physical space than women do when they sit and stand—and that's not just because they tend to be taller and weigh more. Most men sit with their legs stretched out away from their bodies and often drape their arms around the chairs—empty or not—placed next to them. They also tend to fidget and shift their body positions more than women do during conversations or meetings.

Second, men sit much farther apart from one another and from women than their female counterparts, unless sexual intimacy is on the table. By positioning themselves in this way, they can visually scope out and assess the entire situation and their place in it. Men will often sit more at an angle and farther apart from the other person than women do, who usually sit directly in front of the other person. When listening, men tend to lean backward, providing less listener feedback through their body language than women, who are in the habit of leaning toward the speaker.

29

In contrast to their sitting positions, men tend to be "close talkers" when standing, often invading another's personal space, which is another way of establishing dominance. When walking, men are usually not the first ones to move out of a woman's way if a collision is about to occur, but rather assume that the woman will make the adjustment in her stride.

Hand Me This!

Men tend to gesture in a forceful, angular, and restricted manner, with their fingers together or pointed. To the average viewer—especially to the average *female* viewer—such an action may appear to be one of anger even if no such emotion exists. Women gesture in a lighter, more fluid manner, with their fingers apart and their hands moving in toward their bodies.

As discussed in Chapter 2, "What Do We Really Know About One Another?" men tend to touch other people more and in a more aggressive manner than women do. Backslapping, for instance, is far more common in men than in women.

Face It!

We've already mentioned the fact that women make more eye contact and smile more during conversations compared to their male counterparts. But what's just as telling is that men don't just sit there with blank expressions. They display more facial expressions that can be interpreted as negative than women do: They squint, furrow their brows, and tend to frown more when listening to a speaker. They may not be angry at all; in fact, their expressions reveal that they are attempting to listen intently. Overall, men use fewer facial expressions, provide fewer emotional reactions in feedback, and exhibit less emotional warmth. They even tend to clench their jaws more often than women do when they're in conversation.

As they did when they were little girls speaking to one another, observing every minute detail, women are more likely than men to make direct eye contact and to lean forward into a conversation. Men tend to cock their heads to the side and look at the other person from an angle, just as studies show that little boys tend to do when they speak with one another. This is evident during positive interaction between the sexes. When the mood or message is negative, on the other hand, men tend to stare more in response, while women tend to avert their gazes.

Communication Breakdown!

Men take note! Clenching your jaw gives the impression that you're angry, so try to avoid this gesture when the goal is to encourage or engage the person with whom you're conversing. Make sure you keep your back teeth from touching and your jaw relaxed while you listen to your companion.

Male Versus Female Conversational Tones

In Chapter 2, I discussed many of the gender differences in communication techniques. In this section, we take another look at those and others.

Have you ever noticed that most men have difficulty with the art of conversation, which by nature involves an exchange of information and a back-and-forth flow of ideas? Studies indeed show that men have a habit of lecturing or conducting monologues rather than having dialogues with their companions—especially their female companions. This approach, as well as the other stylistic techniques discussed in this section, allow men to come across as far more self-confident and direct than their female counterparts, who appear more tentative and less sure of themselves.

Indeed, men tend to be less verbose than women, and make more direct, simple statements such as, "Open the door," rather than beating around the bush or cloaking their needs in artful language, such as, "It would be nice if you would open the door for me, please." Men use fewer intensifiers ("so," "very," "much"). Instead of saying "This is so fantastic. It was a very exciting night," most men would simply leave it at "This is fantastic. It was an exciting night." Unlike women, men tend to utilize fewer verbs that define their psychological states ("I hope," "I wish," "I feel"). As discussed in Chapter 2, men use more declarative sentences, which come across as far more confident and secure than the sentences with tag endings that women use.

Another way men's speech patterns indicate confidence is their use of more quantifiers such as "always," "never," "none," or "all." Women, on the other hand, may use more tentative qualifiers such as "kind of" or "a bit." And men rarely turn what is supposed to be a declarative statement into a question by making an upward inflection of the last few words.

Men make simple, straightforward commands, such as, "Hand me that book," while women will usually couch their requests with more endearments, such as, "Honey, hand me that book, would you?" Men rarely use adjectives of adoration when describing things, whereas females often use terms such as "precious," "adorable," "charming," and "sweet." Men tend to engage in more cursing vocabulary and use stronger expletives, while women might use milder ones ("crud!" "darn it!" "shoot!"). Men also use more slang and jargon than women do.

Because men do not open their jaws as wide as women do when they speak, they tend to sound a bit more nasal than women. They also speak louder than women and have more monotonous tones. In fact, as mentioned in Chapter 2, men use only three vocal tones and pitches, while women use more than five. This pattern of speech and tonality fosters the perception that men are more authoritative than women, especially since the higher-pitched breathiness of some women's speech can sound grating to both male and female listeners. On the other hand, men tend to have more choppy staccato tones, often making them sound abrupt and less approachable, while women have breathier and more flowing tones. Men use loudness to emphasize points, whereas women use a higher pitch or a vocal inflection to emphasize points, especially when they become emotional.

How We Act

"It's not what you say that counts, it's what you do," and "actions speak louder than words," are adages we've all heard and taken to heart. Well, even in our behavior, men and women send and receive very different messages. For instance, men offer fewer compliments but joke more, while women give compliments routinely as a form of bonding, especially with other women, and rarely joke with one another.

In fact, men will perform more practical jokes and tease in an attempt to show affection, while women are much more direct in their efforts to be warm, open, and friendly. Although in some cases the use of humor to show affection is appropriate, often it is a distancing technique, allowing men to avoid getting close to other people.

Communication Breakdown!

Don't overreact when a man teases you. It may be his honest attempt at showing you affection; or, on the other hand, it could be his way of distancing himself from you to avoid getting too close before he's ready to form a deeper relationship with you.

Men tend to be more task-oriented, asking what specific action needs to be done, whereas women are more maintenance-oriented, asking if everyone is all right. Thus, in a business meeting, men will be more concerned with what is being done, while women will be more concerned about how people feel about what's being done. Men talk more about what they did, what they are going to do, and where they went. Women instead tend to talk more about how they feel about what they did or are about to do.

Men will tend to talk more about themselves and their accomplishments, while women will talk less about or even minimize their accomplishments. This can be a problem between the sexes, because women can misinterpret men's discussions of their accomplishments as obnoxious, whereas men can misinterpret women's tendencies to minimize their accomplishments as a lack of ability. Men look at things more critically and analytically than women, who tend to view problems and solutions from a more emotional perspective. There is no right or wrong way to look at issues, but because men and women approach problems in different ways, it may be more difficult for both parties to reach a conclusion and a solution.

One of the most problematic differences between men and women is the way they first react to a problem. Men will immediately try to solve the problem, while a woman will first be empathetic and talk through the feelings surrounding the problem. Men may misinterpret a woman's empathy as competing and not listening or even going around in circles and not dealing with the relevant issues at hand, while women may misinterpret men's immediate solution attempts at direct and immediate problem-solving as men being bossy and controlling.

Women tend to hold grudges more than men and shed tears more when they feel hurt or frustrated, while men tend to yell and shout when they feel under fire. In arguments, women will usually bring up things from the past, while men will usually stick to the problem at hand. This tendency makes it difficult to fully resolve conflict because a man feels that a woman will always haunt him with his past mistakes or problems. When a woman turns on the tears during an argument, most men don't know what to do. They look at it as the woman "hitting below the belt" and gaining an unfair advantage. Most women don't usually cry for effect in order to get their way, but instead cry out of frustration and anger. Most women are not verbally equipped to defend themselves, which is why they resort to tears.

Women will often apologize after a confrontation, even if it isn't their fault, while men usually will not. Women are not admitting defeat but are merely stating that they are sorry that a fight and argument ensued. When men do apologize, they will often use less emotion. Women also tend to take verbal rejection much more personally than men do, which makes many men feel as though they have to walk on eggshells around women and can't really tell women what's wrong or what they don't like. The fact that a woman takes rejection more personally has a lot to do with her upbringing and conditioning as a child.

Finally, men have more difficulty expressing intimate feelings, whereas women have less difficulty. Once again, this has a lot to do with childhood conditioning. Men tend to be a lot more blunt, while women tend to be more diplomatic when they make negative statements to another person or break bad news.

The Power Is Yours

Well, there you have some of the major differences in communication techniques—physical, emotional, behavioral, and verbal—between men and women. Now you can see why it's so difficult for us to communicate with each other, why it seems so very apt, in the now infamous words of author John Gray, Ph.D., that *"men are from Mars and women are from Venus."*

Let's take a look at some of the things we've learned so far:

Men	Women
Take up more physical space	Sit close together in groups
Fidget and shift	Sit still
Lean backward while listening	Lean forward into conversations
Look at companions sideways or often from an angle	Make direct eye contact
Gesture forcefully	Make more gentle gestures
Speak more monotonously, frequently mumbling	Have a wider range of vocal intonations
Make declarative statements and commands	Use qualifiers and make requests
Clench their jaws	Smile more often
Tease and joke to show affection	Use endearments to show affection
Rarely use tears to show emotion	Become teary more often when in emotional situations

continues

continued

Men	Women
Leap to solve problems quickly	Empathize first, then seek solutions
Rarely apologize for any interaction	Apologize for confrontations, no matter who instigated them

I hope that you, like so many of my clients and readers, will find it comforting to realize that so much of what comes across as negative communication is really just a matter of gender-related communication style. On the other hand, if you feel a twinge of guilt over starting an argument or getting mad at someone unnecessarily, you don't have to beat yourself up about it. Instead you can easily move on.

Don't forget what you've learned in this chapter, however. Take a look at the list of men's and women's communication characteristics from time to time to remind yourself of how different you are from members of the opposite sex. By doing so, you'll not only help yourself avoid misunderstandings, but you might even be able to help others see the truth about men and women. When friends tell you about disappointments, arguments, fights, and disagreements, you'll be ready to show them how much of those kinds of upsets are really matters of man/woman differences in communications rather than personal affronts.

Knowledge is indeed power, and knowledge of the differences between the sexes gives you the power to see through a lot of confusion. You can see how easy it is to misinterpret members of the other sex if you don't fully understand what they are doing. In the next section of this book, I'll show you some of the reasons—biological, cultural, and social—that help explain why men and women look at the world and communicate their emotions and viewpoints in such different ways.

The Least You Need to Know

➤ Men often use body language—such as leaning away or glancing around the room—that seems to be dismissive. In fact, it may just be habit.

➤ Men take up more space than women do when they sit, and they stand closer to others when standing and talking than women do.

➤ Men tend to clench their jaws and use fewer facial gestures when speaking. Women are more facially expressive.

➤ Knowing the differences in communication styles can help men and women understand one another better and form more productive relationships.

Part 2

Understanding the Great Nature/Nurture Debate

The argument is as old as humankind: Are we born with all of our attributes intact, including our style of communicating and our way of looking at the world? Or is more rather than less of who we are as adults dependent on the way our parents and society molded us as we grew up?

In this part of the book, we'll look at the nature/nurture debate as it stands today. You'll see how much of our personalities scientists believe is "hardwired" and how much is malleable and changeable throughout life. We'll also explore the ways in which our innate characteristics may affect the way we communicate "trans-gender."

Chapter 4

The Role of Mother Nature

In This Chapter

➤ The science of genetics

➤ How hormones influence development

➤ The brains of boys and girls

➤ Myths and facts about "male" and "female" brains

So far, you've read about some of the differences between men and women that make life and relationships in the twenty-first century quite a challenge. When you argue with your spouse or your best friend of the opposite sex, you might blurt out, "You're just like your father," or, "Isn't that just like a woman?" What you in fact may really be saying, in your angst, is that you recognize some specific traits that just might be hereditary, and thus something beyond our control.

Is there something biological that makes men and women so seemingly different in their approaches to communication and to life in general? Could there be something in our DNA and in our basic physiological make-ups that causes girls to want to talk things over and boys to want to fight it out? Is there something hardwired into our brains that determines the way we think as men and women? That's what we'll explore in this chapter. We start with a look at the brain and then move on to a discussion of how genetics might influence this crucial communication organ's development along gender lines.

The Human Brain: Male and Female

The human brain is a remarkable communications network. Every emotion we feel, action we take, and physiological function we perform is processed through the brain. The brain itself is divided into several large regions, each responsible for certain activities. The brain is made up of billions of neurons (brain cells) that communicate with each other and with nerve cells throughout the body, through a complex interaction.

The World of the Brain

The largest components of the brain are the cerebrum and the cerebellum. The cerebrum consists of four lobes: the parietal, the frontal, the occipital, and the temporal. It is further divided into the left and right hemispheres. The cerebral hemispheres control such functions as speech, memory, and intelligence, and—thanks to remarkable advances in medical technology—scientists have been able to identify specific regions within the cerebrum responsible for specific activities and functions.

Briefly, the right hemisphere of the brain controls the movement of the left side of the body. It also has been reported to control analytical and perceptual tasks, such as judging distance, size, speed, or position, and seeing how parts are connected to wholes. The left hemisphere controls the movement of the right side of the body and controls speech and language abilities for most people.

Until recently, most scientists believed that men and women pretty much used the brain in the same way, and that any differences in communication skills or preferences came as a result of social conditioning. But more recent research shows that the story is a bit more complicated than that. Recent studies have shown that men use certain parts of one part of their brains for speech and language function while women use several specified parts of both sides of their brains for speech and language function. In essence, women use more of their brains for the same function than men use.

Gender Pathways

For instance, one study performed at the Yale University School of Medicine revealed that men and women may use different parts of the brain for the same purpose. Using high-tech scans to measure brain activity, the scientists asked men and women to perform a certain verbal task. They found that men used one region—the frontal lobe of the left hemisphere—while the women tended to use parts of both hemispheres. Other studies hint that biological differences also may help explain why men are better at reading maps and women are better at remembering details, among other gender-specific preferences.

As you'll see in this chapter, such gender differences may arise because of the way male and female brains develop in utero, under the influence of genetics and hormones. Then the existing neural networks are fostered and maintained as the socialization process reinforces certain behaviors. For instance, a biological factor in the brain may make it easier for boys (in general) to learn math, and then the methods used to teach math reinforce the biological trait by working the neural pathways already in place.

XX and XY: Genetics 101

In the most simple terms possible, a new life begins to develop when a sperm cell merges with (or fertilizes) an egg cell to create a new cell called a zygote. The zygote further divides over and over again until it develops into an embryo. From the very moment of conception, the zygote contains within it all of the genetic information it needs to grow and develop into an embryo, a fetus, a baby, and finally a full-grown adult. This information is stored in our cells in structures called *chromosomes*.

What I Mean Is ...

A **chromosome** is a microscopic long, thin, threadlike substance that carries the genes that convey hereditary characteristics.

Each normal zygote has 46 pairs of chromosomes: 23 from the female and 23 from the male. While 22 of these chromosome pairs help determine eye color, hair color, height, and other characteristics, the twenty-third pair of chromosomes is solely responsible for determining sex. These are called sex chromosomes, or "X" and "Y" chromosomes. A female has two X chromosomes; a male has one X and one Y chromosome.

Interestingly enough, the sperm cell carries the information that determines the sex of this new life: All eggs contain just X chromosomes, so if a sperm contributes another X chromosome, the embryo will be female, and if it contributes a Y chromosome, the embryo will be male.

During the first few weeks of development, the embryo is sexually undifferentiated and has the basic structures needed to develop as either sex. However, if the embryo has the genetic information of a male, the embryo begins to produce testosterone, the primary male hormones, at about six weeks. These male hormones then bathe the organs and cells of the body—including the brain—helping the embryo develop male characteristics. In the absence of male hormones, the female embryo develops female characteristics. Later in the development process, female hormones, including progesterone and estrogen, are produced that will affect development as well.

The Role of Hormones

As you can see, the presence or absence of certain hormones is crucial in sexual differentiation. If a child is to develop as a male, he must have not only the genetic makeup of a male embryo, but also the hormones. A fetus that is genetically male but lacks male hormones may be born looking like a female. The reverse is true for genetic females influenced by male hormones.

Researchers have discovered that hormones not only influence physical characteristics; they are responsible for "masculinizing" or "feminizing" the developing brains in utero, which predisposes little boys and little girls to look at the world differently as they grow up. At UCLA, researcher Roger Gorski found that when female rats were injected with testosterone, they became more aggressive. Similar results occurred with female monkeys at the University of Wisconsin primate laboratory. They were injected with testosterone when they were in the womb. When they were born, they behaved more like male monkeys than female monkeys—they fought more and were highly aggressive. Studies also show that about one in 10,000 females has a genetic condition called CAH (congenital adrenal hyperplasia) that causes them to be born genetically female but bathed in male hormones. When interviewed, most of these females report that they preferred "boyish" or "aggressive" play behavior as children. Psychological studies also show that these girls prefer more male-oriented toys as well.

As we'll discuss in Chapter 5, "The Role of Mother Nurture," and throughout the book, it's clear that environmental and social factors also influence behavior. But even when the two influences overlap, the hormonal influence can be dominant. For example, many parents who report never having given their children toy guns have observed aggressive behavior in them anyway. Reports are common that four-, five-, and six-year-olds make toy guns and ammunition out of carrots and other pointed objects, even if they haven't been exposed to weapons or violence in the past. These findings lead many to believe that there may be a neurological or hormonal element that causes males to engage in such play activity.

These differences in the ways male and female embryos develop are not just abstract biological facts, but rather may have a direct impact on adult behavior. For example, men and women may handle stress and aggression so differently as adults because of the way their brains developed in utero. Men may become more physically agitated than women during stressful situations because of an increase in testosterone levels. Women may become more emotional and may even have greater memory loss when there is a lack of the female hormone estrogen.

He Says, She Says

While aggression has both a hormonal and behavioral component, studies show that nurturing is not related to hormones; it is primarily learned. Men can be capable nurturers if raised in a nurturing environment. And women are not necessarily inherently good nurturers. Harry Harlow's famous experiments at the University of Wisconsin confirmed that female monkeys raised in isolation were less effective at nurturing their young than those who weren't raised in isolation, regardless of their hormone levels.

There's Only One Brain!

Lately there has been a lot of talk in the media about the "male brain" and the "female brain." Labels like these make great fodder for talk shows, but the truth about the matter is far more complicated.

As I mentioned at the beginning of the chapter, the brain is not a simple organ. It is a highly evolved and complex integrated structure composed of neurons that run deep within its numerous layers. Certainly, the brain has a right side that is largely responsible for cognitive thinking and a left side that is mainly responsible for receptive and expressive language, but the brain is an integrated unit. There are so many deep interconnections that it is difficult to say that one side of the brain is responsible for only one function. Its intricate operations cannot be adequately described by lumping them into two categories like male/female or left/right.

However, thanks to the scientific advances that make studying the intricate inner workings of the brain possible, we can now see that there are gender differences in the ways our brains work.

Male Brain Development

I have often counseled mothers who panicked because their young sons have not developed the speech and language skills to the level their daughters had already developed at the same age. The mothers are relieved to learn that boys tend to develop their speech and language skills at a slightly slower rate than girls do. As research shows, the left side of a girl's brain grows a little faster than does a boy's, causing increased development in verbal functioning.

Bridging the Gap

Don't be upset if your son starts speaking later than your daughter does. It may be because the left side of the girl's brain, which contains the centers for speech and language, has developed a little faster than your son's did. The good news is that he will eventually catch up!

As infant and toddler perceptual studies show, boys tend to be more interested in objects and nonhuman visual patterns than girls are. They have a tendency to fixate longer on visual displays and have a greater aptitude in manual dexterity and perceptual motor skills than do little girls of the same age. In terms of brain function and development, as measured through standardized testing, two-year-old boys seem to be better than girls at "visual decoding": pointing at objects when they hear the name of the objects. The visual component is paramount in the boys' brain development.

The other side of the coin is that boys tend to develop the right side of their brains faster than do girls, which means that their visual/spatial, logical, and perceptual development occurs earlier. As a result, young boys tend to be better in mathematics, problem-solving, building things, and putting puzzles together than are girls of the same age.

Female Brain Development

Numerous studies have shown that newborn girls make sounds more often than newborn boys do, and during the first few years of their development, little girls make a larger variety of sounds than little boys do. Little girls tend to have better pronunciation, read earlier, excel in memory at a younger age, and have a higher aptitude for foreign languages than boys do, because the left side of their brains appear to develop more rapidly than their male counterparts'.

As infant girls develop, they tend to be interested in toys with faces. They tend to smile and point to facial features and prefer to play with stuffed animals and dolls, while infant boys of the same age tend to be drawn to blocks or any toy that can be manipulated.

Research into this fascinating area of study continues at a rapid pace—and nothing is yet settled when it comes to fully understanding male and female brain development and physiology. Several studies show that female and male children eventually catch up with one another in their neurological development and thus should have no differences in function. However, other studies suggest that women continue to use the left side of their brains to a larger extent than men do even as adults, while men utilize the right side of their brains more than their female counterparts. Studies also show that there is less specialization in the visual-spatial skills, which, in girls, overlaps between the two hemispheres (usually up until age 13, possibly continuing even later). Boys, on the other hand, have visual-spatial skills localized in the right side of their brains by the time they are six years old.

He Says, She Says

Brain differences are prevalent when males and females are children. Studies using electrical sensors show that, when listening to music and stories, boy and girl babies use different sides of their brains. Differences in brain responses may continue into adulthood as recent research has further discovered.

Neurologists who specialize in the structural differences between male and female brains have found that the *corpus callosum* (a band of fiber connecting the right and the left sides of the brain) is larger and wider in women than in men. Although much more research needs to be done in this area, the implications with regard to the neurology of sex differences may account for why men and women are better at different cognitive tasks.

What I Mean Is ...

The **corpus callosum** is a band of fiber connecting the right and left sides of the brain.

Why do these differences matter? According to some neurologists, they may explain why men and women use different parts of their brains even while performing similar tasks. This tendency is particularly evident when looking at how men and women stroke patients recover. Apparently, women tend to use both the right and left hemisphere equally after a stroke, whereas men rely almost exclusively on the left hemisphere, which may explain why men tend to take longer to recover than women.

Baby Doll Versus Keep on Truckin'

Once a baby is born, the gender differences in behavior and development continue. In one study, a group of boy and girl infants were given a special toy consisting of a doll's head placed on a set of four wheels. There was a significant difference in the boys' and girls' reactions to the toy. When the girls were shown the toy they smiled, cooed, and pointed to the facial features of the doll. Conversely, the boys paid little or no attention to the doll's features. Instead, they rolled the toy across the crib or threw it out of their crib.

This study clearly illustrates how the male and female infants' brains operate on a neurological level. Because of hemispheric development, the left side of the brain, which processes facial discrimination and the ability to communicate, appears to be more developed in girl infants. The right side of the brain, which processes visual-spatial components, appears to be more neurologically developed in male infants.

From the ages of six to eight, boys also show neurological advantages in terms of their visual-spatial aptitudes. In boys' drawings made at this age, we see objects and the beginnings of three-dimensional structures (such as airplanes and cars). This is not the case with girls, who have a greater tendency to draw faces and body images and animal figures.

As most people know, chromosomes are the most basic determinant of sex, but hormones also play a significant role in defining behavioral development within genders. Because behavioral differences between the sexes are present so early on in human development, scientists conclude that they are the result of biological differences, not culturally based. But of course nurture is important, too, and that's what we'll turn to in the next chapter.

The Least You Need to Know

➤ Chromosomes are one factor in defining sex differences, but not the only factor. Hormones also play an important role.

➤ Although there are distinct differences in the way men and women use the brain, there is no definitive "male" or "female" brain.

➤ Boys tend to have better aptitude in three-dimensional and mechanical perceptions than girls.

➤ Girls tend to have better aptitude for memory, pronunciation, and speech and language skills than boys do.

Chapter 5

The Role of Mother Nurture

In This Chapter

➤ The power of cultural expectations

➤ Double standards in males and females

➤ Nursery rhyme stereotypes and sex-role expectations

➤ Toys for boys (and girls) and how they influence socialization

---

In the last chapter, we made a good argument for the role of "Mother Nature" in the differences between the sexes. It seems reasonable that one's biology, genetics, hormones, and neurochemistry would exert some influence—perhaps even a great deal of influence—on how men and women grow up viewing the world. Some scientists, however, reject the idea that men and women are biologically hard-wired to be different. According to this theory, it is the environment and our culture that creates the most profound differences between men and women, at least when it comes to the roles we play in society and the way we communicate and relate to each other.

Feminists and others, for instance, feel that the way parents treat boys and girls encourages or discourages certain traits in children and thus allows these differences to continue. Why, they ask, aren't boys allowed to cry much? Why aren't they hugged, kissed, caressed, or fondled as much as girls are? And why are girls often discouraged from performing physically demanding activities, even when they show talent for them? That's what we'll explore in this chapter.

Cultural Sex-Pectations

The differences in how we perceive boy and girl infants are illustrated by several studies that show, among other things, that infant boys are handled more, and more roughly, by their fathers and other males, than are female infants, who are often barely touched by the men in their lives. Infant boys more often receive nicknames related to their potential physical prowess such as "little football stud" or "big strong boy." Infant girls, on the other hand, are spoken to in more gentle tones and given attributes related to their physical beauty, such as "my little beauty queen" and "my sweet angel." Parents and others tell little girls that they're "pretty," "beautiful," "adorable," and "sweet," while boys don't usually receive such compliments.

Communication Breakdown!

If you are the parent of an infant or toddler, it's not too early to teach yourself about how your behaviors can limit your child's possibilities. Pay attention to how seemingly innocent and well-intentioned actions and words can cause real pain in your children's lives.

In fact, a study at a major university shows how differently we all perceive boy and girl infants. A group of adults were placed in a room with infant boys and girls. In every trial, both men and women spoke in louder voices to boy infants than they did to girl infants. When they spoke to the girl infants, their voices were softer. They made more cooing sounds to the infant girls and used phrases such as "you are so sweet," "look at you, little doll," and "you're a little sweetheart." The girls were stroked and caressed much more, while the boys were handled more roughly. Boys were also told things such as "hey, big guy."

Preconceived notions of a child's sex role are clearly illustrated in the classic Rodgers and Hammerstein musical *Carousel*. When the main character in the play, Billy Bigelow, learns that his wife is about to give birth to a child, he sings a song about "My Boy Bill." His voice is loud, vibrant, and full of energy as he belts out what he and his future son will do together. All of a sudden, realizing his child might be a girl, Billy Bigelow starts singing in a soft, delicate tone.

Even though we don't always do it on a conscious level, it is common for us to react like Billy Bigelow and the people in the university study. We don't mean to treat either group of infants unfairly, but we've been conditioned to do so throughout our whole lives. To change our viewpoint and our reactions will take years.

Numerous studies have shown that girls smile more than boys do, just as women smile almost twice as often as men do, probably because they've been conditioned to do so. Researcher Carol Malatesta, who videotaped facial expressions of mothers and their infants during play, observed that when baby girls showed anger, their mothers showed greater facial disapproval than when baby boys showed anger. The message this sends? Little girls learn early on in life that they shouldn't get angry even though it is a natural emotion.

He Says, She Says

One of the most difficult issues women professionals face is anger management. Because so many young girls have been conditioned to keep their anger in, act "ladylike," and be "good little girls," they have suffered the consequences, including developing stress-related ailments like cancer and heart disease. The bottom line is that it is okay to get angry and even yell at a person if appropriate. See my book, *The Complete Idiot's Guide to Verbal Self-Defense* (Alpha Books, 1999).

Boys Will Be Boys

A three-year-old girl is playing on the playground and ends up biting another child. The mother and father are informed of her actions. What happens? A three-year-old boy is playing on the playground and bites another child. The mother and father hear what he did. What happens?

Would you be surprised if the parents' reactions were different for the same misbehavior? Well, don't be. It's not uncommon for parents to ignore or minimize what the little boy did. They might say, "Boys will be boys," or "Well, he's just teething." In fact, they might even blame the other child for having his or her leg in front of their son's mouth in the first place.

Now, if their daughter had been the little criminal, the parents would react quite differently. They'd probably scold her a dozen times by telling her that her behavior was "not ladylike" and that "little girls don't act like that."

In our society today, boys have a completely different set of rules to follow and, from early on, their parents and teachers generally tolerate behavior they wouldn't tolerate from girls. In grade school, boys can push one another. They can shout, make noise, and even say bad words, but are usually just considered rowdy or overly energetic. Let a girl exhibit the same behavior on the schoolyard, however, and she is immediately labeled a behavior problem, a "bad girl," or "emotionally disturbed." Little girls are simply not supposed to behave like little boys. As a result, what is a little girl to do when she wants to roughhouse and play around? Why should she be conditioned to keep it in and hold back, all for the sake of being a "lady"?

Communication Breakdown!

Beware of using certain phrases with young children. It's appropriate to hold your little boy or girl to good behavioral standards. But when you say that she should act "more like a lady" when she's doing something a boy would be praised for (like adventurous behavior), or that he should act "more like a boy" when he is showing emotions, you are crossing a line.

The Crimes of Nursery Rhymes

Nursery rhymes—little ditties indiscriminately passed down from one generation to the next—are responsible for creating perhaps some of the most unacceptable gender stereotypes. Not only do they play a role in the way parents perceive—and thus treat—their children, but also, finally, in the way children perceive themselves. Often these rhymes provide a child the first opportunities to identify and relate to his or her gender. For example, the child hears:

> *There was a little girl who had a little curl*
> *Right in the middle of her forehead.*
> *And when she was good she was very very good,*
> *And when she was bad she was horrid.*

Experts agree that what most children who hear this rhyme relate to is the concept of being "good" or "bad." More than likely, the first question the child asks is: What did the little girl do that was so horrid?

Did she exhibit "male" behavior such as yelling or pushing? Did exhibiting stereotypically male behavior make her appear horrid as a little girl? What if the character in the nursery rhyme was a little boy? What would he have had to have done to be termed "horrid"?

Without our even realizing it, these rhymes are continuing to reinforce our stereotypic sex-role expectations.

Little Miss Muffet, Get Off Your Tuffet

The same applies to other nursery rhymes, such as the famous one about Little Miss Muffet:

> *Little Miss Muffett sat on her tuffet*
> *Eating her curds and whey.*
> *Along came a spider*
> *And sat down beside her*
> *And frightened Miss Muffet away.*

What message does this send to little boys and girls? Is it that it's alright—in fact expected—that girls will fear creepy crawling spiders? If Master Muffet was sitting on his tuffet, he most likely would be expected to act more aggressively and smash the spider with the spoon, and not flee from the spider. If he ran away from the spider, he would be considered a "sissy," and that was something he wouldn't be conditioned to be.

Or think of the popular rhyme:

> *What are little girls made of?*
> *Sugar and spice and everything nice.*
> *What are little boys made of?*
> *Snakes and snails and puppy dog tails.*

This rhyme continues to feed the notion that little girls are made of "good" things like sugar and spice, but that little boys, in turn, are made of things that are not as good as the girls. In fact, they are made of creepy crawlers, slimy creatures, and animal parts. How does it impact a child's early perception of their self-esteem?

Here's another rhyme that puts boys in a bad light:

> *Georgie Porgie Puddin Pie*
> *Kissed the girls and made them cry.*
> *When the boys came out to play*
> *Georgie Porgie ran away.*

I believe that this little ditty contributes to several stereotypes we'd rather our children dismiss. Little boys who grow up hearing it may end up thinking it's okay to disrespect girls by kissing them and making them cry. And why did he run away when the boys came out to play? Was he afraid of them? Was he feeling guilty that he did something wrong to the girls and that the other boys would beat him up when they found out? It is very disturbing to a child to know that another child upset some little girls and made them cry.

Here's another one of equal distaste:

> *Peter Peter Pumpkin Eater*
> *Had a wife and couldn't keep her.*
> *He put her in a pumpkin shell*
> *And there he kept her very well.*

This nursery rhyme shows how a wife has been relegated to the status of an object that can be kept prisoner by a husband. I sincerely believe that parents should not teach such derogatory stereotypes. They do not engender positive self-worth, identification, and esteem in the children who hear them.

Bif! Boom! Bad Cartoons!

Another way society perpetuates inaccurate—and ultimately undermining—gender stereotypes is through the cartoon images it produces for its children. A study at the University of California, Davis, found that female cartoon characters often perpetuated such obvious and unflattering stereotypes as the ...

➤ Frumpy housewife.

➤ Damsel in distress.

➤ Sexpot heroine.

➤ Helpless senior citizen.

➤ Swooning cheerleader.

Most male cartoon characters, on the other hand, tend to be violent and aggressive, use firearms, try to hurt the other characters, or try to escape from a character who is attempting to harm them.

Furthermore, there are few story lines within "'toon land" that depict men and women as equals, or in which women have positions of responsibility or leadership. Even in the most popular—and potentially progressive—children's programming, such as *Sesame Street,* few of the main characters are female.

Bedtime Brainwashing

Perhaps one of the most popular bedtime stories is "Snow White and the Seven Dwarfs," in which Prince Charming finds a "beauty" sleeping in the forest, only to kiss her for no reason at all. She wakes up, kisses the man, and voilà—she finds her man. No fuss, no muss! The two live happily ever after! Another fairy tale that has ruined the lives of little girls who have grown up waiting for their "Prince Charming" is "Cinderella." Little girls have bought into the fantasy of becoming a combination of Snow White and Cinderella, not because they work hard or do something constructive with their lives. No, a girl gets her Prince Charming because she happens to be beautiful, has the right size body, and the perfect feet to fit into the "glass slipper."

These are negative stories for little boys, too. They suggest that the boys have to do all the work in relationships. Why can't the boy dream of having his own Princess Charming to come along and sweep him off his feet? And should little girls think that as long as they are beautiful, they don't have to do anything else to live "happily ever after"?

Guess what? It's about time these stories are stopped, updated, or modified because they give false hope to both men and women. That is why psychologists' offices are filled with people who are still holding on to the illusions and unrealistic, idealized expectations of finding the Prince or the Princess Charming they read about in the pages of their fairy tales as children.

Toys Are *Not* Us!

Even the toys our children play with hold open the gap between the boys and the girls. In fact, even within the stores themselves the gap exists, with "boy" toys against one wall and "girl" toys against the other. Why aren't the electronic video toys that are so popular with boys popular with girls, too? Is it because they aren't being promoted properly? Are girls still encouraged through a barrage of advertising to play with their "dollies" and "make-up"? Is the peer pressure so strong to play with appropriate toys? Clearly, yes. And subliminal parental messages scream out for boys to play like boys and girls to play like girls; violating this would cause parents discomfort.

Perhaps all of us—but especially the parents among us—need to make a better effort to raise children who will hold both genders in equal esteem and understand one another more clearly. That means we have to allow girls and boys to share in each others' experiences as children. While girls and boys will gain a great deal from playing with members of their own gender, exposure to and acceptance of the games members of the opposite sex play—and the toys they use to play them—may foster greater understanding and perception throughout life.

She's Pretty as a Picture!

Interestingly enough, by the age of two or three, little girls concentrate on their appearance, including their clothing and, if mommy lets them into their vanities or purses, even their make-up. Unfortunately, when you look at how obsessive some girls have become about their physical appearance—note the rising levels of anorexia in girls of just four and six (according to *Newsweek*)—we have really gone overboard. But this concern about a female's physical beauty stems from girls' environment, from how girls are nurtured by their parents and other caregivers, as well from the media.

As I mentioned in the study earlier in this chapter, the people who were not initially aware of their child's sex and were told the infants were females practically all described their girl babies by saying, "She's so beautiful," "Look how gorgeous," and "She's so pretty." Certain ideals of beauty are established from infancy and are at a premium. As girls grow into women, they look to men to receive that reinforcement. The prettier girls are, the sooner they learn they get more men, and so physical appearance becomes girls' most valuable commodity.

If you're a woman, think back to your own experiences as a little girl. If you're like most of your sisters, you played "dress up" and "princess." You wore your mother's make-up and jewelry and tried to look beautiful—or at least to live up to the ideal of beauty promulgated by society. As you grew into your preteen and teen life, you went even further to live up to that ideal. But it all starts in the crib. It is all about approval and basic classical conditioning.

Talkin' Just Like Her Mom

And now we come to the crux of the matter—at least when it comes to how men and women relate as they get older. Studies show that by age three and four, little girls have incorporated several "female" traits into the way they speak. In one study of 35 nursery school students, linguists found the presence of "female" patterns of speech in the little girls on a consistent basis. Some of the female traits little girls showed were the presence of tag endings for what should have been declarative statements. For instance, a little girl was more likely than a little boy to say, "She has a pretty dress, doesn't she?" rather than, "She has a pretty dress." Girls were also more likely than their male counterparts to use terms of endearments, such as "my sweet" or "baby doll."

Such usage may be due to the fact that a mother is more likely to use "female" terms when talking to her infant baby girl than she is when talking to her son. Thus the little girl identifies with these terms from very early in her life and incorporates them into her speech as she grows older.

He Says, She Says

Some speech patterns found early in life among little girls are the use of terms of endearment ("sweetie," "honey") and tag endings (ending statements with questions such as "doesn't she?" or "right?"). This may develop as little girls play together and seek approval and engage in continuous verbalizations that reinforce how one another feels about specific play situations. In essence, little girls engage in very polite play with one another while constantly checking in with one another and making sure the others are okay. They engage one another in mutual conversation on a continuous basis.

Improving Gender Role Models

The good news with regard to understanding one another is that, as children get older, they become more exposed to appropriate gender role models, both in the media and in real life, and we will continue to see this more and more. We rarely see "typical" housewives like June Cleaver from *Leave It to Beaver* or Laura Petrie from *The Dick Van Dyke Show,* who stay at home looking after the kids, appearing crisp and clean, while waiting for their husbands to "bring home the bacon and the paycheck."

Today, more and more women are the breadwinners, both because they desire the stimulation of outside work and because economic necessity demands their membership in the workforce. Many fathers are staying at home full-time and looking after the children, which represents a dramatic role reversal in our society. We are a changing society, with men and women taking on different roles personally and professionally.

And this change doesn't just start in adulthood. There are so many options available to boys and girls that were previously unavailable to them because of sexual stereotypes. For example, there are more and more girls involved in sports than ever before with the advent of soccer teams, baseball teams, and other athletic opportunities directed at women. In addition, girls are being more and more exposed to computers and technology than ever before. Boys, on the other hand, are taught that it's okay to play with dolls and stuffed animals.

As we can see from this chapter, there is indeed a strong environmental influence on the way we develop into our gender roles. In the previous chapter, I made a pretty convincing argument for the role of genetics in this matter. So which is correct? Is it nature or nurture that defines the roles we play in society and mitigates how we communicate with one another? Or is it, as researchers are discovering, a wonderful, integrated combination of the two? In the next chapter, we'll discuss the influence of both nurture and nature on male and female behavior and interaction.

The Least You Need to Know

➤ Cultural stereotypes have a tremendous impact on how boys and girls are treated and the behaviors they exhibit.

➤ Anyone who doubts the power of "nurture" should consider how differently boys and girls are treated when they swear, act in an aggressive manner, or play with dolls.

➤ Nursery rhymes can reinforce incredibly negative and limiting stereotypes (especially about girls).

➤ Toys are not just playthings; they can powerfully affect children's behavior.

Chapter 6

Nature Meets Nurture

In This Chapter

➤ When nature and nurture combine

➤ How infants develop language

➤ The role of intuition and the interrelation of nature and nurture

➤ The biology and environment of choosing your profession

So how do we explain these differences between men and women? Is it all hardwired into us? Is it all about training after we're born? Perhaps the argument that makes the most sense is that Mothers Nature and Nurture work together to create "typical" men and "typical" women. In this chapter, I will present some important issues relevant to gender differences that might be best explained by a combination of the nature and nurture theories. We'll start with a look at the way infants develop language and language skills.

The Root of the Problem

As I discussed in earlier chapters, girls develop language skills more rapidly than boys do, at least in early childhood. One reason is that the left side of the female brain, which is responsible for language acquisition, develops more rapidly than the left side of the male brain does. At first glance, it might be tempting to assume that this biological advantage explains completely the reason why girls learn language more quickly than boys, but that isn't necessarily the case.

One study, conducted by psychiatrist Michael Lewis, for instance, indicates that nurture—the way girls and boys are treated by their parents and caregivers—may play just as important a role as nature in this area of development. Specifically, Lewis noted that mothers repeatedly looked at and talked to their infant girls more often than they looked at or talked to their infant boys, at least until the children were two years of age. Could it be, then, that the mothers' increased level of interaction with their daughters—both their initial communication and the *positive reinforcement* they give them as they respond—is actually what spurs language development to occur more quickly in girls?

In fact, it's probably a combination of the two: Daughters obtain language skills early, and mothers may interact with them simply because they are thus more likely to get more of a response from their daughters than they are from their sons. And so the combination of genetics and environment may well play a major role in language development here.

What I Mean Is ...

Positive reinforcement refers to the positive response given to wanted behavior in order to promote that behavior in the future. If a baby receives a positive reaction from others when he or she smiles, the smiler quickly learns to associate smiling with happy behavior from others.

Aggression in Boys

As I've discussed, boys and girls develop different communication skills, language patterns, and behavior from an early age. You know already from Chapters 4, "The Role of Mother Nature," and 5, "The Role of Mother Nurture," most girls tend to look right at you and face you directly when they talk to you, and notice every detail in the world around them. Such tendencies have evolved because of an innate biological drive to do so based upon years of evolution (according to anthropologists) and because girls' behavior is reinforced by their parents and by society. Most boys, on the other hand, are quite a different story.

Listen to any conversation between little boys when they're playing together and you'll hear lots of phrases like "Gimme that" or "Go away!" Little girls, on the other hand, tend to use much more polite language, such as, "Please give that to me" or "Please stop bothering me." In part, this difference in gender communication styles comes from environmental influences, as discussed in Chapter 5. These influences include boys' own fathers, who speak to them using more command terms and fewer terms of endearment and politeness, as well as their peers, who reinforce this behavior and style of communication, as research has determined.

At the same time, however, we also know that males are more aggressive by nature (perhaps due to the influence of the male hormone testosterone), which is one reason why it appears to be difficult for many parents to teach young boys to cooperate and use proper manners on a consistent basis. In fact, many single parents in my practice have told me that, no matter how hard they try to drill manners into their sons and to get their sons to open up more and be more verbally communicative, they often fail to do so.

As well as being verbally more aggressive than are girls, boys also tend to play rough and to mimic violence in their games. Indeed, studies show that even when parents are careful to prevent their sons from owning toy guns or even viewing violent movies, boys end up playing war games by using guns made out of crayons, spoons, or other harmless toys. As is true for the use of aggressive language, this more aggressive play of boys probably results from a combination of nature—especially hormonal factors—and nurture, the examples set by their peers and from the media.

Bridging the Gap

Relax a little when it comes to choosing your children's playtime activities. It's natural for most little boys to play rough and for most girls to play house. To force them to do otherwise would be going against nature. However, a little gentle encouragement can go a long way in opening up your children's worlds to new activities and possibilities.

In the past, aggressiveness in the males of our species may have been a good quality to develop, because males traditionally fought wars, protected communities from enemies, and—even in the more modern business world—expected to compete for jobs and status. As a result, men also tend to take more risks than women do and, according to studies, are therefore 15 times more likely to die in an accident than women. Both aggressiveness and risk-taking may represent a continuation of the kind of behavior necessary to survive in the early days of man's evolution.

No matter how natural aggression may seem in our sons, it is best to teach them how to verbally communicate their aggression and anger as opposed to exhibiting it physically. In doing so, you'll help your son develop into a more communicative and verbally sensitive and caring individual. If more and more people did this, we'd eventually create a generation of men less likely to become violent and more likely to create open, communicative families and children of their own. This is especially true as more and more men stay at home and take a more active, intimate role in raising their children.

He Said, She Said

Is it toy makers who steer children to engage in stereotypic behavior by marketing dolls to nurturing girls and guns and violent computer games to aggressive boys? While it would be easy to blame toy companies, the innate traits that drive children to play with particular toys are so strong that when companies try to create different types of toys and market them in different ways, they lose millions of dollars. For example, toy companies have tried for years to sell computerized doll games for girls. Unfortunately, they have failed miserably.

Directions, Please!

If you're a woman reading this book, you've been there. You've been with a man who clearly gets lost on his way to some destination or other but insists on two seemingly contradictory ideas: First, he isn't lost at all and second, he can find his way out of this mess. While it's all too easy to blame this attitude on egotism and machismo, the fact is that biological factors may also have an influence. For instance, men tend to navigate through north and south and make mental maps to judge distance, while women tend to navigate via landmarks.

The truth is, when the man in your life says, "Don't worry, I can find it," he truly believes that statement. Because he uses mental maps to judge his progress, he truly thinks he's on the right track and that he'll end up where he wants to go.

In addition, however, there is an environmental, social component to this age-old tendency: Men are raised to be independent, to never need to ask for anything, and to be able to keep their families safe and on the right path, literally and figuratively. To ask for directions would make them look helpless and useless; thus, they'll go to great lengths in order to avoid what to them is humiliation. Perhaps that'll help you to become more tolerant the next time you're lost with the man in your life.

Details, Details, Details

Just as many women find a man's inability to ask for help frustrating, many men find it inconceivable that a woman can seemingly remember every little detail and fact that passes her way, including such things as birthdays and anniversaries. To most women, forgetting a birthday is an indication that the day doesn't hold any importance.

The truth is, men really don't remember as many details as women do, as studies have shown. In fact, a study at York University in Toronto, Canada, revealed that women could remember things in greater detail than men could. When men and women were put into a room individually and removed from the room after a few minutes, the women could recall more of the items inside the room than the men could recall. So when a man doesn't remember important dates or events in your life, it may not be deliberate or careless or a personal affront to you.

This tendency also spills over into the ways each gender tends to communicate. While women tend to load their stories and conversations with details, their male counterparts are much more terse. Part of the reason could be environmental, because women receive more encouragement for language and communication as infants and toddlers than boys do. And part of it may be genetic since, as we just discussed, men simply do not remember as many details and therefore cannot share them with others in conversation.

The Gender of Professions

Although more and more women are becoming doctors, lawyers, and business executives every day, and male nurses and teachers are more common as well, there are definite gender preferences when it comes to choosing professions. Consider these statistics: Eighty percent of all grade school teachers are women, close to 60 percent of all pediatricians are women, and the majority of real estate agents are women. Close to 95 percent of all architects are men and, until recently, most attorneys were men as well.

Why is gender such an issue when it comes to choosing professions? Well, as is true for most things, biological and environmental factors both have roles to play. Historically, both men and women have chosen professions that em-

Communication Breakdown!

Don't make assumptions about profession and gender, especially when it comes to encouraging your children to explore their futures. Every day, more and more professions open their doors to members of the opposite sex—just observe the increase in the number of house husbands and female business executives.

phasize or rely on their innate abilities—for instance, verbal skills for women (such as teaching) and aggressiveness and the ability to think in three-dimensional spatial terms for men (such as the law and architecture).

In addition, men have also tended to choose jobs that require upper-body strength that women—who even when fit are much physically weaker than men—are less able to perform. That includes athletics as well as jobs in the armed services, construction industries, and others. For example, the Los Angeles Fire Department secretly recorded female recruits in training and documented just how difficult tasks involving a great deal of upper-body strength (lifting heavy objects, climbing walls, carrying equipment, and chopping logs) were for most of them.

However, that doesn't mean these professions should forever be off-limits to women who may not have the physical prowess of men. For instance, while a female police officer may not be able to physically subdue a stronger male suspect, she may be able to talk him safely through a potentially violent situation better than her male partner. The best of all possible worlds would be one in which men and women learned to cooperate and work conjointly in performing jobs like these.

The Voice of Gender

For very definite biological reasons, women tend to have higher-pitched voices than men. For one thing, women have smaller vocal cords and *vocal tracts*. The greater the size of the vocal tract, the deeper the voice quality. Since the vocal tract is usually larger in males, men tend to have deeper and more resonant voices than women.

Unfortunately, if women's voices are too high, they can annoy and grate instead of soothe or inform—a fact that creates tension and disappointment among everyone involved. It can even lead to lower job performance and career expectations. Fortunately, with proper speech retraining, women can learn how to redirect their tones to sound more powerful and thus advance in the business world. Indeed, studies show that both males and females listen with greater attentiveness to women with lower voices than to women with higher voices.

What I Mean Is ...

The **vocal tract** is the modifier of speech sounds and contains the cheeks, lips, teeth (the buccal cavity), tongue, roof of the mouth, soft palate (oral cavity), vocal cords, pharynx—a muscular membranous tube that extends from the base of the skull to the sixth vertebra (pharyngeal cavity)—and nasal area (nasal cavity).

Reading Between the Lines!

As I discussed in Chapter 1, "Finding Common Ground in Gender Differences," women aren't really more intuitive than men—they simply notice and then recall details better than their male counterparts, for both biological and environmental reasons. This attention to detail makes women seem more intuitive because they often notice characteristics others might miss, such as a person's facial and vocal expressions and body language.

In addition, women develop certain neurological pathways earlier than men do, and thus become more sensitive to sounds that men can either ignore or do not appreciate. A woman is more likely to hear a baby cry from a distant room, for instance, and, by looking at the visual clues the baby gives about the source of his or her distress, a woman can usually discern what kind of care and comforting is needed. This trait dates back to our primitive ancestors, according to anthropologists. Women also tend to be more attentive and more aware of others' emotions and feelings than men, which may be due to early childhood conditioning. Little girls, and then women, are encouraged in this behavior by receiving positive reinforcement from their parents and caretakers throughout their development.

Nods of Approval

Their attention to detail and innate sensitivity to the needs of others combines in women with a tendency to display almost constant signs of approval and understanding—such as nodding and offering praise—during conversations. Of course, in addition to the biological imperatives that often trigger this behavior, women also do so because they were brought up to react that way. They received that kind of praise and attention when they were little girls, and learned to return it in order to boost their self-esteem and self-worth. Because they are more often interested in relationships and how they are perceived within those relationships, women want to make sure their conversation partners—especially if they're male—feel that they are well-perceived and comfortable. This learned behavior, established at a very early age, is based on the neurobiological differences between boys and girls; that is, girls develop their communication skills well ahead of males.

In the next chapter, you'll see how these biological and environmental factors influence the way girls and boys, women and men, develop their unique communication skills from early childhood through the teen years.

The Least You Need to Know

➤ Most behavior develops out of a combination of nurture and nature influences.

➤ Boy and girl infants develop language skills in different ways and at different times.

➤ Girls are especially adept at encouraging conversation in others.

➤ When we discuss how men and women choose professions, we should be aware of both inherent biological differences and social factors.

Part 3

"Mr. and Ms. Understanding"

When we deal with people of the opposite sex, misunderstandings seem to crop up all the time. Why? That's what we'll cover in the chapters that follow. First, we'll take a look at women from a man's perspective, and by doing so see the classic errors in interpretation he makes in interpreting what women want from a relationship and expect from communication. And then we'll turn the tables and show you women where you go wrong when it comes to understanding man's true nature and intentions. Finally, I'll put it all together for you in a chapter that gives you tons of tips on bettering your communication skills with the opposite sex. Be ready for a challenge, but I'm sure you won't be disappointed with the results!

Chapter 7

Learning the Language of Gender

In This Chapter

➤ Little boys talking big

➤ Girls have their secrets

➤ The need for respect

➤ The fine art of teasing

We have considered factors that cause a male or female child to behave in certain ways: his or her genetic or biological makeup and the environment in which he or she was raised. It seems pretty clear at this point that a combination of nature and nurture makes each of us into the people we are as adults.

Now it's time to look quite specifically at the ways we learn to communicate with one another—gender to gender—as we develop language skills. Again, although there are no absolutes and everyone is an individual, studies show that males and females do develop (or fail to develop) certain communication techniques and skills in this process. Because of these differences, we can end up saying things that members of the opposite sex hear as hurtful. In some cases, of course, our comments are intended this way. But in many other cases, the words are simply misinterpreted.

If we want to communicate effectively, we'll have to be equipped with some guidelines for becoming aware of the differences in how each sex speaks. The differences in how we speak arise from our upbringing, especially what kinds of communication each sex is allowed to get away with. As we'll see, what's most important to both sexes is to be accepted and respected by one another.

Socialization: Male and Female

Studies show that, even quite early in the socialization process, children learn to speak differently to and about one another depending on their gender.

For instance, boys tend to not look directly at the person to whom they're speaking, but instead will look off to the side or into the distance. Boys use commands rather than requests when they speak, such as "Gimme that" instead of "May I have that?" and "Sit down" rather than "Have a seat," far more than girls do. According to researchers Daniel Maltz and Ruth Borker, boys tend to play in larger groups than girls do, and in groups led by one member who organizes the members and tells them what to do. Boys also more often have winners and losers within their group activities. As a result of this kind of play, young boys learn far more than their female counterparts to communicate using the terms and style of competition.

Communication Breakdown!

Attention, parents! Keep an eye on the way you speak to and around your children. Often the way a mother speaks to her daughter is the way the daughter will speak to other girls. The same is true for the father, his son, and his son's friends. If you want your kids to communicate in an effective way, you'll have to set the example yourself!

In fact, such behavior may stem from the evolutionary need for organization that the males of early civilizations developed in order to survive the hunt for food. In addition, such hunting groups required a strict hierarchy, with each man on the team having a specific function. Finally, these groups also tended to reward the man who made the kill for food, thus promoting a competitive edge among the males of our species. Throughout the generations, these tendencies have been reinforced.

Because of this competitive edge, many little boys tend to be more self-centered than girls in their speech patterns. How often have you heard your sons, nephews, or male siblings yelling about who is best, biggest, or strongest?

An interesting study, which further supports the environmental aspect of communication development, examined how men spoke to their sons as compared to the speech patterns and language they used to talk to their daughters. As their sons grew older, fathers used more command terms with their sons, which in effect reinforced the style of communication boys learned with their peers.

On the other hand, as we've seen in earlier chapters, mothers tend to speak in more affectionate, polite terms with their daughters, which reinforces the ways girls communicate with each other.

The results of these socialization patterns are clear to any parent who tries to talk to his or her youngsters. Here is a typical conversation between a mother and her eight-year-old fraternal twins—a boy and a girl—who are in the same class together at school.

Mom:	What did you do in school today?
Boy:	Nothing.
Mom:	Nothing?
Boy:	Yep.
Mom:	Well, you had to do something. How were your classes?
Boy:	Okay.
Mom:	Just okay? Did you do anything or learn anything interesting?
Boy:	I dunno.
Mom:	What do you mean you don't know?
Boy:	[Shrugs his shoulders without speaking]
Mom:	Well, you had to do something?
Boy:	[Annoyed and shrugging his shoulders with his face contorted] I don't remember.
Mom:	How could you not remember what you did in school all day? You were there six hours!
Boy:	Mom, I don't remember. I wanna go play video games.
Mom:	Not 'til you tell me what you did at school.
Boy:	[Now really agitated] I told you I don't remember!

His sister, on the other hand, responded this way when asked the same series of questions:

Mom:	What did you do in school today?
Girl:	When Julie's mother dropped her off at school today, Julie showed us that her mother was pregnant and had a big stomach. Her mom let us feel the baby kicking. She knows it's gonna be a boy, and they are going to name the baby Sam. Then we had an announcement over the loudspeaker reminding everyone not to forget to have their parents sign their permission slips so we can go on our field trip so, Mom, you have to sign Tommy's and my permission slips before we go to school tomorrow.
	Oh yes, Lisa lost a tooth and she looks so funny and had this pink skirt on that looked like a ballerina skirt today with a striped stretch blouse that was yellow. She had her hair all mussed up

69

(I think her baby-sitter from Sweden fixed it for her). She looked so silly today. Everyone was laughing at her. My best friend Jenny and I felt bad for her. Lisa was crying in the bathroom. She told us a secret. I'm not supposed to tell anyone but I am going to tell you. Okay, Mom, so you can't tell anybody. Her mom and her dad are getting a divorce and all. She is so sad. We both cried for her. Jenny doesn't have a father and she told us a secret that she didn't know who her father is, even though she told everyone her mom and dad were divorced, so it wasn't so bad not having a dad.

In math class I sat next to Mitchell. He was so cute. I really like him, but I don't want too many people to know except Lisa and Nancy, otherwise everyone is gonna tease me. He's so nice to me. I got a C on the test, probably because Mitchell makes me nervous every time I sit next to him. Oh yeah, I almost forgot, we found out that Mr. O'Brien has a fake leg because Ted dropped some books and hit Mr. O'Brien's leg. Mr. O'Brien didn't say ouch or anything. It didn't even hurt him. We heard a funny sound when the books banged against his leg. That's when he told us he had a fake leg and he lost his real one when he was a soldier in Vietnam.

What a difference between the responses of an eight-year-old boy and an eight-year-old girl when they are asked the same question. Already, at this young age, boys and girls are so remarkably different. Girls' answers are filled with detail, observations, compassion, feelings, and personal information about relationships. Boys' conversation is much more terse, without detail, and concentrates on the here and now.

Now let's take a more in-depth look at the difference in styles between little boys and little girls, starting with the boys.

Boy Style

As I've reiterated several times throughout this book, studies do show that boys and men communicate in a way that's different from girls and women—which is why there remains a gender gap of confusion, resentment, and misunderstanding that many of us face. However, it also bears repeating that we remain individuals, with individual styles, challenges, and talents. Not all boys are closed-mouthed competitors and not all girls love to chat. That said, it's interesting to explore just how different the genders tend to be, especially when they're communicating in single-sex groups.

As you can see from my earlier example, getting little Tommy to talk is like pulling teeth. Boys have to be coaxed and coerced to tell you what they did. Why? Research suggests that they provide such terse answers to questions about their activities because, in most instances, they simply don't recall the details of their days. It's not that the boy is necessarily stubborn or hard-headed, it's just that his genetic and neurological "hard-wiring" doesn't allow him to remember details, and his conditioning isn't geared to pay attention to such minutiae. Unfortunately, the combination of these neurological and genetic differences, combined with a lifetime of conditioning, leads many men to retain this very same difficulty with the art of conversation.

The Gross-Out

Boys, far more than girls, use horsing around and joking to communicate with one another—it's the way they bond. I'll never forget a young client of mine who was born with a birth defect called a cleft lip and palate, which left him with an unsightly scar and a speech impediment—not an easy burden to bear at any age. At this time, he was in fourth grade and brand-new to his neighborhood, and thus the perfect target for teasing. No matter what he or even the teachers did, the other boys would bully him and humiliate him.

One day, he managed to turn his life around by giving as good as he got. Instead of feeling ashamed or embarrassed when a sixth grader shoved him and said, "What's that ugly scar on your lip?" my client simply retorted, "Oh, I cut myself shaving!" The older boy thought the reply pretty funny and laughed when he told his buddies about it. And then they all laughed together. By showing that he could kid as well as be kidded, my client got himself accepted by the very group who had so abused him. He passed the test.

This shows how, in some situations, what really bonds boys together is not necessarily prejudice and malice, but having a common communication style; when the child who is the target of humor uses humor himself, he is accepted in the group.

Bridging the Gap

Humor is one of the best communication tools available. In many cases, you can make a difficult situation—gender-related or not—easier to face if you make a joke or at least smile instead of reacting with anger, shame, or disgust.

As most parents and grade school teachers can attest, little boys are fascinated with all things gross and disgusting. They love to talk about bodily functions, especially those that take place in the bathroom. Because of their competitive nature, they often derive pleasure out of seeing who can tell the grossest and most uncouth stories. They talk about morbid thoughts. And they especially enjoy using their humor on little girls, who tend to find them utterly disgusting and repulsive.

The Thrill of the Curse Word

Little children often love to use socially unacceptable words. Just say the word "poo-poo" to a four-year-old and watch his reaction. He will often be hysterical with laughter to hear that word coming from you. Oftentimes little children use curse words because they hear them so often, from their parents or siblings or even in the media. They will often use them to test the waters, so to speak.

Foul language between the genders is a hot topic these days—and it affects everyone from little children to teenagers, to adults. A recent case in Minnesota involved a young boy who constantly directed foul language to a little girl on the school bus, continually calling her a "b - - - h." The girl told her mother, who ended up suing the little boy and his family in addition to the bus company and the school. The mother's action may seem a bit extreme, but after gaining no cooperation from the boy or school authorities, she felt she had no recourse. It does send a message that little boys should not speak that way to little girls; they have to learn early on what's acceptable and what is not. Girls need to be treated with respect, just like boys, and they need to learn this message early on in life.

As a songwriter and a member of the Board of Governors of the National Association of the Recording Arts and Sciences (the organization that gives out the Grammy Awards), I find that issues about free speech come up all the time. My own view is that we should permit the recording and sale of all types of music as ways for people from all walks of life to express themselves. Everyone has a right to their music, just as they have a right to their free speech.

But there is a difference between what we permit legally and what we as a society should condone as appropriate. Let's not pretend that hateful music has no negative effect on our culture. In my opinion, there is no question that it does. As studies have repeatedly shown, music and lyrics are very powerful vehicles that affect the psyches of listeners.

Therefore, songs that use vulgar language to describe women, for example, in my view reflect the artists' psychological inner hostility toward and disrespect for women. Unfortunately, after hearing such offensive lyrics over and over again, many young men adopt the attitudes about women the lyrics espouse. Oftentimes, many young listeners may believe, even on an unconscious level, that if the song says it, that's the way it must be, and so be it!

So it is up to some role model in the child's life to set that child straight when it comes to how they perceive the opposite sex and not refer to them with the "B" or "W" words.

Communication Breakdown!

Watch your language in front of your children and monitor theirs as well! If there's one thing we learn from communications studies, it's that words are never "just words." This is especially true of violent and hostile language.

We too often let boys, but not girls, get away with a lot of bad language. So much of the profanity is directed toward women and about women. Unfortunately, adults all too often don't intervene to stop or discourage such language in the early years of a boy's development. Instead, adults write it off as boys "just being boys," and boys' peers encourage the disrespect as well. Although we shouldn't need the threat of lawsuits (like the mother in Minnesota used) to encourage us to do right, perhaps the Minnesota sex discrimination case of the seven-year-old boy may serve as a wake-up call about the need for respect between genders.

The Female Side of the Equation

As we have seen, little boys are given a lot of leeway in what they say and do. Little girls, on the other hand, tend to be more closely monitored by adults and by their female peers. When a little girl curses or uses four-letter words, for instance, she usually is immediately scolded by whoever is present to hear it. Studies show that little girls usually cannot continue such "unladylike" behavior because neither her peers nor the adults in her world will tolerate it.

Researchers have found that, as early as four years old, little girls incorporate "female" traits into their speech patterns. They learn much of this imprinting from their mothers, female caretakers, or female educators. Linguists who have studied such speech patterns have observed such typically female speech patterns as:

➤ Ending statements with questions, such as "That's a pretty dress, isn't it?"

➤ Using terms of endearments, such as "sweetheart," "darling," and "baby," especially when playing with their dolls.

In addition to these tendencies, which we'll discuss further throughout the book, little girls also have other communication techniques specific to their gender.

Talk, Talk, Talk

The image of chatty girls and silent boys is an accurate one. Believe it or not, girls even talk a lot when they're alone, conversing in complete sentences when playing with their dolls and stuffed animals. They ask questions of their dolls such as "Would you like some more milk? Are you hungry?" Or they tell them what they are about to do: "I'm going to sit with you in the chair" and "It's time for our naps now." When boys of the same age are at play, they mostly simply make sounds and noises, even when playing with action figure dolls. Part of the reason for this difference is that, as we've discussed, girls' biology predisposes them to being more verbal in their early developmental years; and girls are conditioned to use verbal socialization in their interactions with others—even if those others are dolls and stuffed animals.

Spilling the Beans

Girls tell all! Why? Because early on, they get rewarded for making you feel as though you were a part of the experience, as though you belonged to the experience. Recall the previous example in which the mother got every detail when her little girl was speaking, but literally nothing from her little boy. The mother felt as if she practically spent the day with the little girl. She knew the color of people's clothing, people's emotional state, and what was going on in the most intimate aspect of their lives. The mother was interested in what she heard. She didn't need to prod her daughter along, or ask repeated questions to get information, as she did with her son.

Because girls are more likely to play in pairs or smaller groups than boys, their play tends to focus more on intimacy and feelings. The way they relate to one another encourages the sharing of details and intimacies, and by doing so, they both include others and feel included in their group. The more details they give, the better their relationships with their peers—a fact they learn early in life.

The need to share so much often works against inter-gender relationships, however, even at an early age. And as girls become women in the marketplace, the need to offer details can interfere with their ability to communicate well in a male-dominated business world. I'll discuss this challenge later in the book.

Keeping Secrets

If you look at what makes girlfriends "best friends," it is the secrets they share with one another. If you're female, maybe you remember what it was like when you were in third, fourth, or fifth grade—maybe even in high school—and you wanted to make a new friend. One of the best ways to bond was to share a secret—a real secret—about one of your peers, even one of your best friends. That secret was the glue that sealed your new friendship.

Unfortunately, it also frequently backfired, hurting the girl you betrayed. In fact, the downside of the telling of secrets is the betrayal of trust and, too often, as girls become women, they unfortunately continue this undermining behavior. In their attempts to bond with other women, they often tell intimate details of their personal relationships, both with other women and with members of the opposite sex.

Although sometimes women can get away with it when it involves other females, most men neither understand nor tolerate such behavior. If you're close to your sister, you might find yourself telling her details about your husband's intimate behavior—maybe he leaves his underwear around the house or uses a baby voice when he is about to make love with you—that he feels are at least private and perhaps even embarrassing. To him, such revelations are not to be taken lightly. To him, they are betrayals of the trust you share.

The Teen Years

When our kids enter their teen years, they face a tough challenge. If they don't have a clue about the latest lingo, they might find it difficult to fit into certain situations and they may even be laughed at. This is true for both male and female teens but for different reasons.

For male teens, there is a strong sense of group dynamics and group interaction because they tend to socialize as a unit in team sports and other groups. Thus, many young men may adopt the lingo of the day (which often contains a lot of curse words) in order to fit in—to belong and sound cool—as one of the group. For teenage girls, the motivation to fit in with socially accept- able descriptive words adds to their sense of belonging by establishing more intimate relation- ships with one another as they in essence "speak the same language" and can therefore better relate to one another.

Bridging the Gap

Although the generation gap is alive and well, you can learn what language is cool with young people by watching program- ming aimed at children and teens, such as MTV. And don't hesitate to ask what a certain word means. Just don't be sur- prised if your teen responds with an "Oh, *puhleeez!*"

Inter-Gender Speak

As they enter their teen years and suddenly want something different from the girls in their lives—acceptance, romance, approval—young boys experience what is often a rude awakening. They learn that the teasing they did when they were two or three years younger will simply not cut it when they are trying to get a girl's attention. Pulling her hair, hiding her pens, or insulting her outfit or hairstyle won't get boys the kind of attention they desire.

As boys begin to talk to girls, they quickly learn that they can't get what they want just by issuing commands. They learn that they have to do a lot of complimenting and a lot more talking than they did with their male friends.

From the age of 12 onward, the main topic of conversation among girls is boys, but boys still focus their activities and their conversations on action: sports, music, video games, and hobbies. Girls want so much to be accepted, to be attractive to one another and to males, that they talk a lot about ways to make themselves more attractive. They usually talk about clothes, makeup, and the social status of others. They continue to talk about relationships as the focus of their world.

Boys and Compliments

Studies show that preteen girls between eight and 12 years old talk primarily about their wishes and their needs and speak more about school, while after the age of 12 their focus is on boys and how to be more attractive to them. This is the age when young girls are the most sensitive, the most insecure about themselves, their looks, and who they are.

At around the age of 12, girls know they aren't little girls anymore (actually it may hit them at an even younger age, around age 10), but they also know they aren't women yet, either. This is the most insecure period of their lives; they feel their least attractive at a time in their lives when attractiveness is at a premium. This is the first time they realize that looks are what boys respond to. In fact, it's even what girls respond to: The prettiest girls are the most popular among the girls themselves. As girls seek solace in their magazines, matters get worse. They realize they don't match any of the pages or resemble any of the models with straight white teeth, slender figures, and clear skin. This makes them feel even worse and adds to their insecurity. To make matters worse, the increased flow of hormones can lead to extremes in moods. Their insecurities can become manifest in self-destructive behaviors such as eating disorders.

This is why teenage girls obsess on boys and their own looks, clothes, and weight. It is a critical period, often the turning point for how they wind up feeling for the rest of their lives. Therefore communication between boys and girls is crucial during this period of time. Boys need to know that girls especially need verbal reassurance about their appearance and who they are. This is where boys need to learn that compliments (especially sincere ones) are essential to breaking the ice and developing open communication patterns.

The message is, if teenage girls and boys learn what one another likes to talk about and how to relate at such a crucial age in their development, they will be setting themselves up for a lifetime of better communication with the opposite sex.

Making New Friends

Considering the challenges teens face, the phrase "friends with the opposite sex" may seem like an oxymoron to them. But not only is such a relationship possible, it is also beneficial for both parties. Young men and women who form such friendships learn and benefit from learning the other genders' communication skills and establishing verbal intimacy.

In this difficult transition period from child to adult, there is a golden opportunity for parents to help their children avoid some of the worst traps of sex stereotypes and socialization. If parents can be open to their children forming close friendships across the sex divide, they'll help their kids get some experience they can carry into adulthood. (Not that parents can force their kids to have particular kinds of friendships, but at least they can get out of the way if their kids show an inclination to form friendships with the opposite sex.)

Mirror, Mirror on the Wall

For both boys and girls, and later men and women, the goal of communication is to foster relationships and to fit in with a group. The fact that men and women continue to have different interests and talk about them in different ways makes inter-gender relationships particularly challenging as we age. To sum up, experts find that there are ...

> ➤ **Female vs. male topics.** Women talk about people and relationships, diet and clothes, and their own appearance. Men, on the other hand, talk about sports, cars, their activities, and current events. According to Adelaide Haas, who conducted a survey at the State University of New York, men talk about things, as opposed to women, who talk about relationships.

> ➤ **Female vs. male tone.** Research shows that both men and women characterize male speech as being forceful, blunt, dominating, authoritarian, and more to the point than female speech, which is characterized as being friendlier, faster, gentler, more emotional, and more enthusiastic.

Despite these obvious and continuing differences in style and content, men and women *are* from the same planet and can learn to communicate with each other beautifully. In fact, men and women become friends, lovers, and intimates every day—despite the challenges they face. You'll see how that all comes together in the next three chapters.

The Least You Need to Know

> ➤ Boys are often socialized to be highly competitive; their language reflects this.

> ➤ Girls are often more open-ended in their speech, giving lots of details to include the listener in the experience.

> ➤ Girls are socialized early on to worry about their appearance, and this anxiety is reflected in their speech.

> ➤ Insulting language, which is more typical of the way boys are raised, has no place in the upbringing of children. Words affect (and reflect) attitudes, which in turn can affect behavior.

Chapter 8

Blue Versus Pink

> **In This Chapter**
>
> ➤ Expressing feelings to bridge the gender gap
>
> ➤ Understanding a woman's powerful memory
>
> ➤ Helping vs. taking charge
>
> ➤ The power of compliments

If the chapters you've read so far have taught you anything, I hope it's that men and women communicate in different ways and that we are not only relatively unaware of why we're so different, we're also fairly oblivious to how these differences affect our behavior and relationships.

In this chapter, I'll be discussing the most common mistakes men make when attempting to communicate with and relate to women. You'll see how men often misinterpret a woman's actions, which results in men giving ineffective and sometimes inappropriate responses, and this can easily lead to the end of what might have been a productive and satisfying relationship.

If you take the time to read through this chapter with care, I guarantee that all of you male readers will be able to improve your relationships with women—and you women out there might gain a better understanding of the ways men think about you. For the purposes of this chapter, however, when I say "you" I mean "you men!" So read on and take heed!

Gaining Emotional Equality

You've already learned from previous chapters that most women tend to express themselves in a more emotional way then most men do. This tendency makes it easy for a man to assume that a woman who expresses herself in this way is simply emotionally insecure. While some women may indeed require more reassurance than others, in most cases, all a woman really needs in order to feel more secure is for you to express your own emotions, to relate to her—at least sometimes—on an emotional level.

It's not easy, I know, for many men to speak in the language of emotion. In fact, for some men, attempting to communicate on those terms is like learning Greek or Latin. In my practice, I've seen countless couples whose primary issue is the husband's inability to express his feelings, which causes intense conflict and frustration. Witness the following example involving Ralph and Andrea, a married couple, who were attempting to communicate with one another.

Andrea:	What's going on with you, Ralph? Are you okay?
Ralph:	I'm fine.
Andrea:	No, really. How are you feeling?
Ralph:	I don't know how I'm feeling. You always ask me that and I always tell you I don't know.
Andrea:	Why don't you know? You should know how you're feeling.
Ralph:	I just don't think about it. I don't think about my feelings.
Andrea:	But I need to know. I need to know how you're feeling about me, about us, about everything.
Ralph:	I'm feeling fine.
Andrea:	No, you're not! You couldn't be.
Ralph:	Look, don't tell me how I'm feeling or supposed to feel!
Andrea	[Begins to cry.]

What in the world went on here? To Ralph, Andrea's first question seemed to be rather casual and he answered it in kind. But Andrea was really asking Ralph for much more. She was asking him to validate their relationship by revealing to her his true inner feelings about it, and about himself. But Ralph, who wasn't really used to checking in with his feelings in that way, was at a loss regarding what to do or what to say. Frustrated, he became hostile toward Andrea because he felt he was being pressured into dealing with his feelings. In fact, he'd been working all his life to keep those feelings at bay and not deal with them at all.

Although you—as a man—may feel inclined to sympathize with Ralph because you, too, would prefer to keep your emotional distance from the women in your life, it's important to understand the danger in doing so. Take Ralph, for instance. Now that he's married, he can no longer keep his feelings under the layer of armor he has created. He needs to allow them to rise to the surface so that he can speak the same language as his wife—the language of feelings. If he wants to stay married and have a harmonious, intimate, and loving relationship with Andrea, he will have to break down and learn the fundamentals of dealing with and expressing his feelings.

As you might imagine, a man's inability to express his feelings is the number-one reason that a woman with whom he is intimate will get angry. When such a failure to communicate occurs, a woman feels ignored and disrespected by the man in her life, even if that's not the man's intention. Most men just don't realize how very important this aspect of the relationship is to women.

Tapping into Your Feelings

But how does a man who's steadfastly clamped down his feelings as far as they'll go learn to tap into them? Although it may sound daunting, it's not so tough. Your first step is to accept the fact that you have emotions and feelings and that they're essential to who you are and how you live your life. According to anthropologists, all human beings share these basic emotions:

➤ Happiness

➤ Fear

➤ Anger

➤ Love

➤ Sadness

➤ Doubt

➤ Compassion

➤ Boredom

➤ Disgust

One great way to get started is to perform what I call a "sense memory" exercise. (Actors practice this exercise as part of their training.) While you are alone or even with your mate (this exercise can help you to become even more intimate), think back to a time in your past when you experienced each one of these emotions. Think of the way you felt and try to translate that feeling into a sound and say the word "Ah" using that intonation. Your tone should differ as you go through each emotion.

Because we all feel emotions in our own way, it's hard to say what your "Ahs" will sound like. Generally speaking, when you're expressing happiness and love, the

sound should be relatively high. Love usually has a soft, breathy quality, while compassion might be breathy but lower in tone. Sadness has a lower tone, too, but more drawn out. People who express disgust often do so with a low inflection in a short burst of tone. Boredom is a lowered inflection that is drawn out in a monotone fashion. Anger is a loud and roaring tone.

Don't be self-conscious when you perform this exercise. It will help you focus on how certain situations make you feel, and how to express those feelings in a vocal—if not quite verbal—way. The more you practice this exercise, the more aware of these emotions you'll become and the more able you'll be to express them in an appropriate and accurate way.

Stop the Blame Game

When it comes to dealing with a negative emotion, do you tend to blame whoever brings it to your attention? If so, you're not alone. It's pretty common for men to blame the women in their lives for "bringing them down" when all the women are attempting to do is either express their own feelings about a situation or to reveal the negative side of an issue that triggers negative feelings in the men.

Once again, it seems that men—through both social conditioning and genetic influences—simply aren't accustomed to focusing on their emotions, especially (of course) when the emotions are negative. Many men work very hard to numb themselves to difficult or upsetting emotions, or they may simply *compartmentalize* negative feelings altogether.

When a woman has caused these feelings to rise to the surface, the man may genuinely believe that she is responsible for the feelings themselves and for the way they make him feel. In many cases, the man will react defensively or condescendingly, causing the woman to feel as if her need for emotional intimacy is being ignored or resented.

Does that sound like you? Do you find yourself blaming the woman in your life for making you feel bad when all she's trying to do is get you in touch with the way you really feel about an issue or situation? If you can answer yes to these questions, it's up to you to change what has probably become a very undermining way of dealing with your honest emotions. Not only will that hold you back in growing and developing as a human being, but it most certainly will interfere with your ability to relate to the opposite sex.

Resist the Instinct to Help!

What's your first response to a woman who comes to you in tears telling you that her boss just yelled at her for being late to work? If you're like most men, you respond by …

➤ Asking her how late she was.

➤ Finding out why she was late and offering solutions to prevent it from happening in the future.

➤ Telling her that tardiness is a growing problem in the business world.

What you don't do, if you're like most men, is tell her that you know how she feels and that it's awful to feel humiliated by a superior, and that you understand completely why she's upset.

Which is exactly what she really wants at this moment. First and foremost, she wants empathy. She needs to be understood and to feel your compassion. Only after she feels secure about this should you even ask if she wants some practical advice about solving the problem. And even if she does want your help, you shouldn't lecture or make demands, but instead talk through the situation step by step with her until you both come up with a way to make things better.

So here's what to do when a woman comes to you upset: First, empathize and comfort; then ask if she wants your advice, and only then work through a solution. Remember, it isn't that a woman doesn't want an answer to a problem. She does. But first she wants to feel understood. You may even want to bring up a situation in your past where you experienced something of a similar nature. A woman will interpret this as your genuine caring—that you have gone out of your way to remember a similar incident so that you can identify with what she is feeling.

Communication Breakdown!

If the woman in your life comes to you with a problem, don't leap first to sorting out the problem and giving advice. First, commiserate with her and lend her your emotional support. Then *ask* if she wants some practical advice.

And then, when it's time for practical advice, she doesn't want you to lecture her or make her feel even more inept than she already does. Instead, ask her what she needs and what she thinks would be a good solution. By doing so, you won't run the risk of sounding condescending or unfeeling.

Her Need for Your Approval

Do you have a burning desire to remake the woman in your life? Ask her to get a nose job, lose weight, for instance, or have a total image makeover? Or change how she dresses, speaks, or behaves? Well, if you do, be warned: Although she may do everything in her power to please you—because she, as most women tend to be, was brought up to be a pleaser by her family and by society—she will most likely end up resenting you for it, and deeply. That's especially true if what you want to change involves her physical appearance, which, as you may remember from earlier discussions, is her most vulnerable area.

Don't Fix Her Up

The irony, of course, is that men are born fixers, so it's perfectly normal for you to want to improve the woman in your life and mold her into a more perfect copy of your ideal fantasy. Unfortunately, your instinct to remodel goes directly against a woman's need to feel loved and accepted for exactly what she is. In the end, then, if you insist on your improvement scheme, you'll only end up losing her, leaving you to feel unappreciated and alone.

Needless to say, the best way to avoid this eventuality is to suppress your natural instinct and be satisfied with the woman you love just as she is at this moment. And if she asks for advice about her physical appearance, offer it gingerly.

The Power of a Compliment

Not only should you temper your desire to criticize and reform, you should also learn to offer compliments and displays of appreciation more often. Women require signs of approval far more than most men, and will end up feeling insecure and even resentful of their mates if they fail to obtain them.

Get over it, you may say. Stop being so insecure. That's easier said than done. As you may remember from Chapter 5, "The Role of Mother Nurture," women are brought up being given more compliments by their mothers, fathers, and their girlfriends than men are—and they never outgrow the need for approval this socialization produces.

Consider this example: I attended a luncheon with a group of women. All of us envied one woman, Nickie, who told us that her husband constantly told her she was beautiful and wonderful and that he loved her very much. Though by all objective standards Nickie was *not* physically beautiful—she weighed more than 300 pounds and had bad teeth and bad hair—her husband loved her for exactly who she was and how she looked. The result was a woman who felt confident and beautiful—and, most important, loved.

Now, is this need for compliments and reassurance a sign of being abnormally needy and insecure? Not at all! It's just a part of a woman's make-up, the way a man's instinct to bury his feelings is part of his. The very worst thing you can do is to withhold compliments in an effort to cure your woman of her need for approval or to stop her from fishing for compliments.

The bottom line is, it's almost impossible to be too effusive with your praise as long as it is sincere and honest. And, as we'll discuss later in the chapter, that's all the more true, the more intimate the compliment.

Forgive and Forget?

I'm sure I'm not telling you anything you don't know already when I say that women take a whole lot longer to forgive than most men, and they *never* forget! In my practice, I've been amazed at how long women can harbor feelings of resentment toward the men in their lives. A woman once rebuffed by a man in whom she's interested, for instance, will rarely be able to get past that initial hurt should the man come around and ask her out at a later date.

The same pattern often occurs in business as well. Let's say Mary, Mark, and Mike have a debate over what the next step in their business plan should be. Mark and Mary agree on an approach, while Mike opposes the plan. The debate becomes heated, involving a great deal of shouting. Passion rules the day.

Noon comes, however, and they break for lunch. Mary decides to stay behind and eat in her office because she's far too upset to break bread with Mike after the things he said. She figures that Mark—her ally in the struggle—will join her to commiserate with her. Is she ever surprised when she sees Mark walking down the hall with Mark, joking as they head off to lunch together. "How could Mark lunch with the enemy?" she wonders.

While Mary holds a grudge, not only through lunch but even after they'd come to an agreement, Mike lets it go quickly, putting it down to just business.

Communication Breakdown!

Never tell an outright lie. Find a way to give honest praise; then offer your compliment with enthusiasm! Remember how you say things is just as important as the things you say!

Bridging the Gap

If you can remember that women hold grudges, you can help yourself and your relationship in two ways. First, you can try to avoid ugly arguments that cause the woman in your life to become resentful in the first place. Second, if such an argument does occur, you can be aware that she may be still seething underneath even if you think she should have gotten over it.

The Long, Long Female Memory

You've been there, I'm sure. You forget to pick up the dry cleaning and the woman in your life not only scolds you for that mistake, but also remembers exactly how many times you've done something like it in the past. Years worth of forgotten dry cleaning gets thrown in your face—sometimes just metaphorically, but sometimes quite literally.

Take Jeff and Laura. They're fighting because Laura has criticized the way Jeff fails to pick up his clothes, instead leaving a trail of them around the house. Jeff protests, saying that he usually does pick up after himself. Not so, Laura says, "You never did, and you never do." They get into a heated debate as she documents exactly when he failed to put away his clothes and exactly which articles of clothing were involved. Her list of misdeeds extends back 10 years, when they had just started dating.

"Ten years ago? What does that have to do with now?" Jeff yells.

"It has a lot to do with now!" Laura exclaims.

"No, it doesn't. What we're talking about is now. You're accusing me of leaving clothes around the house all the time *now*. And I don't. What does 10 years ago have to do with what we're talking about now?" shouts Jeff.

"A lot! It shows a pattern. It shows that you never pick up after yourself," Laura screams in return.

He Says, She Says

Study after study shows that women have a finer eye for detail as well as for retaining incidents in their memories. Add to that their need for discussion on the emotional plane and you can see how difficult it is for men and women to communicate sometimes. When a woman asks her husband how the meeting went and he merely answers "Fine" or "Okay," with no detailed explanation, it drives her nuts. She wants details. If asked the same question, she would explain why the meeting was fine in order to include the man in her world, to share her experiences. In the end, because of this ability to retain and to recount the details of certain incidents, women can remember them better for longer, which is why they can bring them up during arguments even years later.

Sound familiar? Well, if you've been in Jeff's position, you know how he's feeling. As Laura continues to bring up the distant past, Jeff gets angrier and angrier. He—like most men—is used to sticking to the problem at hand and staying in the here and now. Incidents that took place five or 10 years ago seem irrelevant and particularly accusatory, which leaves him feeling defensive and confused. Laura, on the other hand, believes what she says: The past truly has a bearing on the present because it shows a pattern of behavior.

Cease Control

As we've already discussed, if you're like most men, you probably think your primary job in any relationship is to figure out solutions to practical problems. If a woman comes to you with a problem, your first instinct is to tell her how to solve it, and you offer advice with the best of intentions.

Unfortunately, if she's like most women, she'll only resent your approach, assuming that you're trying to control her. Women want to work through the problem with the men in their lives, not have their men lecture them or tell them what to do. They want men to act as sounding boards for their frustration and their angst, so that they can figure out what they want to do for themselves.

Such issues of control extend even further into a relationship. As you may remember from Chapter 3, "Communication Breakdown, Gender Style," most men use command terms far more easily than most women, because that's the way they learned to play and communicate with one another as little boys. Instead of asking for something politely, you may well do as your male brethren do and simply order it. You don't mean to sound demanding and insensitive. In your mind, you *are* asking for something—you're just not asking for it in the form of a question.

Because most women bristle at the mere thought of being controlled by a man, however, the woman you request something of in this way is apt to feel resentful and angry.

Consider the following scenario. Peter is in the living room watching television while his wife, Beth, is in the kitchen.

He says:	Get me a beer.
She says:	Get you *what?*
He says:	[In a louder voice, thinking she didn't hear him] *Get me a beer!*
She says:	Get it yourself. You have legs. You can walk. You can get up off that couch and do it yourself. I'm not your maid.

He says:	What's wrong with you? Is it too much to ask you to bring me a beer?
She says:	I'm sick and tired of being ordered around by you.
He says:	I never order you around. What are you talking about?
She says:	Yes you do. Do this! Do that!—I'm sick of it!

She slams the bedroom door in anger, he feels confused and impatient, and it's days before they're back in tune with one another.

All of this happened because Beth felt that Peter was ordering her around, but Peter had no idea what she meant. He thought of "Get me a beer" as a request, while it sounded like a command to her. When she reacted in a hostile manner, Peter was confused and defensive.

Want to avoid such unpleasant confrontations? Hammer these words into your vocabulary: "Would you mind?" "Please could you?" "When you get a chance …" Those simple phrases—which are the hallmarks of courtesy—change what a woman might consider a rude demand into a simple request. Add a term of endearment such as "honey," "sweetie," or "baby," and watch yourself getting even more than you requested.

Bridging the Gap

Learn to preface commands with phrases of courtesy such as "Would you mind," "Could you please," and "When you get a chance." Although such efforts will be appreciated by both genders, they are especially helpful to women, who otherwise might feel controlled or put upon by what she considers to be demands.

The Need for Closeness

You're in a relationship. You're in love. You trust one another. You share most things. But the woman in your life seems to want more. She wants to be closer, she wants to be with you always and to share everything with you.

Is she abnormally needy? Again, not at all. She's just doing what comes naturally. As you may remember from Chapter 5, girls are conditioned to have one best friend and to play in groups of just two. And when they marry or mate as adults, the same rule applies. Their mates become their other halves, their best friends, their playmates. It's not neediness—it's something they consider absolutely natural. They want to bond with you the way they bonded with their best girlfriends in high school. And they want you to show your loyalty the way their best girlfriends did as well.

And by the way, the desire for their mates to be their closest companions as well as their lovers may explain why women have so much trouble with the concept of boys' night out. To you, a Saturday night out with your buddies is just a way to enjoy male companionship. To the woman in your life, such an activity is a sign that you don't feel as close to her as you should, which leaves her feeling alienated and betrayed.

It's Not About Nagging

Questions, she's always asking me questions. It feels like she's interrogating me, not asking me how my day is.

Is that how it feels to you when the woman in your life asks questions about your day or about your feelings or about any issue that you both face? If so, you're not alone. This feeling that a woman asks too many questions too often is pretty common among men.

Women ask questions—and lots of them—for two reasons. First, they do so because they love details, a characteristic I've discussed before. When they ask you how your day was, they actually want to know how it was and why it was the way it was. Men, we know, aren't necessarily interested in such details, but women certainly are.

Second, women ask questions because it opens up a dialogue with you, a dialogue that helps them feel close to you, connected with you, and part of your life.

My best advice to you: When the woman in your life asks you a question, answer it as fully as you can. You'll both gain from the conversation it opens.

R-E-S-P-E-C-T

It's easy to take other people for granted. All of us—men and women—can fall into bad communication habits, especially as we get used to one another's company. The truth is, however, men are more likely to communicate in a way that undermines and dismisses if it's a woman they're communicating with. And here's how:

➤ **Men tend to monologue, not dialogue.** While you may want to impress women with your acumen and insight, when you lecture or demand, you're actually turning them off. You must let women in on the conversation. Listen to what they say, ask some questions yourself, and relax. Conversation doesn't have to be competition.

➤ **Men tend to dismiss, not reach out.** Although it's true that women are far more self-deprecating than men and do things that put them in a lower position, such as speak in a girlish voice thinking she sounds more flirty, men too quickly jump on the bandwagon. Instead of simply assuming that a woman who says "I'm fat" wants you to agree with her, or that a woman who flirts in a breathy voice has the maturity or intelligence of a 14-year-old, take the high road and be more open-minded and objective.

➤ **Men tend to avoid eye contact, not to connect.** When communicating with a woman, it is key to look at her directly, face to face. Don't size up her body during your conversation and try not to look off to the side when either speaking or listening. Although such movements may be appropriate when talking to other men, women may interpret them as a lack of interest in what they have to say.

If you always remember that respect and dignity are of paramount importance when dealing with a woman, you can never go wrong.

The Least You Need to Know

➤ What seems like insecurity in a woman may simply be her need to be close to you and to feel understood and accepted by you. It's important for you to be responsive.

➤ When a woman needs help, offer your compassion first; then ask if she'd like practical advice.

➤ Always remember: A woman never forgets and may take a long time to forgive.

➤ Women seek approval from the men in their lives. When you can give a genuine compliment, do so. It will be rewarded by growing trust and mutual respect.

Chapter 9

Pink Versus Blue

> **In This Chapter**
>
> ➤ When an insult isn't an insult
>
> ➤ Correcting a man publicly—don't!
>
> ➤ Control issues and taking charge
>
> ➤ Time for himself and still adoring you

Okay, all you women out there—listen up! You just read a chapter (or at least I hope you did) in which I revealed all of the misconceptions men have about what women need and the ways that they communicate. Now it's your turn to find out how little you really know about what men need and want from relationships with the opposite sex, and how they communicate—or fail to communicate—those needs and desires. You'll see how you, like so many other women similar to you, may be completely misinterpreting a man's actions and words. What you're about to read will help you foster more positive relationships with men and learn more about yourself at the same time. So, read on and take heed!

He Isn't (Necessarily) a Jerk!

In case you hadn't noticed, men are different from women. They don't communicate in the same way as women do, and they have trouble relating on an emotional level to each other as well as to the opposite sex. As such, they may seem completely foreign and strange when you first meet them—unless you know from the start what they mean by the way they behave.

Take this typical example of a first meeting. Steve, a handsome young man, sees Marie, a pretty young woman, from across a room at a party. Their eyes meet, and both of them sense a chemistry between them.

But when they meet, Marie notices that Steve barely makes eye contact with her. Instead, his eyes flit about the room as he utters the commands: "Sit down. Let's talk," in a monotone while pointing to two empty seats on a couch. He sits down, sprawls his arms across the back of the couch and keeps his knees spread widely apart, thereby taking up nearly the entire couch. As he continues to glance around the room, barely giving Marie a glance, he continues to talk about himself, describing his job and recounting his achievements.

When Marie tries to engage him in a dialogue by asking questions about other topics, he virtually ignores her and continues to talk about himself, in his attempts to impress her. Marie has had enough. She finally gets up and leaves, assuming disinterest in her on Steve's part. In addition, she's extremely annoyed and disenchanted with him.

Now, it's true that Steve failed to communicate in a giving, open way with a woman who interested him, but it isn't because he was being a jerk. He was just communicating in, unfortunately, a very male manner—a manner he learned through conditioning early on in life.

Accept His Need to Boast

Like Steve, many men have a tendency to talk about themselves and their accomplishments, which is one of the biggest complaints I hear about men from women in my practice. This tendency makes them seem not only self-centered by egomaniacal as well. But the truth is that, once again, nurture has taken over. They're just trying to impress you, which is a goal they learned as children when they competed with each other over who was the biggest, strongest, and smartest boy in town.

Just as girls who have one or two best friends grow up to be women who long for one-to-one closeness with their mates, boys who vie for the top spot among their friends grow up to be men who brag and boast.

If you want to really get along and communicate well with a man, you need to recognize his need to impress. Instead of trying to shut him down by saying he's too full of himself, you can first reassure him of your admiration (if it's heartfelt) and gently—very gently—let him know that he can relax and be himself with you.

Humor Him

Quips. They're supposed to be cute and funny but to many women, a man's attempt to make a little joke can seem like a deliberate attempt to either reveal his true feelings or to simply be cutting and rude.

Here's an example: As happy, upbeat Louise reached for another jelly-filled donut, Carl, her boyfriend, remarked with a smirk, "Go ahead, take another donut. You wear it so well. Ha, ha."

Louise was shocked! Horrible thoughts raced through her head. How could Carl talk to her like that? Did he think she was fat? Was she turning him off? Was she too overweight for him? Was he trying to tell her something? Maybe it was that trip to the beach when he saw her thighs that did it? Maybe he wanted someone else, or to be with someone thinner, someone different?

In the meantime, Carl never once related his comment to anything real about Louise. He said it off the top of his head, just to be cute. He loved the way Louise's body looked, even though she was technically a bit overweight.

When he saw that he had upset Louise, he simply said, "I'm only kidding." But it was too late. Louise continued on her downward spiral and ended up convinced that Carl perceived her as overweight, unattractive, and—thanks to her desire for another donut—undisciplined. The truth is that Carl would have said the same comment to anyone.

And this is the important part—the part that you as a woman must understand. Had Carl made that remark to one of his male friends, he would have laughed it off good-naturedly and gone ahead and eaten the donut anyway. That's why it comes as such a surprise to men when women are offended by their humor, which is, admittedly, often very cutting and sarcastic. Indeed, making fun of another person is a major source of male humor that often dates back to their early childhood development.

Remember, school-age boys learn early on that when it comes to teasing they either fight back or laugh along with the teaser. Humor consisting of cut-downs and put-downs is key to the survival of a grade-school boy. Unfortunately, the use of insults often continues into adulthood, when it tends to hamper men's abilities to form strong and trusting relationships with women. Too often, men don't realize that women simply don't respond well to this brand of humor and, in fact, take it very, very personally.

In the end, it's important that you—as the female partner in this relationship—let some of these attempts at humor roll off your back. Let them go. Don't read into them what isn't meant. Think of it instead as your man's way of letting you know that he's comfortable joking with you in the same way he'd joke with the guys.

Taking Up Space

As I discussed earlier, men naturally take up more room. They take full advantage of the space they're in, even if that means horning in on your space. You may even see this tendency come to the fore in the bedroom (when he hogs the covers) as well as in the boardroom (when his work takes up the lion's share of the conference table).

If you're like most women, you find this behavior demeaning and annoying. Or maybe you're not even sure that it's this need to take up room that makes you uncomfortable. In studies that instructed men in one-on-one settings to sit in highly aggressive ways—taking up space and sitting in an open posture—women tended to express the belief that these men were more "pushy," "aggressive," and "bossy." But when the men sat in more conservative postures, where they paid more attention to a woman's space, women tended to feel less overwhelmed by the men.

The lesson for you women here? Pay attention to how a man's physical demeanor makes you feel, and understand that if he tends to take up more room or invade your space, it's usually only because he was brought up to establish a powerful presence. Don't take it as an attempt to belittle or control you.

Resist the Desire to Nurture!

I know it's in your nature, as it is for most women, to want to make things right for the man in your life, to nurture him, to please, to give of yourself to better the relationship. You were born with an innate tendency to nurture that was reinforced by your upbringing and societal imperatives. You mean well, you really do.

Communication Breakdown!

Never correct the man in your life in front of others. It will make him feel like a child and perhaps cause a spat of bickering between the two of you that's both unattractive to others and unproductive for you as a couple.

However, the problem is that most men will interpret your nurturing tendencies as attempts to smother and control them. To them, you're not simply being supportive, you're trying to "mother" them. Take this mothering quality just a little farther, and they'll think you're trying to treat them like children—like your own children, in fact.

John Gray talks about this concept in detail in his book *Men Are from Mars, Women Are from Venus*. While it's perfectly acceptable—in fact appreciated—to offer support and love, be careful not to smother or mother the man in your life—to do too much for him—to go overboard. If you do, he'll run for cover and perhaps never return.

You know how it makes you feel when you sense that a man is trying to control you by tossing around commands or dismissing your questions or hiding his emotions? Well, a man feels the same way when you go out of your way to do things for him that he's used to doing for himself, or trying to anticipate and meet his every need, or attempting to "better" him by correcting his grammar or straightening his tie. A steady diet of such talk and such actions will end up turning off a man quicker than you can say, "Honey, don't *do* that!"

Another Word for Control Is ...?

More women in my practice than I can count complain of being involved with controlling men. In some cases, of course, that's absolutely true. But more often than not, the men aren't trying to control—they're just communicating in a very male way which, as you've learned so far from reading this book, means that they tend to give commands rather than make requests.

Women, on the other hand, tend to be very inclusive, using "we" more than "I," and using words of possibility, such as "might" and "could," rather than giving ultimatums. Men, however, tend to blurt out imperatives and directives.

Women often report feeling as if men are backing them into corners and badgering them during negotiations, which often forces women to take stronger stands than they actually hold. When men become more cognizant of how their way of communicating makes women feel, they are often taken aback. It's not that they didn't mean what they say, but they have no idea that women hear their words as commands. Since men have been socialized mainly around other men, they tend to use the resources familiar to them for communication. So they fall into the language of imperatives, and communication—real give-and-take—suffers as a result.

Another way a man's perfectly natural behavior can make a woman feel as if he's trying to control her is when he gives unsolicited advice when she comes to him with a problem. You want sympathy and empathy, and men want to solve the problem in a practical way. That's why men will appear to bombard you with questions just at the moment you want to be held and comforted. It's not that they're insensitive to your feelings—in fact, they may understand better than you think—but the only way they think they can make things better is by solving the problem themselves.

When you find yourself in this position, don't shut down or turn him away. Take a moment and ask him for what you need simply and directly. And thank him for his concern, which, if he's worth your attention in the first place, he feels very deeply.

"I Want to Do It Myself!"

As you may remember from Chapter 5, "The Role of Mother Nurture," men are brought up to be in charge, to be the responsible ones, to be in control. No matter what the challenge, men are expected to meet it without fear, without tears, and with efficiency. They learn to deal with whatever life throws at them "like a man."

Once you take that kind of social conditioning into account, you won't be surprised that the man in your life finds it difficult to ask for directions when he gets lost on his way to a party or to collaborate with others when a problem arises at work or at home.

When I deal with men who have trouble engaging with others in a team way, asking questions from others, I sometimes have them work on an assigned problem, letting them choose how they want to go about solving it. Even if I tell them that others in the room are available to help them, most men insist upon working it out themselves.

The good news is that, once shown how much more quickly they can reach their goals if they work with others, men will indeed start to collaborate. It is possible to retrain your man simply by showing him—not just telling him—that another approach will work better than his own in meeting the challenge at hand.

Another thing to keep in mind is that the man in your life may well ask for your help in an indirect way. He may offer up a challenge "just for discussion." It's up to you to resist the impulse to offer a simple solution and instead listen and empathize first— just as you'd like him to do for you when you come to him with a problem. The next step is to ask him questions about the challenge in order to get him to look at it in new ways. If he's under too much pressure at work, ask him what quitting his job would do to the way he feels about life. If he's thinking about buying a new car because the old one has been giving him trouble, ask him to describe the options he has (leasing, repairing the old car, buying used vs. new, and so on).

By asking questions, you'll help him feel like he's still in control and not being told what to do—something most men resent. You may well be instrumental in the decision-making process, but by doing this in a way that isn't challenging to his way of working, you won't risk putting him on the defensive.

What I Mean Is ...

Narratives are simple stories that have identifiable beginnings and move straight through to middles and endings. If you can speak in pure narrative form, without digressing or sidetracking in your story, a man can understand you more fully.

Bridging the Gap

Let's face it: It's really annoying when a man looks at you with complete confusion or annoyance as you tell him a story, stuffing it full of details and side issues. It's not that he doesn't want to follow what you're saying, it's just that he and his male brethren approach *narrative* storytelling in a very different way. They tend to speak in a linear fashion, with sentences and stories that have identifiable beginnings, middles, and endings. So when you go off on all of these tangents, it is very difficult for them to follow you and to grasp what you're really trying to say. Men appreciate it when you get to the point. Then, after they get the message of the entire story, you can go off on any tangent you please.

I Just Want to Be Loved

Irony of ironies: Although men aren't terribly comfortable with giving *compliments,* they sure do like getting them! Just like women, they need reassurance and support, and they need to feel accepted and admired. When it comes to fostering a healthy, positive relationship, women would do well to mitigate their criticisms with reassurances as much as possible—even when the criticisms are deserved—and to remember to offer compliments as often as possible.

Now that may seem unfair, considering how difficult it is for men to do the same for you. However, here's a tip: If you offer encouragement to them when they do compliment you, then you'll be reinforcing this behavior, making it more likely than ever that they'll continue it in the future.

What I Mean Is ...

A **compliment** is a gift. When you give a man a compliment you are giving him a gift. Make sure you mean it and are sincere. Do not be overly effusive. Compliment him often and enthusiastically. If you compliment him on his good behavior and how well he treats you every time he does something you like, you will be reinforcing good habits in your relationship.

Don't Fight Him, Join Him!

When it comes to romantic relationships, men want women to be their allies, not their competitors. As a woman, your first instinct may be to empathize, to compare whatever problem or experience he brings to you with one that you experienced yourself. You want to share with him how it felt to you, what it meant to you, and how it all turned out.

Unfortunately, when you respond in that way, most men will think you're trying to compete with them rather than support them. They'll translate your kind commiseration into hard-nosed rivalry.

Therefore, although you probably would love a man to respond this way to you, you must avoid this absolutely natural inclination to share and empathize. Instead, you must first listen, then listen some more, then ask questions that allow him to express his own views about the matter. Although it may seem that you're holding back on support or practical help, the fact is, if you're able to ask the right questions, you can direct his actions and his feelings about the situation at hand.

The Space Race

You love him. You feel that you're his best friend and he is yours. You want to be with him always, and, though you need your own friends and time for yourself, you could be happy spending most of your time with your man.

Communication Breakdown!

Even though they may love you more than anyone in the world, men still need time with others and by themselves to be totally fulfilled persons. When they feel smothered by you and feel guilty about seeing others or spending time alone because you resent it or pressure them about it, they will end up trying to escape from you. Or when they are around you, they will end up being miserable or making you feel miserable.

If you feel that way, you're just doing what comes naturally to most women, who are—as I've discussed—brought up to play in pairs and have just one best friend throughout childhood and into adulthood.

Most men, on the other hand, need to be with other men. Within a group of his peers, a man speaks almost another language that only he and his brethren understand. He doesn't have to edit their thoughts or their language, and he can reconnect with his own male identity.

At the same time, a man also needs time alone, on his own, away from his colleagues, his friends, and the woman in his life. He uses this time to recharge and regroup.

If you, as the woman in his life, think that by insisting he break off his relationships with other men or stop taking time for himself you'll get more quality time with him, your plan will only backfire. You'll only end up engendering resentment, anger, and distance.

He Said, She Said

Men have gotten a bad rap throughout the years for being terrified of commitment ("commitment phobic" in the lingo). In most cases, the man isn't really afraid of commitment, he just doesn't want to be smothered. He wants to know he has a certain freedom, and once he feels he has it, he may very well come around. When a man feels comfortable around you, he feels that he can do anything, say anything, and be anything as far as you are concerned. He feels special. That in turn makes him "want" to be around you more, and he automatically becomes committed to being around you more and more.

In addition, men don't feel comfortable talking about their feelings and emotions. As children, they were brainwashed into believing that boys don't cry or share their feelings. If boys do cry around other young male playmates, they often face merciless teasing from their friends and, often, their own fathers. To be called a sissy or a crybaby is a curse worse than death for little boys, so they learn early on to keep their emotions in check.

In fact, men often feel more comfortable being physically intimate with women than being emotionally open and accessible. This is why it may oftentimes be hard for a man to shower you with compliments or to say that he loves you all the time. Hopefully, some men will become more aware after reading this book, and that will all change!

Bridging the Gap

Always remember that actions speak louder than words, and this is especially true when it comes to interpreting how a man really feels about you. If a man treats you with kindness, shares his time with you, and looks at you with love and kindness in his eyes, he may be "saying" more than he is capable of expressing with words.

Actions Speak Louder ...

As discussed in Chapter 3, "Communication Breakdown, Gender Style," men have a tendency to frown, scowl, and fidget when they listen—and it's up to you to not take these natural expressions personally. They do not mean that the man you're talking to is angry or bored or irritated. And again, if he speaks to you using command terms—saying "Get me a beer" instead of "Would you mind getting me a beer, sweetheart?"—it isn't necessarily that he takes you for granted or that he's rude. It's simply the way he learned to communicate with his buddies when he was a kid, and these are habits that are tough to break.

Now that you've learned the inside scoop about communication from a man's point of view (the previous chapter) and a woman's point of view (this chapter), you're ready for the next step. In the next chapter, you'll learn some basic communication tips that will help resolve these challenges in the most efficient and fun ways possible.

The Least You Need to Know

➤ Be sensitive to a man's sense of humor. Insults are often meant simply as attempts to bond and be playful, not as put-downs.

➤ Men use imperatives in their speech, but that doesn't necessarily mean they are trying to take charge.

➤ Men need time alone.

➤ Don't treat your man like a child, unless you want your relationship as adults to end.

➤ Realize that just because a man needs his space and his friends doesn't mean he doesn't need you, too.

He-llo?

Chapter 10

Learning the Basics of Good Communication with the Opposite Sex

---

In This Chapter

➤ The value of changing your communication skills

➤ Being aware of his interests to improve communication

➤ Monologues vs. dialogues to eliminate hard feelings forever

➤ Speaking up once and for all!

Although you may be well aware of the fact that men and women don't always get along, what you might not know is *why* there remains a very real "war between the sexes."

Having traveled around the world giving seminars and lectures on the topics of gender differences and closing the communication gap between the sexes, I'm convinced that the reason men and women don't get along in their business and private lives is because they really don't know how to communicate with one another.

One problem is what seems to be a widespread societal resistance to hard work—at least when it comes to relationships. Today, it's all too easy for some couples simply to discard a 10- or 20-year relationship because they "aren't getting along" or "can't seem to communicate." To them, such lack of immediate and simple "chemistry" means that they've inexorably fallen out of love.

But is it really as simple as that? Did love just vanish from their lives? Probably not! If many of these couples took the time to look beyond the surface, beyond the fights and the stony silences, to really examine the true issues that they face, they might just have a chance to come through it stronger than ever—individually and as couples.

Sadly, though, even couples who go that extra mile and seek therapy to resolve their differences may fail to see the root of the problem. This is partly because some counselors aren't well trained in communication skills, and partly because the couples spend so much time on superficial problems that they don't allow the counseling sessions to cut to the core of the issues involved. In this chapter, we'll start to cut to the core.

Change Is Good

Believe it or not, all it takes to save a relationship is learning simple communication skills. I can't tell you how many marriages I've been fortunate enough to help save in my practice simply by teaching people to mean what they say, say what they mean, and listen to their partners. I start by giving them the information about very real differences between the genders that I've laid out for you here. I show them how to be sensitive to the "buttons" they push—purposely or inadvertently—that may perhaps distress or anger their partners. In essence, I explore with them techniques to bridge the gap between the sexes—and these techniques work equally well in business or in romantic relationships.

However—and this is a big however—for many people, this means changing their behavior in order to achieve the ultimate goal of improving their relationships. And changing your behavior isn't always so easy, as you may well have discovered for yourself already.

Why Should I Change?

Are you bristling over that last concept? Are you thinking to yourself, "Why do I have to change my behavior? That's the way I am. As a man (woman), why do I have to change the way I present myself to a woman (man)?" Well, step back and think of the big picture: You want to get along, don't you?

And so, with that desire to get along, and to stop all of the agony that comes with bad interactions with the opposite sex, comes change. What I am suggesting is that we compromise and learn how to use communication skills. I am not asking you to risk anything. These skills that I discuss have been proven to be effective and have worked time after time.

Applying the skills I discuss in this chapter will make you the best communicator you can be because they allow you to reinforce the positive qualities associated with your gender and eliminate (as much as possible) the negative ones. By doing so, you'll go a long way in maintaining good relationships or repairing damaged ones.

Finding Common Ground

It may seem like a strangely obvious mistake to make, but millions of men and women do it every day. They simply don't make the effort to learn what really interests the other one or they don't take the time to talk about it (even if it isn't a favorite subject of their own), or both. Dale Carnegie, perhaps the first "self-help guru" ever, established several rules for helping millions of men avoid alienating women (and vice versa) by not really knowing what to talk about. They have difficulty having fulfilling conversations and are often left with little or nothing to say. This can further alienate a relationship because without shared topics of interest, there is no bond, so many couples can become bored with one another. This can all change if you speak in terms of your mate's interests.

He Says, She Says

Over 75 years ago, the late and great Dale Carnegie said that for a person to be successful in getting along with another person he or she has to speak to that person's needs. How right Mr. Carnegie was!

Here's a great example of what I'm talking about. I knew a couple named Terry and Mike. They'd been dating just a few months before Terry decided that Mike—a financially successful, attractive, and sensitive man—was "boring." All he wanted to do, according to Terry, was talk about his Corvette, a subject that bored her to tears. She just wasn't interested in cars, and nothing—not even this pretty neat guy—could get her to open up to this subject. Instead, she found it easier simply to break up.

Terry made two mistakes in coming to that conclusion. First, by dismissing the subject of cars off-hand, she closed herself off from learning something new. Second, and perhaps more important, she failed to explore what this hobby meant to Mike and how it affected him. The fact is, if she'd taken the time to really talk to Mike about his car, she'd have seen a remarkable change come over him every time he talked about his passion. His eyes lit up, he became animated and excited, he was thrilled. As you may well know, such excitement is often quite contagious and chances are Terry would have learned to love Mike's Corvette—if not for her own reasons, then for what it did for Mike.

I met another couple—very much in love and very attentive to one another—who had a similar problem, but learned to solve it in a beautiful way. When I asked the woman what the secret was to their relationship, she replied, "I learned early on that you have to give in order to receive."

She told me that they had nothing in common when they met, but she made it a point to learn what in his life excited him and, if possible, to take an interest in it

103

herself. Even if she didn't take part in the hobby herself—she never learned to play golf, for instance—she at least understood it well enough to be happy for him when he did well. He also loved sharing with her his interest in fast cars, including—yes, you guessed it—his Corvette. Although it wasn't obvious to her before, she could appreciate the car's fine lines and powerful handling when she saw them through his eyes.

Bridging the Gap

Embrace change and the positive things it can bring to you as an individual and to your relationships.

And it worked both ways. Though he never cared for dressing up tuxedo style or attending benefits, for instance, he loved the way *she* loved such events and so was more than happy to accompany her. He also made a special point of understanding the finer points of her career in advertising. In short, the couple felt connected in ways that Mike and Terry never did, because they made the effort to look at life through the other's eyes.

What a lesson in both the art of love and the art of communication. Indeed, taking the time to meet each other halfway provides marvelous benefits both to each individual and to the couple.

Mix and Match Interests

If you and the man in your life haven't figured out a way to bring your own interests into the couple relationship, here's a tip I learned from another couple in my practice. One weekend the couple would do something that interested her, like going shopping, seeing a romantic comedy, or going to antique shows. The other weekend they would do something that interested him, such as watching baseball games and wrestling matches.

Although it may sound stereotypical, studies show that men enjoy sports, current events, cars, and technology more than women do. Women tend to be interested in relationships, self-improvement, fashion, the arts, and music. So expand your horizons and journey into the world of interests of the opposite sex.

Don't Hog the Dialogue

As we've discussed, men grow up learning to lecture rather than dialogue, especially with women. Women, on the other hand, tend to ask lots of questions, change topics often, and ramble through their stories. In order to communicate better with one another, therefore, it's urgent that you learn to dialogue, to listen and speak in a relatively orderly fashion.

This is especially true as men and women first get to know one another. So often, the man will talk too much about himself. He might come off as obnoxious when in reality he is just nervous and uncomfortable, wanting to impress the woman. The woman, on the other hand, may ask a lot of questions in an attempt to get to know the man. This may make her appear as though she's interrogating him.

In order to avoid any of these wrong impressions from forming, it's essential to do two things:

➤ Ask *open-ended questions* of the person, ones that don't require only a "yes" or "no" answer.

➤ Monitor how much time you are talking, so that you give the other person a chance to engage in what you said and say what he or she has to say.

Communication is a two-way proposition. It is a give-and-take phenomenon. When both parties practice these two simple tips, they'll find that they're able to get to know each other much faster and stay in touch with each other much better.

What I Mean Is …

An **open-ended question** is one that encourages the respondent to expound on an answer, as opposed to answering just "yes" or "no." Instead of asking something like "Do you believe in gun control?" which would require a "yes" or "no" response, say something like "Why do you think gun control is a good or a bad idea?"

Look and Listen and Stop Missin'

Eye contact and other direct, physical forms of communication are essential when it comes to establishing and maintaining a good relationship. As we discovered earlier in this book, most people have habits that interfere with the fine art of communication.

For instance, although women seem to be much more polite listeners than men, they often don't react with appropriate gestures that express how they really feel about the conversation. They'll often smile and nod in order to make the man feel comfortable and encourage him to keep speaking, whether they truly agree with him or not. As you might imagine, this is both confusing and disconcerting to the man.

Instead, a woman needs to respond with gestures that more accurately reveal her true feelings. In addition, if the man is one of those bulldozer lecturers and she can't get a word in edgewise, her desire to be polite shouldn't stop her from breaking into the conversation to say, "Excuse me, I would like to say something." If he ignores her, she needs to say it again, this time a little louder. If he ignores her a third time, he can be tapped on the hand while she says it. If he still doesn't respond, she can be sure that she is listening to a person who's totally unconscious of his surroundings. Such a technique is also useful if you're constantly interrupted or ignored while you're speaking.

Unfortunately, a man is often guilty of interrupting a woman by bulldozing into her conversation as she is speaking or by changing the subjects that she brings up. A Gallup Poll I conducted shows that interrupting is the most annoying of all habits, leaving women to feel frustrated, angry, and ignored. Men often have no clue that their constant interrupting makes women furious.

In addition, men have a tendency not to maintain eye contact with female conversation partners, which means that they often miss the woman's hostile facial and body language that stems from her frustration at not being able to speak.

Here are a few simple tips to improve your physical communication skills:

➤ **Concentrate on the face.** In order to be a good observer, it is essential to establish good eye contact. If you're not used to looking at someone's face and into her eyes while she speaks, try this the next time you launch into a one-to-one conversation with a member of the opposite sex: Look at the entire face of the person to whom you are speaking for two seconds. Then look at her forehead for two seconds, eyes for two seconds, nose for two seconds, and mouth and chin area for two seconds. Once again, look at her entire face. By doing so, you'll be sure to pick up clues about the person's feelings as well as make her feel comfortable and desired. She'll know you're interested in what she has to say and how she feels about your end of the conversation.

➤ **Avoid interrupting.** These simple steps should help people to break the very bad habit of interrupting:

1. Pay attention to the whole idea being expressed and stop focusing on the small details. Rein in your urge to correct.

2. Physically control your impulse to interrupt. Start by sucking in a breath of air, holding it, and then slowly releasing it as you let the person finish what she is saying. This technique not only helps you gain control of your interrupting impulses, but it also gives you time to plan more carefully what you're going to say next and how you're going to say it.

3. If you still can't manage to control yourself, *bite down on your tongue* until it hurts. Sound silly? Well, it works. It gives you the clear and painful message to shut up while the other person is speaking her mind.

Speak Up! Be Heard

Believe it or not, the way you sound to members of the opposite sex determines how well they will communicate with you and how they will perceive you. All too often, people give the wrong impression by the way they sound. Women may come across as lightweight, dumb, or even ditzy by how they speak. The same holds true for men, who may come across as arrogant, mean, or even boring based on their vocal intonations.

In order for both men and women to have a clear advantage and not give off an erroneous "vocal image," they need to use good tonal techniques when they speak. Here are three simple techniques for you to practice:

1. Take a small breath in through your mouth and hold it for a second, and then speak on the exhalation of air. In essence, all of your words need to be spoken on that breath of air you previously inhaled. Doing this allows for more resonance in the voice so that you can be heard.

2. Keep your back teeth apart at all times when you speak so that you never clench your jaw. Doing so will also allow for greater vocal clarity and reduce mumbling or a nasal quality in your sounds.

3. Whenever you speak, you need to tighten your abdominal muscles, pushing them out as you speak on the exhalation. This allows you to project your voice more so that you can sound more confident.

The more you do these three things when you speak, the more control you will have when you speak to anyone of the opposite sex. This will also help you to alleviate nervousness and anxiousness.

I trust that you've learned a great deal about the misconceptions men and women have about their opposite genders and about the ways we can all improve our communication techniques. In the next part of the book, we'll explore a touchy subject for all of us: anger and the way we communicate it. Read on!

The Least You Need to Know

➤ Change is not about defeat or giving in—it's about compromise.

➤ Learn about the interests of the other person if you want to build successful connections.

➤ Communication is not built on monologue. Back-and-forth dialogue is the key.

➤ The other person can't understand you if your vocal style interferes. Speak up and speak clearly.

Part 4

Battleground of the Sexes

Anger is a perfectly natural emotion, but one that can damage a relationship beyond repair. In the chapters that follow, we'll explore some of the most common sources of anger between men and women, then learn some important coping skills. By learning to deal with anger and to communicate through the anger, you can avoid the hurt feelings and hidden resentments that often remain long after the arguments are over.

Chapter 11

Basic Madness: Unmanaged Anger

In This Chapter

➤ The undermining nature of words spoken in anger

➤ Learning to guard against verbal abuse

➤ Toxic behavior and its harmful effects

➤ Rules for healing toxic relationships

Anger is one of the most natural but also one of the most potentially undermining of all emotions. Poor communication between men and women triggers more anger, and thus is at the heart of more arguments and hurt feelings, than almost any other issue.

As I'll discuss in this chapter, we're particularly vulnerable to the damage that angry words expressed by members of the opposite sex can cause. Sexual tensions and insecurities are part of the reason for our vulnerabilities in this area, as is the fact that our styles of communicating remain so different from each other.

Of course, this is even more true when intimate partners are involved. Ironically, the very people who deserve our respect the most are those we tend to take the most for granted. And the very people who can make us feel so good also have the power to undermine our confidence and hurt our feelings.

When such a pattern of behavior exists, our relationships can become what I like to call "toxic"—almost poisonous to both individual self-esteem and to the future of the partnership. In this chapter, I'll discuss ways to recognize toxic behavior and then to avoid it in the future.

Is Your Relationship Toxic?

Here's a little quiz I've devised to help you figure out if you're involved in a toxic relationship with a member of the opposite sex. Answer "yes" or "no" to the following questions:

1. Do you feel that you often take offense or issue with whatever seems to come out of his or her mouth?

2. Does he or she always seem to be criticizing you or putting you down?

3. Do you often feel tense and nervous around him or her, as if you're walking on eggshells?

4. Do you usually feel angry and irritable whenever you are around him or her?

5. Do you get sad or depressed or feel uncomfortable whenever you are in his or her presence?

6. Do you feel emotionally numb after being around him or her?

7. Do you feel devalued—less than who you are—after you have been around him or her?

8. Do you constantly feel judged by him or her?

9. Does the person sabotage you behind your back or do you feel betrayed by him or her?

10. Do you want to get away from him or her physically?

11. Do you feel emotional relief whenever you are away from the person?

12. Do you usually cringe whenever you are around the person?

13. Does he or she constantly speak in a harsh or aggressive tone toward you?

14. Does he or she constantly use foul language around you and vice versa?

15. Are you always at a loss for words when speaking to him or her?

16. Do you often feel weak and lack energy when you have been around him or her?

17. Do you usually feel aches and pains and physical tension before, during, or after you've been with him or her?

18. Have you ever had the urge to punch or do bodily harm to the person?

If you've answered "yes" to any of these questions about a relationship with a member of the opposite sex, then it's likely you're involved with a *toxic person* in a *toxic relationship*. However, keep in mind that even in the healthiest of relationships, you may feel like slugging your partner on occasion!

If you think you're involved in a seriously toxic relationship—one that constantly undermines your self-esteem or that has already erupted into physical or emotional abuse—I urge you to either remove yourself from it or obtain help from a marriage counselor or therapist as soon as possible. Such relationships are undermining to both your physical and mental health. If you work with such a person, try to resolve your differences using whatever resources available to you, which I discuss in my book *Toxic People*. In addition, use legal outlets that your workplace offers. For example, you may wish to contact your human resources department or your superiors; they can help you resolve the issues at hand. If you can't, it's time you thought about getting a new job— one that doesn't undermine your sense of self-esteem and confidence.

However, most relationships, even those that engender occasional bouts of anger and resentment, are workable if you simply learn how to communicate more clearly and directly. Let's take a look first at how these relationships can develop. Then, at the end of the chapter, I'll show you how to heal the "toxic" relationships in your life, if that's what you decide is best for you.

Bursting Out of the Cage

When it comes to dealing with other people, what makes you the angriest? Is it when someone makes an honest mistake that throws you off or takes you by surprise? Probably not. If you're like most people, you feel the most anger and resentment when someone treats you with a lack of respect by ridiculing you, putting you down, or belittling you. And when that happens, you react both physiologically and psychologically, and the effects can be both internal and external.

Internally, for instance, intense anger can cause a temporary rise in blood pressure that, over time, can become chronic hypertension. Feelings of resentment can actually burn in your gut, triggering the production of excess acid that can cause indigestion and ulcers.

What I Mean Is ...

A **toxic person** is someone who doesn't support who you are, who makes you feel bad about yourself, and who brings out the worst in you. I coined the phrase in my best-selling book, *Toxic People—10 Ways of Dealing with People Who Make Your Life Miserable* (St. Martin's, 1998).

What I Mean Is ...

A **toxic relationship** is a relationship that does not bring out the best in you. It depletes your energy, it makes you feel less than you are, and it takes away from you as a person, as opposed to adding to your self-worth.

When feelings of anger and resentment flow outward, they can be just as "toxic"—to our relationships rather than to our bodies. We end up saying things we don't mean to say or, more often, saying things without thinking about how our partners will hear and perceive them. When a woman hears a man tell her something that sounds like a cut or a slam, or when a man hears a woman's request as a nag, their intimate relationship ends up damaged. Hurt feelings innocently persist, even if no intention to hurt existed.

Indeed, all too often we don't realize what words are particularly hurtful to the opposite sex or what words will push the anger buttons in our partners. Without even realizing it, then, we end up chipping away at the self-esteem of the very people we most want to communicate with.

Words are the most powerful weapon you can use against another person, and if you fail to use them with care, you can end up maiming someone you actually do love and respect. That can happen the moment you start to take an intimate partner for granted, feeling that you're so close to one another that you can take the liberty of saying whatever you want to the other person without thinking of the consequences.

Consider the case of one of my clients, a woman named Chelsea. Chelsea left her lover David simply because she grew tired of his constant "teasing" about her weight, a particularly painful and sensitive subject for her. No matter how often she explained how much his teasing, which he considered to be just good-natured ribbing, hurt her, he just kept at it until she felt she had no other choice but to leave him. She had no choice because she began to negatively associate him with hurtful comments. Although he thought it was no big deal, she did. By not taking heed and stopping the teasing, he was actually saying he didn't respect her feelings.

In order to avoid being on either end of such a "toxic" relationship, you should take extreme care with the words you choose and be sensitive to how you say them. You have to know what hurts the other person, listen to that person when he or she reacts negatively, and stop doing it immediately. And if someone you love starts to use words that hurt you, you need to find a way to make him or her understand what his or her words sound like to your ears. By working together to bridge these communication gaps, you can actually end up strengthening your relationship. Your first step is to understand what words are particularly hurtful to members of the opposite sex.

Words That Hurt Never Heal

If you curse your mate out or insult his or her parents in the heat of an argument, you might end up kissing and making up, but those words will never be forgotten. Women especially have long memories and do hold grudges. Remember that! If you tell her, "My mother thinks you're a b - - - h, too!" your partner will probably never be able to look at your mother the same way again. When, in the heat of anger, you tell him "You're a loser, and you'll always be a loser," you'll damage his ego in a way that may be impossible to repair. Whenever he's having a bad day or things aren't going well at work, rest assured that your horrible words will resonate in his head and in his heart.

The lesson here is, *think before you speak,* no matter how angry you get. Remember that hurtful words can never be taken back—they are there forever. Indeed, *verbal abuse* is one of the most painful forms of abuse because its scars last forever. If you are a woman, when your male boss, your male colleague, your husband, your lover, or even your son continually and consistently answers you with a curt "Yep" or "Nope," or ignores you, he is verbally abusing you and disrespecting you. If your female partner belittles you or nags at you, she's verbally abusing you—and hormonal imbalances or biochemical problems are no excuse! There is therapy and medication available today for these female verbal abusers, so no one has to suffer their verbal wrath.

Here are some verbally abusive phrases that people typically use and that often inflame tempers and trigger animosity:

> ➤ You should have ....
>
> ➤ You didn't ....
>
> ➤ That's stupid.
>
> ➤ You'd better ....
>
> ➤ Why didn't you ...?
>
> ➤ How come you never ...?
>
> ➤ Why do you always ...?
>
> ➤ How could you ...?
>
> ➤ Why don't you ever ...?

Verbal abuse can also take the form of silence: If your partner simply ignores your need for a verbal exchange, it's another form of disrespect. Of course, as I've discussed in other chapters, this type of behavior is apt to be displayed more by men than by women, and often is not meant in a negative way.

What I Mean Is ...

Verbal abuse occurs when someone consistently speaks to someone else with a lack of respect and with an aim to belittle or demean. But it doesn't involve only shouting or cursing at the other person. It also may reveal itself through hostile, curt, or demeaning tones. Noncommunication—the proverbial "silent treatment"—may also be a severe form of verbal abuse.

The Source of the Toxins

Why does it appear to be so easy for anger, resentment, and miscommunication to enter into our inter-gender relationships? There are many reasons for what seems to be a pervasive male-female antagonism. Many of us, for instance, develop hidden resentments toward the opposite sex because of the way we saw our mothers and fathers interact and the way we related as children and adults to our parents as individuals. In addition, we bring to every new relationship with the opposite sex our past experiences with people we have been emotionally involved with.

If you're a woman who's learned not to trust men because your father was a womanizer or you were molested by an uncle as a child, unless you have undergone therapy or worked out these serious issues, you often come to any new relationships with men with a certain undermining bias. If you're a man who's been taught on a subconscious level by your father or your peers to believe that women are second-class citizens or that women are unpredictable and emotionally unstable, you're apt to treat women with disrespect even if you're unaware of your motivations.

Bridging the Gap

Think before you speak. You can never take back hurtful words once you express them, and they can cause some of the longest-lasting and painful scars of all. No matter how angry or frustrated you are, take a deep breath, hold it, blow it out, and then decide what you want to say and who you want to say it to with care.

Clearly, it's important for you to explore any biases you might have against members of the opposite sex as quickly as you can. You may be able to do this through private reflection or through conversations with trusted friends and/or siblings. Or you might benefit from seeking help from a therapist or a counselor who can help you delve into what may be painful memories in a safe and supportive environment. No matter what road you take, however, you're sure to find that once you take those biases into consideration—and work hard to compensate for them—you'll be able to improve your relationships with the opposite sex.

That Old Green-Eyed Monster

One source of anger and resentment among men and women is another perfectly natural but utterly undermining emotion: jealousy. Both men and women are vulnerable to such feelings, but men seem to be at particular risk. That's perhaps because most men have been raised to be particularly competitive and are conditioned to strive to win and to be the best at what they do. When such men meet equally accomplished and capable women, they often feel the need to put the women down in order to get the upper hand.

Vanessa, an accomplished attorney, met Jim, another accomplished attorney, at a party. Vanessa responded to Jim's stories about all of his successful cases appropriately. Truly impressed, she asked him questions about his work, smiled with praise, and encouraged him to continue. When he discovered that she, too, was an attorney, however, he was unable to handle what he perceived as competition. In essence, he put on his verbal boxing gloves and came out fighting. He started interrogating her to see how much she knew. At first, she gave back as good as she got, but finally grew tired of his verbal attacks and decided it wasn't worth talking to this hostile man any more.

What happened was that poor Jim was threatened by this confident woman who also happened to be a partner in one of the most prestigious law firms in the country. Even though he was a qualified attorney himself, in his own mind he thought she was no match for him. And, thus threatened, he tried to cut her down to size. When Jim realized that Vanessa had more than he did—more prestige, more high-profile cases, and more money—he was envious. As Sigmund Freud once said, "Envy seeks to destroy," and thus Jim's envy of Vanessa caused him to try to destroy her verbally.

He Says, She Says

Many psychologists and family counselors, including Sigmund Freud, who stated that "envy seeks to destroy," believe that more spouses who are jealous and envious of one another end up committing physical violence due to their feelings of inadequacy. They resort to violence because they feel impotent to do anything else in their desperate attempt to gain control over the relationship. If you are experiencing jealousy and envy toward a spouse or a mate, it may very well be in your best interest and in the interest of the relationship to seek professional counseling to help you understand these feelings and deal with them appropriately without "seeking to destroy" the other person.

All too often I have seen men who perceive themselves as less successful than the women they marry try to destroy their wives' self-esteem, and in the end destroy the relationships themselves. Obviously, this isn't the case with every situation, but surveys consistently show that when a woman earns more than a man, the relationship rarely works. Why? Because of the ingrained competition factor that so many men have, which is often reinforced by society.

Of course, professional success is not the only source of jealousy for either men or women. Many people feel jealous because they feel that their partners are physically attractive to—and attracted to—other members of the opposite sex. Some people are envious of other relationships of all kinds—of friendships, of parent-child bonds, even of the attention paid to a pet or a hobby.

Whatever the source of the jealousy, the emotion causes a fairly standard set of reactions. Angry words, resentful actions, and even violence may erupt. In many cases, the object of these reactions is control: The goal becomes not to relate to the partner or coworker, but to control his or her actions. And what happens then? The relationship disintegrates in resentment, fear, and anger on both sides.

Unconstructive Criticism

One of the most common ways for anger and resentment to enter into a relationship is through criticism. Men will often criticize women by either putting them down or making absolute declarative statements with a lot of conviction. Women usually criticize by asking questions with a certain tone in their voice—often a whiney or grating tone—that they know push men's buttons because it makes women sound like victims in whatever scenario they're attempting to live out.

The Groucho Marx Syndrome

Legendary comedian Groucho Marx used to say in jest that he would never want to belong to a club that would want him as a member. Unfortunately, all too many people feel that way about their relationships with the opposite sex. "If he likes me," you think, "he must not be great." And if she doesn't respect a man because he likes her, then she'll automatically—if subconsciously—treat him badly. Then, only when he decides to leave her will she respect him enough to want to make him stay. Sound unhealthy? It is. But it happens more often than you might think.

Exhibiting a related syndrome are the girls who go after the "bad boys"—men who don't treat them well—and shun the "good guys" who respect them. At least in part, this attraction to such men reflects a woman's own lack of self-esteem. What they don't realize is that these "bad boys" who treat them poorly probably don't like themselves either, and suffer from the "Groucho Marx Syndrome" as well. So now you have two people who don't like themselves playing havoc with one another's emotions and further diminishing each other's self-esteem.

118

The bottom line is that in order for any male/female relationship to work, there has to be mutual respect. You need to treat the ones you love better than you treat anyone in the world. You need to use sweeter words and kinder tones, and exhibit more giving actions.

Understanding Toxic Relationships

At the beginning of the chapter, I offered a quiz designed to help you decide if the relationship you're in is troubled because it's truly "toxic," or if you just need to understand the source of your anger and resentment better in order to move forward.

What did you find out about yourself and your relationship? What do you think now that you've read the rest of the chapter? The truth is, there really are people who will simply bring out the worst in you and you in them. They make you do things and say things you would not do or say to anyone else. They bring out a side of you that you can't stand seeing—often a side that you don't know exists before it comes to the forefront.

I know it's difficult, but it's essential that you be brutally honest with yourself when it comes to making a decision as to whether or not you can rectify a toxic relationship. If you know deep inside there is no hope, then you know what to do. If you really believe you can do something about it, do it. Don't just read about what to do about it in this or any other book—go ahead and do it!

You've taken the first step by reading this book and, perhaps, in seeing yourself in it. If you keep reading, you'll find out how to break out of formerly undermining patterns of behavior and learn to communicate more fruitfully with members of the opposite sex. You'll gain a more complete and thorough understanding of the other person's needs, as well as your own.

Communication Breakdown!

If your relationship has turned violent, leave it immediately! It's over! The relationship has deteriorated to the point where there is no more respect for one another. Chances are, you'll never break free from what has become a vicious cycle of violence unless you get out immediately. Nine times out of 10, it will happen again.

Healing Toxic Relationships

If you've decided to try to heal a once-toxic relationship with the opposite sex, you both have to start fresh by forming a brand-new line of communication. Here are a few tips to get started:

➤ Readily apologize if it's your fault or let the person know you want to work things out if it isn't your fault.

➤ Don't hold back when it comes to revealing your true feelings.

➤ Don't attack.

➤ Don't threaten.

➤ Never belittle or use sarcasm.

➤ Stick to the issues at hand.

➤ Monitor the tone of your voice.

➤ Try to see things from another point of view.

If you can manage to keep these pointers in mind and follow through with them as often as possible, you're sure to find your relationships with the opposite sex to be less fraught with anger and resentment than ever before.

In the next chapter, all you men out there will get some special advice about dealing with anger in your relationships with women. So, read on!

The Least You Need to Know

➤ We need to be sensitive to the words we use when talking to members of the opposite sex.

➤ Verbal abuse comes in many forms.

➤ Think before you speak. The pain of hearing bad words hurled at you stays forever.

➤ Men and women can repair a "toxic" relationship only if they establish a new set of rules.

Chapter 12

Mad About Women

In This Chapter

➤ Women's behavior that makes men crazy

➤ Getting to the point

➤ Privacy acts

➤ Making yourself understood

Okay, all you women out there—this chapter's for you! If you've ever wondered (and there's no doubt in my mind that you have) just why the men in your life react so badly to your attempts to communicate and to share your feelings, you'll now have at least some of the answers. And if you're a man, don't stop reading now. You'll finally learn why the women in your life act the way they do—and it really isn't just to make you insane!

As you read some of the "whys" I offer, you'll probably see yourself in some of the scenarios. You may want to laugh, and you may even want to cry as you recall how many of your arguments might have been avoided had you known some simple facts about the way men and women communicate their needs.

However, once you've learned to analyze the patterns of miscommunication involved and explore the different assumptions that both men and women bring to these particular conversations, you'll be able to decode the true underlying message in the next such conversation.

What's Wrong? Nothing! No, Something!

Many of the issues I will be discussing in this chapter are the source of things you hear stand-up comedians talk about all the time. Perhaps there was no funnier Broadway play than *Defending the Caveman,* which comedian Rob Becker performed all over the country. In one of the acts, he devotes an entire dialogue to the concept of the "What's Wrong? Nothing!" issue. These two words uttered by men and the one word uttered by women is the most common communication that leads to a) hurt feelings followed by b) frustration followed by c) tears followed by d) silence followed by e) a full blown-out battle.

If you could weigh every issue that makes men feel that women don't understand them and frustrates them to the degree that they don't care if they ever speak to a woman again, it is the word "nothing," when they know very well that "something" is the matter.

So men, when women say "nothing," what they want is for you to grovel, to cajole, to sweet talk—to give them some love and to figure out what you did wrong. Even if you aren't a mind reader they expect you to figure it out anyway. So start guessing! Basically, they want you to *pay attention* to them and to how you behave toward them. If you figure out what you did wrong, the woman wants you to apologize to her and really feel that you are sorry for what you did.

What I Mean Is ...

"Nothing" said with either a blank expression or pinched face means that something is definitely wrong and that you had better figure out what's bothering her on your own. You are not going to be told what is wrong, unless you a) guess it, b) reverse your negative behavior, or c) apologize profusely and mean it.

When a man asks "What's wrong?" a woman needs to realize that it is his way of breaking the ice. He's obviously sensitive to his environment, feeling the woman's repressed hostility that "could be cut with a knife." When the tension has become too much for him to deal with and things feel too uncomfortable, in an attempt to resolve the issue and get to the bottom of the problem, the man will ask, "What's wrong?" This is a good sign because it indicates that the man cares. He wants to make an inroad. When he hears "nothing," he feels rebuffed. He gets angry. Hence, the war begins.

So, if a man asks "What's wrong?" he's opening up a dialogue and showing that he cares. The woman has to tell him and stop playing the immature game of punishing him. Help him along and tell him what he did that bugged you. After all, he's not a mind reader!

On the other hand, men, if you are going to open up the dialogue, think back—and think hard about what you might have done to cause her to feel bad. Try to see things from her point of view.

But be honest, women. When you tell a man "nothing" when something's really the matter, what you really want is for him to care enough about your feelings to press you to discuss what's really on your mind. Basically, you want him to *pay attention* to you. And if what's bothering you is something he did or failed to do, you need to tell him what it was.

So women, here are two things you need to know about this approach. First, if a man asks you what's wrong, assume that he really wants you to answer his question. Do not answer him with silence or vague answers, but explain what's on your mind as clearly and directly as you can.

Second, don't let your anger and resentment build up for too long before spilling the beans about the truth of the matter. Otherwise, you're apt to answer with that curt "nothing" that the man in your life will only take as a sharp rebuff to what are probably his honest good intentions to help you.

Accuse Me!

Another anger-provoking, undermining approach to conversation is the use of what I call "victim talk." That's what you use when you whine and accuse your man of some minor transgression, hoping to trigger guilt, but more often eliciting defensiveness and anger.

For example, have you heard, "Well, I was just busy!" or "Why are you always bugging me?" after you've practically spat out, "Hey, you didn't call me!"? See how easy it is to start a fight without knowing it? If you use a whiney or accusatory tone, a man will almost always react defensively and, before you know it, you've got a nasty, negative situation on your hands.

Take a look at some other examples:

She says:	You never call!
He thinks:	Yeah, and keep it up and I'm never gonna call.
She says:	We never go anywhere.
He thinks:	What do you call going to the movies last week?
She says:	You think I'm fat.
He thinks:	I never even thought about it, but now that you mention it ....
She says:	I saw you flirt with her.
He thinks:	I was just being friendly.

If you didn't use the victim tone and became more conscious about making generalized accusatory statements toward the men in your life, it's likely that they'd be able to react in a positive, empathetic, caring, and loving way. Let's take a look:

She says:	Honey, I was worried when you didn't call.
He says:	Oh, I am sorry. I just got so carried away with my meeting. I really apologize.
She says:	I know how hard it is for us to find the time to go out. But let's see if we can make it to the lake this weekend.
He says:	Sounds like a good idea.
She says:	Honey, when you said I could stand to lose weight, it hurt my feelings.
He says:	I never said that. I just agreed with you. I love you the way you are. If you choose to lose weight or not, it's fine with me.
She says:	Did you think she was pretty?
He says:	She's okay, but I think you're even prettier.

You see how a fairly simple change of tone can foster communication instead of hinder it? Try it in your own inter-gender relationships and see if they improve.

What Are You, My Keeper?

There is nothing that turns a man off more than to feel that the woman he loves is turning into his mother. No matter how much he may love and respect his mother, he doesn't want another one, at least not if he's psychologically healthy. Such motherly behavior usually centers on "checking in to see what's up," which most men interpret as "checking up to undermine my privacy."

Keep in mind that, as a little boy, the man in your life probably already had a mother who insisted he talk about the details of his life, even though remembering such details is innately difficult if not impossible for most boys to do. As discussed previously, most little boys aren't as verbal or detail-oriented as little girls of the same age. Trying to answer their mothers' questions, then, puts them under an extraordinary amount of pressure. They usually resort to "Yep," "Nope," or "I don't know" answers. Because of their sons' lack of verbal openness, many mothers believe that their little boys must be hiding something from them, so they check up even more closely on them.

Most little boys resent this and often rebel by playing a little game called "How much can I get away with without Mom finding out?" They seek out ways to escape their mothers' prying eyes and ears and to gain a sense of independence.

Now segue into adulthood. Once on his own and independent, the last thing a man wants to hear is a barrage of questions about the daily details of his life. This drives men nuts! I know—you don't ask such questions because you're nosy or because you're truly suspicious. It's simply because you're curious and detail-oriented. But if you want to avoid instigating a full-blown battle or another round of the silent treatment, don't barrage the man in your life with a series of questions. Instead, let him know you're interested in what happens in his daily life because you want to grow closer to him, not because you suspect something or want to nag him.

If your man admits that he doesn't know quite *how* to tell you about what happens during his day, you can suggest he use the journalist's tool of "who, what, where, when, and why" in preparing a story. Ask him to describe the people involved—how they looked or what they were wearing. Try to remember what they said and how they sounded when they said it. Try to remember details, colors, textures, smells— things he never thought of until now. Let him know that this is exactly what you want to hear.

Otherwise, you might end up having this conversation-cum-argument one of these days:

She says:	Did you have a nice lunch?
He says:	Uh huh.
She says:	Where did you go?
He says:	To the Steak House.
She says:	What did you have for lunch?
He says:	A sandwich.
She says:	Who did you go with?
He says:	A group of people.
She says:	Oh, who?
He says:	Just people.
She says:	No, really, tell me who was there.
He says:	What's with you? Are you so suspicious of me? Why don't you trust me? Lay off already!!! I wasn't cheating on you. I was just having lunch!

Clearly, this miscommunication occurred because the man gave too few details. The woman was simply trying to elicit more details about her husband's lunch so that she could enjoy it with him vicariously. But her husband perceived her attempts at sharing as jealousy and suspicion. She didn't even think that he might have been cheating on her. All she wanted was to feel a part of his day. Their ensuing fight could have been avoided had the husband known that women communicate using a lot of description and detail and want to hear the same from men.

The Caveman Cometh

Although you, like most women, need a "room of your own," too, the man in your life has a special need for very personal and private space—away from you, away from the office, just away …. As Rob Becker writes in his play, *Defending the Caveman,* when a man retreats into his cave (personal space), it means only that he wants to be alone—which translates into "he doesn't want you in his cave." What it doesn't mean is that he doesn't love or care about you or that he never wants to be with you. It does mean that, for the moment (whatever length of time that moment is), you're not welcome in his space. Do not take it personally, and above all, do not force the issue.

John Gray, the author of the best-selling *Men Are from Mars, Women Are from Venus,* refers to this phenomenon as the "rubber-band effect," in which men have a need to retreat before they can come forward. This is especially true, Gray says, during times of commitment and other emotional events.

Bridging the Gap

When you see a man retreating, give him his space! If you don't push him, he'll come to you when he's ready. Allow him to take his time to work out whatever issue he's dealing with in his own way. As difficult as it may be for you, be patient and understanding, and that often means keeping quiet for a little while.

If you're like most women, however, you usually want to talk out your emotional problems—in fact, you'll do so ad nauseam if you've got an audience. Men, on the other hand, exhibit behavior that is 180 degrees opposite to that of their female counterparts. Men retreat. They tend to shut down and think about things. Men do not freely ask for help. In fact, we know that men can drive around for hours without ever asking for directions, even when they are obviously and hopelessly lost. Think about it this way: If a man is squeamish about asking for directions, how is he going to feel comfortable asking someone (especially someone of the opposite sex!) to help him figure out the issues in his life? Initially, most men retreat, but after a while, they do come around and ask for help from others—especially if the loneliness and pain become too much to bear.

At the same time, you're right to feel a little hurt if your man is too abrupt with you as he withdraws into his cave. If you sense he needs to retreat, urge him in the most gentle way possible to let you know just a little bit about what's going on. He really should find a way to tell you that he's going to be uncommunicative for a while as he works out whatever issues are troubling him.

By knowing about these different coping mechanisms, which are indigenous to each sex, we can better see things from each other's perspective, not be angry anymore, and perhaps even compromise with one another.

Keep the Change!

Another thing many women tend to do that drives men crazy is to involve themselves in other people's lives. While you find it fascinating that Jane is going out with Scott when she really should be dating Fred, the men in your life wonder how in the world you have the time or energy to care. They also wonder how, based on a friendship you made with a woman only hours ago, you can tell her how to dress or wear her hair and even change your own look depending upon what she shares with you.

Of course, men will put up with such perceived "interference" and "female bonding" as long as it doesn't apply to them. At first a man may go along with it, especially when it occurs at the beginning of the relationship. However, when you insist that he wear the red suspenders with the butterflies and he decides against it, don't push it! Unless he specifically asks for help in changing his image, or in improving his relationship with his mother, or in moving up the ladder at work, hold back on your efforts to make him over. Otherwise, the man in your life will feel as though you don't accept him the way he is and end up resenting you.

No Competition Allowed Here!

A man comes home from work so angry that there's practically steam coming out of his ears. His face is red and he looks as though he is about to burst. As he walks through the door and sees you—his wife—he lets loose about an incident that occurred at the office. It seems that his office mate stole his idea that would have made him the perfect candidate for an important business trip.

You feel just terrible about his plight—so terrible, in fact, that you conjure up a similar experience you once had. Here's what's likely to happen if you share that experience with him:

She says: I know exactly what you mean. When I was in my sorority, Chi Omega, back in college, I told one of my sorority sisters and best friends about this great girl I especially liked during Rush. Rush is the time that freshmen come to visit our house and we decide who we want to let into our sorority. Well, my best friend "stole" her away and the two of them became best friends, started a clique, and I was left out in the cold. I was devastated because it was my idea to have her in the sorority in the first place!

He says: What! Why are you telling me that lame story? I'm the one in pain here, not *you!* Why do you always have to compete with me whenever I try to share anything with you?

She says: Compete with you? I'm just trying to help you—to relate to you.

He says: Well, you're not relating to me. You're making me crazy. I wanted you to listen to me.

Communication Breakdown!

Don't try to fix your man or make him think he doesn't know what he's doing, especially in business situations. Instead of saying, "You should have told that creep off—he's a lowdown, dirty scoundrel. Tell the boss what he did!" you might say, "Honey, what do you think you're going to do?" That way, he comes up with the solution on his own.

Now, it may seem unfair to you that he would react in such a negative way because you know that's *exactly* what you'd expect to hear from another woman, and what you'd really want from your husband if you came home to him with such a story. You would want him to identify with you—to feel your pain and anguish. You would know how he felt if he related a similar experience that he may have gone through.

But that's because you're a woman, and you react in a way that's different from your male counterparts in such situations. Men view this as competition! So, as tempting as it may be to share your experiences, don't. What a man wants to hear is how right he is and how wrong the other person is. Be on his side. Stick up for him. Say, "Honey, I don't blame you for being so upset. That's just awful. What a horrible jerk he is to do that to you!" You can support him by being on his side and sticking up for him.

Get to the Point Already!

Whenever I give my lecture "He Says, She Says: Gender Differences in Communication," I always get a huge laugh from the audience whenever I bring up the topic of male-female differences in getting to the point. I will usually ask five or so men about what they did that day, and they will briefly tell me of certain specific events. When I ask the same question of women, the answers I get are completely different. Here's an example:

He says:	I made some calls, went to breakfast, read the paper, and came here.
She says:	I got up at 8 A.M. and got upset because the desk was supposed to wake me at 7 A.M. I guess they got confused with so many people attending this convention. I just didn't want to miss your talk, so I rushed to get ready. I got dressed in a hurry but then I couldn't find my shoes. My aqua dress needed the right shoes, and I had no idea where they were. So I put on these ugly brown ones, and I hope nobody is looking at my feet. Then I came down on the elevator and ran into so many people I haven't seen in such a long time—so many good friends I have made through the years by coming to these conferences. I realized it was late, so I grabbed a Danish and I am eating it now, and here I am.

These two very different responses to the very same question might seem amusing in my lecture environment, but I can assure you that it is not so funny when men and women are engaged in a dialogue and trying to get their points across. It can be maddening and thereby lead to miscommunication and inevitable verbal battles.

So, the bottom line for women is: Get to the point first and then go into more detail later. Limit the details and sidebar comments of your conversation and don't go off on tangents when you tell men something. Otherwise men tend to get bored with what you're saying or get annoyed with you.

Tell Me You Didn't Say That!

Burt had been sick in bed with the stomach flu for a few days. He finally felt well enough to drag himself downstairs to get something to drink when he heard Kendra on the telephone telling her sister that he threw up all over the bed. Here's the conversation:

Burt says:	How could you tell her that? My illness is nobody else's business.
Kendra says:	She asked how you were so I told her. Besides, she's my sister.
Burt says:	I don't care who she is. I don't want anyone knowing my personal business.
Kendra says:	I tell my sister everything.
Burt says:	Well I don't want everything about me told to anyone. How can I ever trust you with anything I ever tell you again?

As you can see, Burt has a point! Nobody likes their dirty laundry aired. Unfortunately, too many women feel that they can tell all and withhold nothing because doing so is a form of female bonding. Are you one of them? If so, you must learn to respect your man's desire for privacy. If you don't, your man will end up feeling betrayed and angry when he discovers that something he wanted to keep to himself is now the subject of gossip among your friends.

Treading on Sacred Ground

Not only is it essential for you and your fellow females to keep your mouths shut about any personal information you know about your men in general, it is equally important for you to know how much detail to give when discussing your mates or your relationships. Again, women tend to be very detail-oriented and thus think nothing about sharing every single detail about what most men would consider very private situations, conversations, or experiences. Indeed, I've heard women go into amazingly graphic details not only in my private sessions with them in my practice, but when I've appeared as a psychologist on the *Rikki Lake Show*. They do so not to embarrass or shame their men (unless the men have done them wrong!) but because they simply want to share, to empathize with one another, and to vicariously experience the lives of others. Most women do this because, by telling all, they are in essence reliving the luscious or disastrous experience they want you to feel, as though you were right there with them!

He Just Told *You* He Loved You!

When was the last time you asked your man, "Do you love me?" If you're like most women, it wasn't that long ago. And if your man is like most men, he was tired of the question the second or third time you ever asked it, never mind the fifteenth or twentieth time. His usual reply is probably, "Of course I love you, or I wouldn't be here," which probably ends up upsetting you rather than calming your fears or feeding your ego. In fact, surveys show that asking your partner if he loves you is one of the most annoying questions a man can hear from a woman.

However, you're asking this question simply because you need some reassurance. And why not? Everyone needs reassurance, men included. However, women are the ones bold enough to ask for what they need in this area. But you and your female colleagues would probably get the response you really want if you asked the question in a different way. Perhaps if you said, "Honey, I love you, and I love it when you let me know how much you love me back," you wouldn't sound so off-putting, whiny, and insecure.

Now men, you're not off the hook! In the next chapter, we'll explore what men say, or fail to say, that makes women crazy! So, read on!

Bridging the Gap

Men, if your woman *is* asking you if you love her, you may not be doing enough to make her feel secure in the relationship. Tell her you love her again and again and again, even *if*—maybe especially *if*—she doesn't ask you!

The Least You Need to Know

➤ Men: When you ask, "What's wrong?" expect an answer.
  Women: When you're asked, "What's wrong?" answer honestly.

➤ Men: Don't assume women are nagging at you or competing with you when they ask you lots of questions or share their own experiences with you.
  Women: Slow down on the questions and listen first before you empathize.

➤ Men: Let women know when you need your space to regroup.
  Women: Give men some room to think things through on their own.

➤ Men: Understand that women have a need to discuss all the details, which means that sometimes they tell too much and sometimes they have a hard time getting to the point.
  Women: Respect your man's right to privacy.

Chapter 13

Mad About Men

In This Chapter

➤ Why "nice" isn't good enough

➤ Letting her finish her thoughts

➤ Keeping your word

➤ Face-to-face communication

In this chapter, all you men out there will learn exactly what you do that drives the women in your life right up the wall—and then learn some tips that will help you avoid that behavior in the future. Although we've touched on some of this information in earlier chapters, I thought you'd benefit from seeing some more in-depth examples so that you can find more ways to navigate through the tricky corners of your relationship with a member of the female gender. By learning from these examples, I can assure you that you'll be able to avoid some of the most common pitfalls men face when it comes to establishing healthy, harmonious relationships with women. Let's get started!

Is That It? N-I-C-E?

It's a big night for you and your girlfriend. You're taking her to a fancy party, and you know she's been spending hours and hours and tons of money on dolling herself up. Now the moment has come. You ring the doorbell and she opens the door. She greets you with a great big beautiful smile, and you say the three most dreaded words (to a woman) in the English language: "You look nice."

Instead of responding to you with a hug and a kiss and walking out the door with you arm in arm for a heavenly evening, your date instead looks absolutely crestfallen. And why? Because "nice" isn't good enough. "Nice" means, well, nice, okay, average—not gorgeous, or sexy, or adorable. "Nice" is bland. "Nice" is boring. "Nice" is how your grandmother looks when she fixes herself up.

You don't even realize your mistake before your date whisks away from you to immediately change her clothes. At this point, there's really nothing you can do to save yourself or her from the pain and frustration of the moment. The damage is done—this time. Chances are, she'll come downstairs, you'll tell her she looks "nice" again (because you don't yet know what you know now!), and then, no doubt, an argument will ensue. The evening is ruined even before it begins, all because of that nasty four-letter word that is clearly not music to a woman's ears. So men, think of some other, more exciting, adjectives when you see how much time and effort a woman has taken to look her best for you.

He Says, She Says

Men, here are some adjectives you can use instead of "nice" to describe how appealing a woman is to you: "stunning," "phenomenal," "sexy," "classy," or "fly." Even though the word "phat" has a positive meaning these days to describe how great someone looks, you are safer not using it because it might be mistaken for the word "fat." To a woman, this is a zillion times worse than saying "nice."

Feelings Are a Girl's Best Friend

We've discussed this before, so it should come as no surprise to you now that emotions form the heart of the female. It's not that males and females don't share the same emotions or aren't interested in the same subjects; it's that we look at things from completely different perspectives and express them so differently. Maybe you and your girlfriend both enjoy football, but when it comes to talking about it, you come at it from two different directions. You'd probably be thrilled to simply trade football statistics back and forth, but your girlfriend wants to talk about how it *felt* to see the winning touchdown or even to imagine how the quarterback felt when he threw the pass that won the game.

Most of the time, you probably don't mind taking the conversation in that direction, at least when it comes to talking about abstractions. However, the hard part comes when your girlfriend wants you to talk about how *you feel*—where you're at, emotionally speaking. She wants to know how you experience your life and your relationship with her, what it feels like to be you. And that's difficult, isn't it?

Here's how it works. Let's say you take a spin around the track in a race car. I guarantee you that your girlfriend doesn't want "just the facts" about the kind of car you drove or exactly how fast you went. She wants to hear about what it felt like to be behind the wheel, how scared you were, how exhilarated you felt, how the speed of the ride made your legs and arms tingle. And do you know why? It's because she wants to *share* the experience with you, not simply hear about it from a distance. She wants to feel as if she were sitting right next to you during that 10 minutes that so clearly excited you. Why? Because she believes it will bring the two of you even closer together, and she's right. Try it and see.

And when you do, here's another tip that might help open up the lines of communication a bit more. Try providing more inflection or vocal excitement and enthusiasm when you speak, using a wider range of tones than you usually do. Just as you find your girlfriend's high tones a little annoying at times, she thinks your voice sounds monotonous and dull, even when you're talking about something that interests you. Also try using what I call *emotional state verbs* that help both of you understand the direction of the conversation. Women want you to match their emotional excitement. So let loose, and let your voice and the words you use show her how you really feel and what's really going on inside you.

What I Mean Is ...

An **emotional state verb** helps define your feelings and sets the sentence (and the conversation) in an emotional direction. Emotional state verbs include: "I wish," "I feel," "I hope," "I sense," and "I appreciate."

Listen and Enjoy

As I discussed in Chapter 2, "What Do We Really Know About One Another?" one of the biggest barriers to male-female communication is a man's tendency to interrupt. What about you? Do you let the women in your life finish their sentences, complete their stories, take their time when they're describing the events of their days? Or are you inwardly (or even outwardly) tapping your fingers against the table, shaking your leg, impatient and bored, simply because they aren't speaking quickly enough in the short, clipped tones you're used to with your male friends?

If what you want is to form close, intimate relationships with members of the opposite sex, then you have to hold your horses and let the women in your life express themselves freely and openly. Don't interrupt, don't roll your eyes in frustration, and don't frown or grimace in concentration. Simply listen, chime in when you have something you really want to share, and ask questions about her perspective and her feelings about what she's telling you. If you fail to do so, you'll be telling her, in essence, that you're judging her, and judging her badly. She may just hurry up and finish what she's trying to say because she senses that you're bored or disapprove of her and what she is saying, and this just makes matters worse.

He Said, She Said

Don't make the mistake of cutting a woman off in the middle of a conversation—even if you simply don't have time to hear her through. Instead, try to briefly summarize what she said and then gently and politely let her know of your time constraints and that you want to continue hearing about what she has to say at another time. Then ask when you can get together to set up another time to continue your talk. That will reassure her of your respect, which will add to a harmonious and cooperative environment.

Remember, women need time when they speak because they love to explore every feeling they had, every detail they noticed, and every path an event may have taken. As I mentioned in Chapter 12, "Mad About Women," women usually get a vicarious thrill when they get to relive a story, either by telling it themselves or by hearing you tell it to them. Watch and see how the more you let a woman talk, the more intimacies she will share with you and the more animated she will usually become. She also wants you to reciprocate and share your own perspective with her. The best advice I can give you, at least when it comes to personal relationships, is to go with the flow and listen, encourage, and share with the woman in your life. Give back as much detail and emotion as you can in what you say and how you say it.

When it comes to business relationships, time is probably at more of a premium. If you have a female colleague who loads every conversation with time-consuming and extraneous details, gently let her know that, as interested as you are in the whole story, you need the bottom line—just the bottom line—for right now. Later, if time permits, let her know that you are interested in having her share the rest of her perspective with you.

Be a Man of Your Word

> *"Oh, please call. Dear God, please let him call. I won't ask anything else of you, truly I won't, only please let him telephone me now. He said he would call at five. 'I'll call you at five, darling.' That's what he said. 'Darling.' He called me 'darling.'"*

What you just read is an excerpt from a 1925 Dorothy Parker short story titled "The Telephone Call." Even back then, it seems, men tortured women with the simple words "I'll call you," and then failed to do so. Seventy-five years later, not much has changed. Although times are changing, and it is becoming more and more popular for women to call men and ask them out and call them when they haven't heard from them, there are many women who still wait by the phone for men to call them just as the men have promised.

It probably seems obvious to you that promising to phone, or promising to do anything, and then failing to do so is rude and shows a profound lack of respect for the other person. But it all too often happens between men and women, and for reasons that have never been made clear. Perhaps men worry that if they call, they'll be rejected. Or perhaps they're not sure that they want to get further involved. Or maybe they just don't want to seem too eager. Or perhaps they have only said "I'll call you" as a nicety—as a way of parting. Well it's not nice! And women don't appreciate it!

There's no good reason for not calling after you said you would. If you aren't sure you'd like to see the woman again, or you'd rather wait to see how you feel before making the next move, simply say, "It was wonderful to meet you. Perhaps we'll see or speak to each other again." That way, if you decide not to call, you won't have made a promise you'll have to break.

Grow Accustomed to Her Face

Yes, it's perfectly normal to want to gaze at a beautiful woman's body, especially her breasts. But it isn't acceptable to do so when you're in the middle of a conversation with her, especially if you're not already on extremely intimate terms. You'd be surprised how many men do this without even realizing it. Even though it may be flattering for some women to see that you're noticing or appreciating their physical attributes, for most women it is offensive, especially if you seem to be constantly ogling their bodies. This makes a woman feel like a piece of meat and that you really don't hear or respect what she is saying. So, it's important to pay attention and to keep your eyes above her neck rather than below when speaking to a woman.

How can you avoid this communication barrier? Do the "face contact exercise" in which you gaze at the woman's entire face for two seconds, then look at each part of her face, from her forehead to her cheeks to her nose and mouth, all for two

Bridging the Gap

When you're in the midst of conversation with a woman, be sure to make eye contact and then to gaze at her face while she speaks. If you let your eyes drift to her body, she may feel that she's being ogled and disrespected.

seconds each. At first, it may seem stilted to do so, but soon it'll become a natural part of your communication technique.

Empathize, Don't Solve!

Karen was feeling depressed, very depressed. She didn't know what to do, whether to take a more prestigious and lucrative promotion or to stay with her current job that she adored. Her present position seemed more like a party than a job because her colleagues got along so well and cooperated when it came time to sharing the workload and meeting their goals.

Confused about what decision to make, she contacted her boyfriend Ron. Hardly waiting for her to finish describing her dilemma, he blurted out, "It's a no-brainer. Take the money. That's it. Case closed! Now let's decide where to have dinner."

Ron's behavior angered Karen. He failed to take the time to see things from her perspective and to work out the issues with her. She wanted him to invite her to sit down and hash out both sides of the dilemma carefully. She wanted him to see her various points of view and to feel her anguish. She did not want a solution. She wanted compassion, understanding, and support for the decision she eventually would make on her own.

What about you? Can you see yourself reacting as Ron did? If so, you're not alone. As a male, you are doing what comes naturally. As you may remember from past chapters, men are problem solvers. They thrive on fixing things. Maybe it goes back millions of years to the time when men were responsible for feeding their entire clan using only their problem-solving abilities. Maybe your brain is better set up to see the connections between the beginning, middle, and end of a problem.

Unfortunately, when it comes to the women in any aspect of your life, it's best to tone down your problem-solving skills and pump up your listening skills. And if you can add some empathy and compassion—not for the problem itself but for how the woman in your life *feels* about the problem—you'll go a long way in furthering the relationship. Of course, she wants your help in finding a solution, but she doesn't want you to take charge and solve it for her. Instead, she first wants you to understand her, and then she wants to work it out together with you.

No Orders in This Drill!

It was Alice's first day on the job, and she was in tears. It had taken her months and months to land this job, and she had to beat out more than 100 other applicants to get it. She felt like she was the luckiest woman in the world when she arrived at the office bright and fresh on Monday morning.

Her world came crashing down pretty quickly, however, as soon as she met her male boss. He insisted on barking out orders, leaving no room for discussion, and refusing to even attempt to add politeness into the equation. He treated her like a cross between a dog and a robot. As far as Alice was concerned, no pay was worth her staying at a job where she was degraded at every turn.

When I heard Alice's story during a counseling session, I suggested that she stick it out a little longer. I could see from what she told me that she wasn't being singled out for any reason, but that her boss spoke that way to everyone and was considered by all of the female employees to be the most disliked man in the firm. However, it was interesting to note that the male colleagues didn't seem to get offended by his command terms. In fact, many of them spoke the same way. Slowly but surely, Alice learned to work around her boss's "orders" as much as possible and to steel herself against what she realized was his male communication pattern, albeit not a pattern she approved of necessarily.

Communication Breakdown!

Never make direct accusations. For example, don't say, "You didn't get the mail," but instead phrase it as a question such as, "Did you happen to get the mail?" By doing so, you'll avoid sounding like an ogre and engendering resentment.

Not every woman has learned this lesson, however. So men, you have to watch carefully the tone and content of your words. No woman wants to hear commands barked at her, especially in her personal life. Make sure you say "please" or phrase your requests in question form in order to avoid engendering resentment in the women you deal with on a personal or professional basis.

Stop with the Jokes Already!

As you read in earlier chapters, women don't use humor as a way to bond with other people the way that men do. When men try to bond that way with women, men often are quite surprised how quickly their efforts are rebuffed.

When Jonathan went away to Boston for college, his twin sister, Maryanne, stayed behind to attend college in their hometown. She kept running into Jonathan's buddies, who really missed her popular jokester brother. He was really a lot of fun to be with—fun to everyone except Maryanne. She was glad he was away from her so she didn't have to listen to his lame jokes every day. Now she had freedom—that is until she ran into any of his friends on the street or in a shop. They would never fail to tell her a joke. Although she laughed politely, she was frustrated that she couldn't escape what she considered to be the "lame" humor hurled at her by all of Jonathan's friends, whom she apparently had somehow inherited.

Even though she couldn't stand the jokes, her brothers' friends were really just trying to tell her that they liked her and accepted her as part of the gang. To them it was a compliment. To her it was an annoyance. If they really wanted to bond with Maryanne, they would have been better off giving her a compliment.

One of the biggest complaints women have about men is that women can't stand men's constant jokes and don't appreciate hearing that they have "no sense of humor." Women do have a sense of humor; but women don't find jokes about other women funny at all, especially if the jokes degrade women (like "dumb blond" jokes), which they consider sexist. Women especially don't take well to jokes that poke fun at them, personally, either. Whether or not it has to do with being conditioned to be "ladylike," most women, as a rule, don't appreciate "raunchy" humor that deals with bodily functions and sex as much as men do. So don't be surprised if the woman in your life doesn't respond to that typically "male" brand of humor.

Also, save your practical jokes that involve scaring someone half to death and then saying "I was only kidding." While most men will laugh after a practical joke has been revealed because they find it hilarious, women will usually get angry or cry or both. Women feel tricked and degraded, and most women take it as a personal affront to them. And unlike men, women are not likely to forgive someone as easily, because they tend to hold grudges a lot longer than men do. Perhaps this has a lot to do with early childhood conditioning. Groups of boys are conditioned to play together and use practical joking as a way of competing (who can out-smart, out-gross, or out-trick their opponent), and women are conditioned more than men to play in cooperative pairs where competition or one-upmanship doesn't exist.

Now that I've outlined some of the ways both men and women can deal better with anger in relationships—and avoid getting angry in the first place—it's time to move on to a cozier subject—sex.

The Least You Need to Know

➤ Men: Use any other word besides "nice" to describe how a woman looks. Women: Try to give your guy a break if he fails to extol your beauty every time you put on a new dress.

➤ Men: Let a woman finish her stories. It's her way of establishing intimacy. Women: Understand that men communicate with each other using far fewer details than you do.

➤ Keeping promises and commitments shows both respect for the other person and self-respect.

➤ Men: Watch your raunchy humor and practical jokes. Women: Lighten up a bit and realize that just as you use emotional talk as a way to bond, men use humor to foster friendship and closeness.

Part 5

The Art of the Turn-On

Without a doubt, good communication is the key to a good love life and to the kind of intimacy necessary to sustain a romantic, loving relationship. Unless you know how to communicate your most attractive attributes and to recognize the potential of the members of the opposite sex who cross your path, your chances of succeeding in the world of love and romance are pretty small. In the chapters that follow, you'll learn the secrets of attraction between men and women and find out how you can make the most out of your own unique qualities and become the most attractive, sexy individual that you can be!

Chapter 14

Playing
(and Winning)
the Dating Game

In This Chapter

➤ The value of compassion

➤ The power of the voice

➤ Let a smile be your umbrella

➤ Learning to screen people and situations

Okay, admit it. If you're single, you've probably been heard to moan "There are no good men (or women) out there!" on more than one occasion. In my private practice, I hear this refrain constantly, and the people who repeat it are completely convinced they're right.

I'm here to tell you, however, that it is not the case. There are lots of decent men and women out there—probably right in front of you, in fact—but you need to learn how to recognize them, and then how to communicate with them, in order for you to fully understand and accept that fact.

Indeed, once you begin to understand the opposite sex a bit better, your dating life will almost certainly improve. In this chapter, I'm going to show you how the gender differences we've discussed in past chapters can influence your dating patterns and strategies for better and for worse.

Compassion Leads to Passion

The first thing you need to do when it comes to your dating life is to start fresh. That means putting aside all the old stereotypes about the opposite sex that you carry around in your head and heart, stereotypes based on both societal messages and your own personal past experiences. Take a deep breath and make a promise to yourself that you'll look at the next person of the opposite sex you meet with a fresh perspective.

When you do meet a new person with this fresh perspective, you'll get off on an even better footing if you can also approach him or her with a sense of compassion and empathy. If you can look at the world from his or her perspective, your own defenses and insecurities may well disappear. Instead of feeling as if you're this person's adversary or opponent, you'll be able to feel as if you're an ally—or at least an equal.

Think of it this way: As far as you know, the person you're about to approach has been through as many "bad" dates as you have, has suffered as many broken hearts, and is just as apprehensive about stepping back into the fray as are you. With that in mind, keep these four points in mind on your next date. Know that your date …

1. Is just as nervous and afraid as you are.

2. Wants to impress you as much as you want to impress him or her.

3. Wants to meet someone with whom he or she has a connection, and if that connection exists, perhaps take it to another level of intimacy (regular dating or something even more permanent).

4. Wants to feel accepted by you and thus able to feel comfortable and relaxed in your presence.

By first having a compassionate frame of mind and then putting yourself on the same footing by realizing that the two of you are probably feeling the same sense of insecurity and fear, you'll at least have a better date, if not a richer potential for a future relationship.

Indeed, when it comes to dating, one of the biggest hurdles both men and women face is the fear of rejection. Yes, indeed, our own insecurity about our own attractiveness is what causes most of our problems, at least at the start of new relationships. Being insecure encourages us to play games, to pretend, and to hide our true selves from the very people we're hoping to attract.

As undermining as this insecurity is, it's also perfectly natural. Face it: No one wants to be at the other end of rejection. And to avoid that awful feeling, we often go to great lengths, including making ourselves as physically attractive as possible and reading books like this one to get the inside scoop about the opposite sex. But not all our protective measures are so positive: Many of us also learn to build some pretty sturdy walls around our true selves, creating defenses to protect ourselves from men or women who may not accept who we truly are, just the way we are. We keep others at arm's lengths—we even say to ourselves, "I hate dating," or "All men are dawgs (cheaters)," or "All women are out of control"—because otherwise we'd risk our own hearts and souls.

So, starting right now, try to let go of your fears by realizing that you and the one you meet on your next date are in the very same boat—both of you fear rejection and want to be accepted.

Finding a Match Made in Heaven

Prince Charming? Princess Charming? Could you be setting your sights a bit too high when it comes to choosing the right mate for yourself? All too often, people become disappointed because they have unrealistic expectations about who the "right" mate would be for them.

Instead of searching for someone who is probably not only unattainable but also inappropriate, look instead for more basic and identifiable qualities that you can assess that are realistic and appropriate for your lifestyle. Your goal is to find someone who attracts you physically, of course, but also someone who comes closest to you on these other levels:

➤ Mentally

➤ Emotionally

➤ Financially

➤ Spiritually

➤ Socially

➤ Morally

Your goal, really, is to find someone who is headed in the same direction as you are and who shares the same basic outlook on life as you do. The most important factor of all is that you share the same moral and spiritual values— without that in common, you'll have little to build upon in the end. Let's take a look at these issues one by one.

Communication Breakdown!

Beware of the pitfalls of realizing your "fantasy mate." If you're a man lusting after a supermodel, think about how little time this "goddess" would have to spend with you, considering her hectic lifestyle. If you're a woman who thinks of a Donald Trump-type go-getter as her ideal husband, consider the energy he'll expend on building his financial empire instead of a cozy nest with you.

In the Eye of the Beholder

Chemistry: That physical connection between a man and a woman so important to the success of a romantic relationship. Without question, such chemistry is as important to women as it is to men. However, by the same token, whether you want to admit it or not, it's also true that physical appearance—body shape and type, hair color and style, and so on—is an important factor. Indeed, our own perceptions about the way we look are at the base of most of our insecurities. As I'll discuss next, however, physical appearance as it relates to the opposite sex seems to be more important to men than to women.

Men and Their Icons

Like it or not, most men will judge a woman by her physical appearance and, often, that criterion alone may be enough for him to determine whether or not he wants to approach her at all. In fact, I've had several male clients who admitted that they've left a blind date in the lurch after catching a glimpse of them beforehand and, finding that their looks were not to their liking, simply left without introducing themselves. As far as these men were concerned, if the physical component—just the way she looks on the outside—doesn't make it for them, there simply isn't any point in even meeting. Perhaps in the long run these men are really doing women a favor by not subjecting them to their superficiality and shallowness.

Bridging the Gap

Start letting go of your anxieties about your physical appearance. A wide range of physical types considered beautiful and attractive exists today in magazines, on television, and in movies. Combined with a confident personality and a well-developed sense of style, you can shine!

What a man finds physically attractive in a woman varies, of course, depending on the man's age, cultural background, and personal preferences. Surveys show that men who grew up with voluptuous women as the sex goddesses of the day, such as Sophia Loren and Marilyn Monroe in the 1950s and early 1960s, tend to be more physically attracted to those curvy body types; while those who grew up looking at Twiggy (in the 1960s) and Kate Moss (in the 1990s) tend to favor super-thin women. And there other types that became popular at different times—the super-fit, aerobically driven Jane Fonda types of the 1980s and the buxom babe lifeguards of the *Baywatch* 1990s, to name just two. Generally speaking, what a man perceives as attractive when he's in his adolescence—and what society reinforces as attractive at that time—is what he oftentimes remains attracted to as an adult.

In addition to the societal icons to which one is exposed, a man's cultural and geographic backgrounds also determine the type of woman to whom he's attracted. Anthropologists have noted that Europeans, Middle Easterners, and Africans tend to favor a heavier-set woman more than do most men born and raised in the United States. And even within the United States, many have observed that such preferences may depend on what geographic area a man is brought up within. Men who are raised in cities such as Los Angeles, Manhattan, and Miami, where industries contain an abundance of models and actresses, and physical looks are considered a premium, often have a tendency to be more attracted to a thinner woman.

Sometimes when a person leaves one of these entertainment meccas where physicality is at a premium, they find that there is life beyond the focus of thinness and aesthetics takes on a different meaning. One of my Los Angeles clients, who was slightly overweight yet proportional, had a hard time meeting men, rarely dated, and felt unattractive and very fat. Now she's moved to Chicago, where men constantly approach her, a far cry from Los Angeles where she was virtually ignored. This scenario is very common among women who go to other parts of the country and are a lot more appreciated.

Finally, ideals of beauty depend on the man's own personal imprinting: If he had a crush on a redhead in junior high, chances are he'll find redheads attractive when he's an adult. Or maybe he fantasized about his older next-door neighbor who had long dark hair and a Rubenesque figure and now finds this type attractive to him. And this imprinting does not necessarily fit into standard cultural ideals of beauty. Certain men will find overweight, excessively thin, or athletic women attractive if women who looked that way were once important to them.

And thank goodness! Such a wide diversity of factors makes it likely that no single standard of beauty will ever prevail—which means that there's a man somewhere out there attracted to almost every type of woman. There are men who like very overweight woman, while others like very tall and skinny women, while still others prefer blondes. It's all very subjective and very personal.

What's important for all of us—men and women alike—to realize is that men are very visual and thus do judge women by their physical attributes. Again, that is *not* to say that all men find the same physical type attractive—far from it. But because physical appearance is so important to men, it does mean that in order to be attractive to men, a woman must be well-groomed and confident in her own physical beauty within her own type.

So if you're a petite woman who feels you'll never find a man because you're not taller, stop worrying! There are plenty of men who love petite women. If you're a curvaceous brunette, go with it all the way instead of trying to starve yourself into a body you'll never have—otherwise you might miss the chance to find a man who'll love the way you look, just the way you are.

Women: More Forgiving

Although it seems that women are more obsessed about their physical appearance than men are, men have their own set of insecurities about their looks. Despite the fact that Roger was an attractive man, he became obsessed with his hair. Terrified that

147

he was going bald, he used all kinds of hair concoctions to try and make his hair grow back, none of which (of course) worked. He wore toupees, which turned most women off, then shaved his head, then decided to have hair transplant surgery. He still wasn't satisfied with how his hair looked.

And do you know what? Nobody much noticed the difference or cared. The reason why women weren't attracted to Roger was because he paid more attention to his hair than he did to the women he dated. Women are more concerned about who men are, what they do for a living, and how they treat women than they are about men's looks. Of course, women, too, grow up with their own preferences about looks and physical attractiveness; but more often than not, women are more concerned about how men treat them, as we'll see further in Chapter 20, "What Women Want and Don't Want from Men."

Accent the Positive: Strategies of Attraction

Now that we've covered the fact that both men and women are insecure about their physical appearance, we can explore some of the best ways to accent some important qualities that will boost your chances of attracting the right people to you better than any diet or exercise plan can do. Those qualities include your voice, your confidence level, and your smile.

The Sound of Music

Studies show that the way you speak is more important than the way you look when it comes to attracting members of the opposite sex. If your voice is annoying to others, or difficult to understand (you stammer or mumble), you may find it hard to get past the first meeting in any relationship. In fact, my own research for my doctoral dissertation showed that the way a person spoke was more important than the way a person looked.

If you cannot stand the sound of your voice, or suspect that it's holding you back from forming new friendships, fix it. You'd spend hundreds of dollars on a new outfit—why not spend less money on something that will really get you results? There are countless resources to help you improve your speaking voice. Read *Talk to Win* (Putnam, 1987) and get my audiotape on the subject, which will give you all the steps you need to develop an excellent speaking voice. You may also contact our offices at info@drlillianglass.com for individual consultations.

Confident and Sexy!

Four seconds—according to studies, that's all the time you have to make that essential "first impression." If you're a woman who's friendly and easy to talk to in those first four seconds, you're likely to attract a man to you. If you're a man who exudes confidence, most women will be willing to spend some more time with you to find out more about who you really are. Remember to be interested in her and not worry about being interesting yourself. You don't have to boast. Just let her know who you are by what you say and how you say it.

Part of being confident is being well-groomed. If you take the time to take care of yourself, you're showing the world that you're worth that care. I'll expound upon this subject in more detail in Chapter 16, "Intimate Misunderstandings."

Smiling Faces Go Places

When I ask a man what drew him to the woman he is with presently, he will almost inevitably say: "Her smile." Why is smiling so important, especially to a man? Because it indicates acceptance. Although the tradition is changing, it's often customary for the man to make the first move in a relationship, and when that move is greeted with a warm smile, the tension and anxiety he has been experiencing simply melt away. A smile is, in essence, the green light that lets the man know he can approach a woman with confidence and hope.

He Says, She Says

According to studies, while women smiled 93 percent of the time when they were around men, their smiles were reciprocated by men only 67 percent of the time. This may indicate that men may not be focusing on the women or paying attention to them, or the men may be feeling a bit self-conscious or awkward smiling back.

This makes for uncomfortable feelings when this happens to women. Men need to be conscious of this. Pay attention and be on the lookout for smiling women. When you see one, always return her smile! Not doing so is interpreted as rude and rejecting!

Warmth Is the Key

One very poor technique that some men and women use when playing the dating game is that once they've managed to finally catch someone's eye, to pretend to not be interested in the very person they've been working hard to attract. Perhaps many people act aloof at this point in order to protect themselves, once again, from possible rejection. They may also enjoy setting up a greater challenge for their intended "catches," figuring that if their dates make that extra effort, their dates must really find them interesting and alluring.

Bridging the Gap

Let a smile be your umbrella, or at least let it signal acceptance and interest if you meet someone of the opposite sex to whom you're attracted. Don't act aloof or disinterested; you'll only turn off the very person you're hoping to turn on.

But this strategy rarely works, and for at least two reasons. First, who wants a man or woman insecure enough to want you only if he or she can manage to "break down" your pretense of resistance? And second, it's likely that this person will remember long into the future the initial feeling of rejection he or she felt when you acted so aloof and uninterested at the start of the relationship.

That Very Important Next Step

Let's say you've gotten past the initial stage of attraction and have managed to put aside your insecurities and stop playing games long enough to actually meet. Now it's time to start to get to know one another so that you both can decide if there's really something worth going after between you. At this stage of the process, there are two very simple but very essential rules that you must follow:

1. Don't lie.

2. Don't be selfish or egotistical.

These tips may seem both obvious and trite, but in fact, too many men and women think it's all right to say almost anything as long as it impresses a member of the opposite sex and to focus all the attention on their own accomplishments in an effort to impress. But in the end, these tactics only backfire and leave those who attempt them alone and lonely. Let's take these major dating offenses one by one.

The Truth Will Out

Lying—either by omission (like failing to tell someone you're dating that you're married) or commission (by pretending you have a job or a salary that you don't)—is not only pointless, since the truth will eventually come to light, but also shows a lack of respect for the other person. Hurt feelings and a profound lack of trust will almost certainly follow.

And it doesn't matter what the lie concerns. Traditionally, women lie about their age and—traditionally—men have ended up resenting it. I've had numerous men in my practice admit how upset they were when they found out that the women in their lives had lied about their ages. "If she lied about her age," these men complain, "what else is she going to lie about?" Getting past this initial breach of trust may be impossible, no matter how benign the lies seemed to the women who perpetrated them. From that point on, as benign a matter she may have thought it was, trust is gone.

Men, on the other hand, tend to often exaggerate about their assets, what they have, how much money they have, or what positions they hold.

While it's important to make yourself sound as appealing as possible, don't go overboard. Never misrepresent yourself. It will *always* come back to haunt you.

Be Interested, Not Interesting

Another strategy you want to avoid is coming across as selfish and narcissistic when you're first getting to know someone. Sounds pretty obvious, doesn't it? But you'd be surprised at how easy it is to cross the line between putting your best foot forward and being obnoxiously self-centered. In an effort to show off your best qualities, you can lose sight of the goal of these initial meetings—to get to know the person to whom you're attracted. Instead, out of very normal nervousness and insecurity, you make the conversations all about you, your accomplishments, and your interests.

Communication Breakdown!

Of course you know the definition of lying, right? Well, don't be too sure. What you consider playful exaggeration or simple joking may be cruel lying to others. Stick with the absolute truth until you can gauge the other person's perception with some degree of accuracy.

If you find yourself talking about yourself too much, stop and take a deep breath. Then start asking questions of your date, questions about his or her interests and accomplishments, his or her family situation and past history.

Always keep in mind the phrase *"be interested, not interesting"* whenever you're talking to someone you might have a romantic interest in. By doing so, you'll gain important insight into his or her character, values, and views. The key is to ask questions, listen to the answers without passing judgment, and then share your own insights. By doing so, you'll open up the all-important line of true communication that is essential if the relationship is to deepen and grow.

In addition, by taking the time to learn about the other person in a more intimate and constructive way, you'll be able to spot some warning signs of a potentially bad relationship before you become too involved.

Flags and Warnings

Red Flag #1: The Married Person. "Oh, but my wife doesn't understand me," he says. "We are going to get a divorce," she says. Those lines have been said to unsuspecting women by conniving men (and vice versa) since the beginning of time. And, much to our disgust, we heard them again when Monica Lewinsky claimed that Bill Clinton uttered them to her during their liaisons in the White House. Needless to say, if the person you're attracted to is married, run—as fast as your legs can carry you.

151

The odds of a fulfilling, long-term relationship emerging out of such a situation are not phenomenally high.

Red Flag #2: The Victim. She says: "My first husband was drunk and violent. My second husband put me in debt by running up all the credit cards, and my last boyfriend, who I lived with for five years, cleaned out my bank account to run off with a bimbo he worked with." He says: "My first wife always harped on me. My second wife was a real b - - - h. The girl I lived with for five years would always put me down and nothing I could do would ever please her."

Needless to say, a woman (or a man) with this kind of history is bound to be trouble. Not only does she or he probably need quite a bit of therapy, but he or she also has a penchant for picking losers and abusers. Since you're neither, it's best to cut your losses and look for someone more stable.

Be a Friend First

Romance. Roses. A wife. A husband. A parent for your children. When you think of dating, chances are your mind wanders to these kinds of fantasy images of the mate of your dreams. As natural and normal as these fantasies are, however, in the end, they're just that—fantasies.

Ask any couple married more than 10 years what the secret to their longevity is and you'll probably hear this simple truth: "We're best friends." They don't say, "It's the great sex we have," or, "We make a lot of money." Instead, the glue that holds a couple together is friendship, a bond made of mutual respect, admiration, the sharing of interests, and simple compassion. That translates into love. The friendship, honesty, and open communication are what make the sex great sex and allow for long-lasting love—true romantic love. Never lose sight of that goal as you learn to communicate better with members of the opposite sex.

The Least You Need to Know

➤ Remember that everyone fears rejection. The other person has many of the same insecurities you do.

➤ When it comes to attracting a member of the opposite sex, the quality of your voice is as important as what you say and how you look.

➤ The easiest and most powerful tool you can use on a date is your smile.

➤ Forming a close friendship, by listening and sharing, is the best way to start and then maintain an intimate relationship.

Chapter 15

Attracting the Opposite Sex

In This Chapter

➤ Learning about physical types

➤ The power of personality

➤ Confidence matters

➤ Learning to listen

In the last chapter, I briefly mentioned physical attraction as one of the important factors in any romantic relationship. In this chapter, you'll learn how the other sex really sees your sex, and what characteristics they find most appealing. Even though it may seem superficial to many of you and may, in fact, anger you to discuss physical attraction, it is a reality. People do relate to you based upon how they are attracted to you, whether it is by the way you look, speak, or act, or by all three elements. It's not fair, but it is one of those unfortunate realities of life we have to cope with.

Who's Type Are You, Anyway?

Since we all come in different shapes and sizes, it stands to reason that not everyone will be attracted to the same physical shape or type of person. Which is a good thing all around, because, otherwise, most of us would spend our lives striving to be people we're not and can never be. Short, petite brunettes will never be tall, buxom blondes. If you're a slight, small-boned man, you'll never look like a championship wrestler. Those are the plain and simple facts, and it's best to accept them—honor them now and truly appreciate who you really are as a person so that others can do the same.

The good news, however, is that we can make the most of what we've got and thus become as attractive and appealing as possible within our own "types." Take Nina, for example, who's a client of mine. Nina is a short, curvaceous brunette with large brown eyes and olive skin. She shared with me how discouraged she was to be going out to dance clubs with her best friend Veronica because Veronica was tall, model-thin, light-skinned, and blonde. As Nina said, "She always gets all the guys. I feel ugly, fat, and dumpy around her."

When she took my advice and stopped comparing herself to Veronica and concentrated on bringing out her own best qualities—her curves, her big beautiful eyes, her sparkling personality—her life made a dramatic turn. About three weeks later, I got a call from a bouncy-voiced Nina, who told me that as soon as she stopped trying to be someone she couldn't be, she freed herself up to have fun and to shine.

Unfortunately, too many people are caught up comparing themselves to others who they feel may have more positive attributes than they do. Perhaps they are brainwashed by Madison Avenue to feel this sense of insecurity. But it needs to stop in order for a person to get the most out of his or her life.

He Said, She Said

Research at Loyola University in Chicago pointed out that only 1 percent of the women surveyed were attracted to a "he-man," muscular body type, even though magazine ad pages proclaim this to be the ideal type male. Most women perceived men with this body type as being "vain" or "abnormal looking." Interestingly enough, what women did prefer were men with body types that matched their own. Fit women liked athletic types, bookish or artistic women liked leaner men, and heavier women liked stockier men.

As discussed in the last chapter, beauty is indeed in the eyes of the beholder. Each of us is attracted to a specific type of person based on our cultural backgrounds, our innate preferences, and our past histories. But what makes virtually everyone—of every type and every background—more attractive is a vibrant personality and an attractive smile.

Take Larissa and Anissa, twins I once knew in Los Angeles. Although these women were identical twins, which meant they shared every gene and every characteristic, one twin (Anissa) was perceived by almost everyone around her as being more beautiful than her twin sister, Larissa. That's because Anissa had more expression in her face and more life and exuberance than did Larissa. She used more of her facial muscles when she spoke and exuded more charisma. This animated facial expression made Anissa not only the more beautiful of the two, but also the more popular because she was more outgoing and, therefore, much more accessible to others than her sister.

Personality and the personal chemistry between two individuals are important factors in the physical attractiveness equation. I'm sure you've experienced this yourself: You're not attracted to someone at first, but as you continue to speak and get to know one another, you find yourself more and more drawn to that person— physically—because of what's happening on an intellectual or emotional level. Although that kind of thing usually happens more to women— men are still highly visual creatures who value looks above personality—it is an important quality to remember as you navigate through the dating world.

Communication Breakdown!

Don't jump to conclusions! Both men and women need to take their time when it comes to assessing their attraction levels to one another. Before turning off someone who doesn't perfectly fit your physical requirements, listen to his or her voice, see how his or her smile affects you, let a touch or a handshake give you another clue. You may find that you become physically attracted to that person after all.

What Attracts You the Most?

A survey I conducted among about 50 people shows that women and men value different qualities when it comes to what they're looking for in a relationship with the opposite sex. Here are my results:

Qualities Most Desired by Women:

1. Financial security (82 percent)
2. Intelligence
3. Personality
4. Physical attraction

Qualities Most Desired by Men:

1. Physical attraction (93 percent)
2. Personality
3. Intelligence
4. Financial security

Now let's take a look at what this survey really says about what women want from men and vice versa.

As obnoxious and superficial as it may seem, according to my survey, women tend to be attracted to men with money while men tend to be attracted to women with beauty. My findings support other similar studies that show that, on the whole, women value economic resources 100 percent more than men do—in Japan, that number jumps up to 150 percent more—while men value physical beauty much more than do women!

Perhaps these two findings validate the evolutionary process. Historically, women have expected men to be the "hunters" and "protectors" while men have looked to women as potential sexual partners who could bear them children. Our early male ancestors had to be attracted to women so they could acceptably procreate with them. Women, in turn, found men desirable if the men could provide for them and their children whom they sired. So today, it's not surprising that these qualities—financial security in men and sexual attractiveness in women—would continue to be revered.

Confidence: The Key to Sexual Attractiveness

What makes a man sexy? Remember the James Bond 007 movies starring Sean Connery? Remember how sexy Bond was as he sauntered onto the screen? Remember how he looked at a woman with one eyebrow raised and purred out his sensuous introduction, "Bond, James Bond"?

What I Mean Is ...

Self-confidence means you feel great about yourself. It is the feeling you have when you know who you really are and feel that you have the world at your fingertips. It is a sense of knowing that you can do things that nobody else knows but you. It is an inner strength and an inner power that people sense in one another and find extremely attractive.

In addition to being physically stunning, Sean Connery as Bond also exuded a *self-confidence* that made him even more attractive. The way he carried himself, the way he walked, the way he talked, his sensuous tone, his accent, the words he chose, the purr of his voice, and the way he deeply looked into a woman's soul are what won our hearts then, and now, which is why he remains on *People* magazine's "Sexiest Man Alive" list today. Men, too, universally found him sexy because of the risks he took and the adventures he found himself in and because of his boldness and self-assuredness.

Confidence is what allows men to be successful, to take more risks, to be bolder, and to become even more successful. It allows people to make more money and have more power—traits that make anyone more appealing to either sex.

And the boost to one's attractiveness gained from self-confidence is available to women as well. An example from the silver screen is Audrey Hepburn, who played her characters with such demure confidence that both men and women were drawn to her. Indeed, self-confidence is the ultimate beauty secret. Why? Because having self-confidence allows women to feel good about themselves and to feel attractive. When a woman knows who she is, and feels good about who she is, it shows on her face. As a result, her muscles become more relaxed and she is freer to express herself. She says what she means and means what she says, not worrying about what some-one else thinks about her. The same holds true for men, too!

Getting Some Confidence and Charisma

Self-confidence isn't something you're born with. It's a quality you develop over time and through experience. It is something that hopefully is nurtured in childhood by your parents, teachers, and peers—those significant people in your life who give you positive reinforcement for being who you are and doing what you do. Unfortunately, it is something that can be easily undermined by bad parenting, difficult relation-ships, or difficult challenges as we go through the hardships of life. In these instances it is not uncommon for a person's self-confidence to become a bit shaky.

Therefore, if you lack self-confidence, you may need some help in tracking down the source of your insecurity. Working with a trained therapist, who can help you resolve any past or current stumbling blocks, is one way to increase your sense of self-esteem.

Another important step to take is to surround yourself with positive, caring, and compassionate people. You need to be around those who truly support you and bring out the best in you. You need to be around those who allow you to be all that you can be. You need to be around people who truly let you shine. Take another look at Chapter 11, "Basic Madness: Unmanaged Anger," in which I discussed the undermining influence of "toxic" people. Evaluate who you choose to have around you, and if someone detracts from your self-confidence in any way, dismiss that per-son from your life as soon as possible, or learn the different ways to deal with that person so that he or she won't burn a hole in your self-esteem.

Bridging the Gap

Don't hesitate to start down the path of personal change, be-cause the rewards are certainly worth the effort. In fact, it may be extremely exciting to start a fresh, new approach to life. Take one step at a time, be patient with yourself, surround yourself with positive people who pro-vide you with reinforcement, and you'll soon see a more confident and "centered" *you* emerge.

The Touch of Attraction

So far, I've talked about the importance of making the most of your physical attributes, the appeal of accepting your personal style, and realizing that not everyone is going to be attracted by it. I discussed the importance of being the best that you can be, and the attraction that one's self-confidence has for others. There are just a few other factors in the equation, one of which is touch. Indeed, that elusive quality called "chemistry" also has a very physical component.

Shake It Up, Baby!

What's the first instance of physical contact most people have? That's right, the handshake. And so, as you might imagine, how you shake hands is very important when it comes to attracting a member of the opposite sex as you first meet him or her. A wimpy fish-like gripped handshake that lacks strength indicates a lack of confidence. A sweaty handshake indicates nervousness. A handshake that's too firm indicates egotism or aggression or vying for power and dominance.

When you shake a person's hand, it is important to not be afraid to touch that person. Place your palm inside their palm. Cup your thumb around theirs and with a firm comfortable grip give three shakes. Make sure that your palms are touching—that skin is touching skin. This shows that you are open and confident and communicative.

At first it may seem awkward to you, but if you continue to practice this way of shaking hands with the opposite sex, it will become more and more comfortable until it becomes second nature. You will also begin to notice how much more receptive men and women are to you when you first meet them.

That First Touch

According to studies, a woman is more likely to let a man know that she likes him or is interested in him by touching his forearm while she is talking to him. Dr. David Givens, an anthropologist at the University of Washington, has studied body language during courtship. He found that if two people are interested in one another, they will mutually exchange a series of "affectionate gestures" by accidentally touching one another during conversation. For example, one person might take hold of the other's wrist while admiring a watch or touch the other's shoulder while brushing a piece of lint off his or her coat.

According to anthropologists, affectionate gestures are bodily cues—often indirect and subtle—that indicate openness, trust, and attraction on the part of the one who gestures.

So, if you want to let someone know that you might be interested in them, the right gestures might very well be your courting signals.

Translating Body Language

In addition to your facial expression, you reveal your personality and your attitude through your body posture. If you stand straight and stiff, you give the impression that you're feeling uptight and unapproachable. A casual stance indicates that you're in a more open and friendly mood. If you're uncomfortable and it shows in the way you carry yourself, you'll find it more difficult to attract members of the opposite sex. In essence, your own discomfort makes them uncomfortable. The posture you want to take is one in which you are relaxed; however, you do hold your head up, square your shoulders, and keep your eyes open and alert to the people around you.

Making eye contact is especially important when you're engaged in conversation. As you may remember from previous chapters, a self-confident, attractive person is not thinking about himself or herself, but instead is looking at, listening to, and concentrating on the person with whom they are conversing. Remember what was said earlier: "Be interested, not interesting!" If you always remember this phrase you will never fail with another person. You will never be at a loss for words, and you will always be focusing on them instead of being so self-conscious about yourself that you act in ways that don't reflect who you are.

When I helped my client Rod to be a better listener by concentrating on his wife's words and looking at her face as she spoke, he took what I said to heart. About a week later, he reported that his newfound listening skills helped him please his wife. "One evening, she started talking all about these designer sunglasses she'd been searching for. I listened to the details about the glasses and the next day found them in a store. She was in complete shock when I brought them to her. She asked me how I knew they were her favorite glasses. I was so pleased to be able to say, 'Because I listened to you.'"

If you're a man—or a woman, for that matter—who needs help to improve your listening skills, take another look at Chapters 6, "Nature Meets Nurture," and 10, "Learning the Basics of Good Communication with the Opposite Sex," in which I give you lots of tips. Being a good listener is one of the most attractive qualities a man or woman can offer.

The Least You Need to Know

➤ By not seeing yourself as a physical "type," you can stop comparing yourself to others and appreciate your own uniqueness.

➤ Looks are fine, but having a warm personality is just as powerful, if not more powerful.

➤ Confidence is the key to timeless beauty and allure and sexual attraction in both men and women.

➤ Listening attentively makes you more attractive to the other person.

John, I'd like you to meet my parents...

Hello!

Intimate Misunderstandings

In This Chapter

➤ Why communication is so important to good physical relations

➤ Cuddling

➤ The power of touch

➤ Making up after arguments

➤ What to do when your partner "has a headache"

Thus far, you have seen how it is so easy to misinterpret someone else's intentions simply because you aren't familiar with how males and females react to and communicate with one another. These differences are far-reaching and can have serious implications if you don't pay attention to them during the most crucial moments between men and women—those moments of intimacy.

Most therapists who counsel people with intimacy problems will tell you there is no question that one of the main causes of today's high incidence of sexual dysfunction and incompatibility among couples lies in the fact that men and women don't know how to communicate with one another in the bedroom. In this chapter, you'll see how and why some of these differences can lead to intimacy problems and how becoming sensitive to those differences can afford you a new and improved love life.

Sexy Differences

It probably comes as no surprise to you that men and women are sexually turned on by different stimuli. Research has repeatedly shown that men, more so than women, are stimulated by the visual, while women find the auditory aspect of intimacy to be of paramount importance. Indeed, Oscar Wilde put it best when he said, "Men love with their eyes, women with their ears." In essence, men love to look at the object of their love while women love to listen to the object of their love. They love to hear those "sweet nothings" and terms of love and affection.

In essence, men are more turned on sexually and are stimulated more by what they see visually. Women tend to be more sexually aroused by what they hear from their partners—what is said to them when they are making love.

No matter how much Viagra or other items (chemical or mechanical) are used to enhance the sexual act, the most essential aspect of the lovemaking process is lost if couples don't know how to communicate effectively with one another. Not knowing what to say and how to say it in an open, honest, and sensitive way can ruin any relationship, especially an intimate one.

Styles of Affection

Touch is the key ingredient in intimacy. We discovered in earlier chapters that men and women touch so differently, with men touching more than women, and women often not being direct enough in terms of how they like to be touched while men are perhaps too direct in how they wish to be touched. This difference can be a huge problem in terms of intimate relations. All too often, couples will remain unsatisfied and frustrated with one another because they haven't communicated their physical needs and desires. Thus, it is essential for both parties to communicate exactly how they want to be touched.

Bridging the Gap

Speak up! When it comes to getting what you need in the bedroom, communication is the essential key. Tell your mate how you like to be touched, then let him or her know when you're satisfied with words or touch. By doing so, you'll reinforce "good behavior."

Cuddling Women

Even though men tend to touch women in a social environment, they often don't practice this positive habit in the bedroom. Columnist Ann Landers took a poll several years ago that revealed that women enjoyed cuddling and snuggling with men just as much as they enjoyed having sexual intercourse with them, perhaps because women are traditionally touched and cuddled more as infants than men are.

Unfortunately, most men tend to find that cuddling doesn't come naturally to them. In fact, they may become very sensitive to sex and actually dislike being touched for some time. This makes for a lot of hard feelings, which oftentimes go unexpressed.

Never let that happen! Discuss it. Discuss when it feels comfortable to be touched. Don't take anything personally without discussing it first. If you're a woman who wants to be held after sex, it's up to you to make your desires known. You can do this by initiating the act of touching and showing him just how you want to be held. You might also simply verbalize what you want by saying, "It makes me feel so good when you hold me," or "I feel so close to you when you touch me."

If you're a man who finds it difficult to remain intimate right after intercourse, tell the woman in your life about this directly. Let her know that you love her and enjoy being close to her, but that you need a little time-out before resuming physical intimacy. Otherwise, you risk making her feel discarded or used after sex.

The good news is that the more you touch your partner, the closer and more intimate you'll become as a couple. According to studies, those who report that they are in happy marriages sit closer to one another than those whose marriages aren't as happy.

Teasing Leads to Hurt Feelings

Remember when I talked about the gender differences in humor, that men like to tease while women tend to take such teasing personally? Well, needless to say, the last place you'd want to see this communication malfunction occur is in the bedroom. Women do not like to be teased about their bodies, especially when they're naked and vulnerable in bed. So all you men out there, resist joking about "cottage cheese thighs" or "cute, round tummies" or you'll risk undermining your woman's self-confidence and damaging your relationship.

Kissing and Making Up

As discussed, studies show that men get over arguments more quickly than women do—and when they do, they're ready for physical intimacy. Men look at an argument as an event—sort of like a contest, with a winner and a loser. They see the argument as having a beginning, a middle, and an end. After the end, most men move on quickly with no hard feelings, and usually think nothing of wanting to make love after an argument. Not so with women. Women often can't understand how their mates could even

Bridging the Gap

If you're a man, you need to make sure that an argument is over in your woman's mind before attempting to be affectionate or sexually intimate with her. Using very soft and even tones, ask her how she feels about what you've just been through, and only when you're both on the same wavelength should you expect physical intimacy to resume.

163

think of physical intimacy after the emotional trauma of an argument. Indeed, the very act of approaching women for sex at this time can cause another argument.

At the same time, it's important for women to learn to either let go of any remaining resentment or express it clearly in order to bring closure to an argument. The very last thing they should do is bring up a past argument in bed, which will only put distance between them and their partners and make true intimacy—physical or emotional—almost impossible.

Speak Up and Speak Out

In a Gallup Poll survey I once commissioned, I asked more than 1,000 American men and women throughout the United States if they were satisfied with what they heard in bed from their partner. Surprisingly, the majority of both men and women were dissatisfied with what they heard—or didn't hear—in bed from their partners. More women than men responded that their partners did not say the things they wanted to hear.

Young men between the ages of 18 and 24 revealed that they thought their partners talked too much, which may indicate that younger men may not yet realize that good communication is essential for quality lovemaking.

When men and women do talk during intimate moments, they say different things to one another. Several years ago, I did an interview for the Playboy Channel where I asked both men and women what they talked about with their partners when making love. Women wanted to be reassured and complimented about their appearance, as well as to be told that they were loved. Women also wanted to hear how good their partners felt while they were making love.

Men, on the other hand, wanted to hear that they were the best, that they were satisfying their women, and that the women liked how the men were making them feel. Most of what men wanted to hear concerned physical, task-oriented praise for their actions. This tendency may stem from the fact that little boys are taught to compete to be the "biggest" and the "best." This need apparently doesn't change much throughout the years as they mature into men. Sexually, men want to hear about the physical aspects of their sexual performance from women.

I also questioned men and women as to whether or not they found "nasty talk" a turn-on or a turn-off. Approximately 70 percent of the women did not like hearing such talk during sex—some even reporting that it made them feel degraded and debased. Most men, on the other hand—about 80 percent of them—enjoyed listening to dirty talk. Other research also shows that men find it very erotic to hear women talk dirty during sex.

No matter what your preferences in terms of cuddling, touching, or talking, it's up to you to make them known to your partner.

No Mind Reading Allowed!

So many couples I've talked to in my practice have relayed to me their frustration over their mates' apparent lack of interest in satisfying their specific sexual desires. However, upon closer examination, it seems that the main reason they're not getting what they want in bed is that they don't ever ask for it. That's especially true for women who—even now as we enter the new millenium—feel uncomfortable talking about their sexual needs and preferences. Men can help their women become more open by making it okay for them to speak up and say what they want.

Although it appears to be easier for men to ask for what they want, they often do so in a way that's off-putting to their partners. Men have a tendency to use "command terms" when they tell women what they want. Instead, they should make requests couched by terms of endearment and use soft, sensual, loving tones. "Sweetheart, take your time" is what a woman wants to hear from a man, as opposed to being commanded to stop or go.

The Intimacy Questionnaire

The key to remember is that if you want something, you need to ask for it in a way that increases intimacy for both you and your partner. For some couples, it is difficult to verbally communicate at first, which is why I designed the following questionnaires. Both the man and the woman fill out the questionnaires together and thus even the process helps foster better communication.

The great thing about the Intimacy Questionnaire is that it gives each partner insight into what the other wants. It gives the man insight into what the woman wants and the woman insight into what the man wants. Before filling out this questionnaire, they may not have even thought of some of the things they might enjoy that are listed.

If you and your partner decide to take this quiz, it's important for you to make a pact to be completely honest and not simply answer in a way that you think will please each other.

After sharing the answers with your partner in writing via the written form or by discussing it, be adventurous and do some of the things on your partner's list that you now know will please him or her. For many of my clients and readers who have answered this questionnaire together, it has greatly enhanced their love lives overnight. Perhaps it can do the same for you.

Intimacy Questionnaire

My favorite romantic fantasy is _____

_____

My favorite sexual activity is _____

_____

The most sensitive parts of my body are _____

_____

If I could do one new thing sexually it would be _____

_____

Touching makes me _____

_____

I like to be touched here: _____

_____

Talking nasty during lovemaking is _____

_____

During lovemaking I want you to _____

_____

When we kiss I love it when you _____

_____

Oral sex is _____

_____

During intercourse I love it when you _____

_____

I love it when you wear _____

_____

My favorite cologne on you is _____

_____

My favorite place to make love with you is _____

_____

I don't like it when you _____

_____

Learning the Right Touch

Since touch is the basic element of intimacy, it's important to communicate how you like to be touched by your partner—and vice versa. Here is a questionnaire I devised to help you do just that.

Touch Questionnaire

I really like the following areas of my body to be caressed, kissed, or touched:

	A Lot	*A Little*	*Not at All*
Eyes	❏	❏	❏
Nose	❏	❏	❏
Ears	❏	❏	❏
Lips	❏	❏	❏
Chin	❏	❏	❏
Neck	❏	❏	❏
Shoulders	❏	❏	❏
Underarms	❏	❏	❏
Arms	❏	❏	❏
Hands	❏	❏	❏
Fingers	❏	❏	❏
Breasts, chest	❏	❏	❏
Abdomen	❏	❏	❏
Navel	❏	❏	❏
Lower abdomen	❏	❏	❏
Genitals	❏	❏	❏
Thighs	❏	❏	❏
Upper back	❏	❏	❏
Lower back	❏	❏	❏
Legs	❏	❏	❏
Feet	❏	❏	❏
Toes	❏	❏	❏
Top of head	❏	❏	❏
Forehead	❏	❏	❏
Hair	❏	❏	❏

Hand this questionnaire to your partner. Study it. Compare notes. Follow it. Take heed. And enjoy. It will open up a whole new world of possibilities toward pleasing your mate and vice versa that you never before dreamed possible!

Not Tonight, Dear

Being refused lovemaking by your sexual partner can be a hurtful thing for either gender. But it doesn't need to be. Therefore, how you say "no" is crucial to the longevity of the relationship. The key element is, when saying that no, to offer your partner an alternative time when you're more likely to be ready for intimacy. "Honey, I'm not in the mood right now because I'm preoccupied," you could say. "But I do love you and want to make love with you. Please, can we make it another time when I can really be there with you and for you?" If you utter such words in an affectionate way, you're more likely to avoid hurt feelings.

Oftentimes when one partner feels rejected in a hurtful and insensitive way, it's not uncommon to punish his or her partner by refusing sex at a later time. Clearly, this immature tactic will only backfire and undermine a relationship.

Communication Breakdown!

Don't expect your partner to be "ready whenever you are" when it comes to sex. That's especially true when you yourself have postponed intimacy. Remember, intimacy is a give-and-take situation. Be sensitive to each other's needs and treat one another with generosity and respect.

Instead, keep the lines of communication open, and try to work together. Men have particularly fragile egos when it comes to sex, so when women constantly turn away their advances, men react by becoming gun-shy and have difficulty approaching their women for fear of getting refused yet one more time.

Your best bet is to work together as partners, to compromise whenever possible, and to always treat each other with affection and respect. The key is to make sure that your partner doesn't take the rejection personally and is reassured that he or she is desirable. It is difficult for most couples to get into sync. So many other factors enter into the equation, from work and family pressures, to medical issues, to hormonal imbalances. If you can figure out what's holding you back and communicate those reasons to your partner, you'll make great strides on the road to increased intimacy—no matter how often you have intercourse.

The Least You Need to Know

➤ Women like and need to be cuddled.

➤ Men and women want to hear different things in the bedroom, so you need to be sensitive to that.

➤ Not being aware of differences in touch can prevent intimacy as men and women must be able to express their needs to be touched to provide for the most comfort and intimacy.

➤ Using the Intimacy Questionnaire, you can help your partner and yourself understand each other's desires and needs.

➤ Postponing physical intimacy doesn't have to be a problem, as long as your partner knows the reason.

Shh...

Top Secret

Chapter 17

Top Secrets About Men

In This Chapter

➤ Commitment phobia

➤ Fear of rejection

➤ Trying to change him

➤ Lying

What do men really want? What turns them off? That's what you'll find out in this chapter.

Men Are Not (Necessarily) "Commitaphobic"

Valerie and Rick dated for two years. Finally she had had enough and gave Rick an ultimatum: "Either marry me or I'm not going to be with you anymore." Rick was shocked. He was angry. How dare she put him under this much pressure when they had been having such a great time together these past two years! Apart for a week, Rick pondered whether or not he could commit to her. He then decided to come see me for help with his relationship and to help him find out why he was so commitaphobic.

During our sessions, Rick told me that he'd also been unwilling to commit to three other women with whom he'd been involved—two he knew in college and one he'd seen just before he met Valerie. As we talked, Rick realized he had good reasons for not committing to the first two women; he was in college, after all, and had no financial resources. The girlfriend he was with just before Valerie was completely inappropriate, having a severe drinking problem and cheating on him to boot.

And when it came to Valerie, he also had a good reason: She was passive-aggressive and he could never really get a take on where she was coming from. They really didn't have that much in common. She also had a rude and abusive teenage son who, in Rick's estimation, belonged in juvenile hall. She also spent way too much money on frivolous items and then was always crying about how poor she was, even though she had a lucrative job and made good money.

It finally came to him that he was not a commitaphobic—he just didn't want to commit to the women he'd been intimate with in the past. He weighed the positives and the negatives, and poor Valerie ended up in the negative column. Six months later Rick met Stella, who was perfect for him. They are now married.

The moral of this story is, if a man doesn't want to commit, it may be that he just doesn't want to commit to *you!* Women who plot and scheme are wasting their time with men who don't want to commit to them. Why would you want to be with a man who doesn't want you?

Men Fear Rejection

Men are not immune to fears of rejection. In fact, they go through turmoil when faced with approaching a woman in a club and asking her to go out on a date. They dread it, which is why "playing hard to get" is so damaging and undermining.

Communication Breakdown!

Thinking about never calling a man back and playing hard to get because you've heard about how successful those "rules" are? Well, think again. Most men won't put up with such behavior, and you'll end up quashing a potentially great relationship without even giving it a chance to begin.

Larry met Kendra at a party. He was really attracted to her and felt that she returned the sentiment. Several days later he called and left a warm message telling her how much he enjoyed meeting her and giving her his phone number. When he didn't hear from her after a few days, he called again and left a second message, but she never returned his call. Assuming she wasn't interested in him for one reason or another, he let it go.

Months later, he met her at a restaurant. She seemed genuinely pleased to see him and asked him to join her for a drink. She continued to make eye contact and expressed how pleased she was to see him again. Then he asked, "Well, how come you never called me back? I left two messages for you." She immediately smiled and very flirtatiously replied, "I'm a 'rules' girl, you know." "A 'rules' girl?" he remarked. "What is that?" "You know—the book of rules about how women should act with a man. It says you should never call a man."

Although Larry and Kendra continued to chat, Larry decided never to call her again. The risk of rejection and of going out with a woman who would play such games was too high. It wasn't out of lack of interest, but she'd shown him she was more interested in game playing and manipulation than in getting to know him.

Men Want to Be the Biggest and the Best

Deep down inside every man, no matter how powerful and successful he is, lurks a little boy filled with insecurities and fears. This little boy wants to belong and wants to feel important, secure, and in control. In order to achieve this, the adult man competes for control in order to feel powerful and important.

When Tim's little brother Jason was bullied by some older boys, it was Tim who came to the rescue and handled the situation—and not diplomatically! He gave his brother's little tormentors a taste of their own terror. When their parents got wind of what had happened, Tim was obviously punished and grounded for taking matters into his own hands. Although he had to suffer the consequences, however, he didn't mind. The punishment he received from his parents was a lot less than the self-punishment he would have endured had he not come to his little brother's rescue and shown him that he was powerful and could protect him.

This "little boy" reaction continues into adulthood. When men are faced with making a decision, they'll choose the one that displays them in the most powerful light. To be placed in this most powerful light means they cannot cry or show weakness. Instead, they're likely to show anger, which allows them to keep some control over their other emotions.

For example, when Jack's girlfriend Penny dumped him, he got angry instead of sad: "How could she do this to me? I'm furious. She was a user. She just tried to take advantage of me. I was gonna dump her anyway." He was enraged at Penny and talked in anger about her to everyone who would listen. His anger distanced him from the sadness, depression, and loneliness he was truly feeling.

Typically, unless they go through therapy or learn from good role models, most men will continue to mask the rest of their feelings and emotions through feeling angry.

Men Like to Avoid Confrontation

Studies show that men do not bring up problems and issues of major concern. It is usually the women who do so. Why? It is so that they don't have to deal with their emotions and bring them to the surface. Oftentimes men would rather ignore the problems, hoping they will either go away or take care of themselves. If men have to confront a problem, it is not uncommon for them to confront it at the latest possible moment.

Men Hate to Be Criticized

As bad as men feel about being rejected, they hate being criticized even more. Criticism tends to validate any doubts a man might have about himself. Although women don't mind giving and getting a little "constructive advice" from other women, men don't behave this way with each other. They usually take a more laissez-faire, live-and-let-live attitude. Thus, when a man hears "Why didn't you throw out the garbage?" or "How come you didn't call me?" he feels as though he is being attacked and that an argument is inevitable. He doesn't know why he didn't throw out the garbage or why he didn't call you when he said he would.

What I Mean Is ...

To **save face** means to preserve one's self-esteem. Certain cultures, especially Asian cultures, emphasize the importance of avoiding embarrassment and emotional discomfort.

He either (a) forgot (and that is something his pride will usually not let him admit to), (b) didn't want to (which he also doesn't want to admit because he doesn't want to come off sounding rude and obnoxious), or (c) doesn't want to disappoint you or hurt your feelings.

So, because of his embarrassment at being "busted," and to get out of the situation with some amount of esteem, he fights back with a verbal attack or becomes angry or sullen. The bottom line is that conflict ensues, simply out of his attempt to preserve his self-esteem and *save face*.

Therefore, it is essential that when a woman tells a man something about himself he may not want to hear, it's important that she phrase the criticism in a gentle way: "Honey, the trash bag in the kitchen is full. Can you please help and toss it out?" Now the man's ears have perked up. First, he hears the word "honey" so he doesn't think he's on the hot spot. Next, he hears the words "please" and "help," which most men are willing to do because they like to fix things and solve problems. Saying something like "When you didn't call me, it hurt my feelings" works in the same way. He wants to fix your hurt feelings and you've given him a chance to do so. When you couch criticisms with terms of endearment and questions, a man can hear you and is now more likely to apologize for his indiscretion.

All Men Are Repairmen

Again, fixing things makes men feel as though they have accomplished something. In fact—perhaps because they're biologically driven to do so—men will often say they can fix things even if they really can't. That is why do-it-yourself home repair is so big these days. It is a male challenge to actually fix something and fix it right.

All this goes to show why, when you tell your boyfriend about an argument you had with your boss, his first instinct is to find a solution to the problem by telling you what to do, what to say, and how to say it. You may resent it and interpret his action as an attempt to control you, but in reality he's just trying to fix things and take care of you.

Men Like Women with Verve!

Most men in this day and age appreciate a woman who takes the initiative, who approaches them, engages them in conversation, and even asks them out, according to a lot of surveys that appear in most women's magazines. In essence, they appreciate not having to put themselves on the line, and they are flattered when a woman approaches them.

Men Prefer the "Natural Look"

Less is more, at least when it comes to makeup. Most men I've interviewed are turned off by women who wear gobs of makeup. They feel as if these women must be hiding something about themselves or must feel terribly insecure. Women who are well-groomed and who use makeup to enhance their natural features are far more attractive to men.

In addition to the aesthetics of the matter, men dislike too much makeup for practical reasons. I'll never forget Zane, a handsome man in his 30s who came into my office and told me about his new girlfriend. "One thing for sure is that with my new girlfriend, my dry-cleaning bills will certainly be a lot cheaper." "A lot cheaper? Why?" I asked. "Because now I won't have stains all over my shirts whenever she hugs me or kisses me!" he joked.

Men Hate Being Changed

Men just don't like being changed. At first, they may go along with your suggestions about changing their hairstyles or styles of dress, but later, they'll come to resent you for it. They may feel mothered or smothered by such attention, which makes them feel more like a child than a lover or partner.

Unless a man comes to you personally and says, "I have no clue how to dress. Will you help me?" stay away. If you try to mold him into some look or another, or into behaving in a way that isn't natural for him, it simply won't work. He may feel better in those worn blue jeans and no amount of cajoling will get him to thrive in an Armani suit.

Unfortunately, it's likely that he won't communicate his annoyance with the woman in his life, because, as we've just discussed, men usually dislike confrontation. But the resentment will fester within him along with the need to get back to being his old self. And if he does, will his woman still love him?

175

The answer to that question is never obvious. As the relationship becomes more comfortable, so does the idea of going back to the man's old ways, which usually upsets the woman involved who thinks, "How could he do such a thing after all the time and effort I spent improving him?" At the same time, the man gets upset because he feels trapped in this new self. When he doesn't see himself as she sees him, the fights begin. Feelings are hurt and nobody is satisfied.

Prior to meeting Linda, for instance, George was a slob. Linda saw a "diamond in the rough" and proceeded to make him into her image of what she thought he should look like—fancy suits, suspenders, high white collars on colorful shirts, and matching colorful ties. She suggested he grow his hair and loved it when he wore it pulled back in a ponytail.

After their divorce, George went back to his military haircut; his simple, drab, uncolorful, conservative outfits he felt reflected who he was and not what Linda wanted him to be. He has now regained his lost identity.

So the moral of the story is that what you see is eventually what you'll get.

Men Like to Be Gross and Irreverent

If you ever want to know how men really think when they want to be "guys," then listen to Howard Stern. The majority of his audience is male and most of his humor is rather on the crude side. Men often use such humor as a way to deflect their true feelings of sadness, hurt, love, and sentimentality—feelings that they're not very comfortable expressing.

As if joking this way with each other isn't enough, men also try to test a woman with gross jokes. They often want to see how she'll react. Will she still like them or respond to them if they use "bad boy" humor? If she doesn't react well, instead of feeling rejected and dejected he can simply say, "I was only kidding. Where's your sense of humor?"

Men Lie for Good Reasons, Too

You ask your husband how many lovers he's had in the past and if you're the best lover of his life. Chances are, if he's like most men, he'll lie in order to save your feelings and to protect himself.

Paul, a client of mine, is very handsome and very personable. He's sincere in his compliments and is also very helpful to people. He always seems to be addressing people's needs and hooking them up with people who can best help their careers or personal lives. Because he's such a great guy, he attracts a lot of women, and a lot of women call to ask him out for dates. Being the free spirit that he is and not wanting to hurt anyone he likes, or ruin a good friendship, he tells them "no" in a very diplomatic way. Oftentimes, some of the women won't take "no" for an answer and get rather persistent.

For example, Paul told me about Theresa, a nice woman but someone to whom he felt no physical or romantic connection. She called him up and said, "Paul, I would like to go out with you." He gave her every possible excuse as to why he wasn't able to make it. Finally she asked, "Why won't you go out with me? Don't you like me?" "Of course I like you," he replied. "You're a good friend." She then said, "Well, I want to be more than friends. I want to hook up with you."

He then said, "Well, I'm just not ready to date at this point. I have a lot of personal things on my agenda." Angrily she blurted out, "What's wrong? Don't you find me attractive?"

Well, he certainly wasn't going to tell her the truth, that he really didn't find her attractive. Whom would that help and whom would that hurt? She kept pressing him, declaring to him that he didn't find her attractive. Was it because she was too fat, or had acne scars, or her breasts were too small? Paul was beside himself.

He got so frustrated that he was tempted to say, "You're right, I'm not attracted to you. I could never get sexually excited around you." But he didn't dare. He would never want to hurt her or anyone by saying something like that. So he lied to save face—her face and his. He said, "I really am not in a dating mode, so don't take it personally. There is nothing wrong with you. It's my issue." So remember, men will lie more than women in order to protect others or to protect themselves.

Men Don't Want to Be Put on the Spot

Kathy and Jeff are in a restaurant when a tall, voluptuous woman with a voluminous full head of auburn hair strolls by wearing a tube top and Capri pants. Kathy turns to Jeff and asks, "Do you think she's pretty?" "Yes," he answers. "Is she prettier than me?" Kathy asks. Now Jeff begins to squirm. If he answers "yes," then he will make Kathy feel bad and he knows she'll start acting insecure. If he says "no," then he will be lying. He decides to go with the "no," but Kathy won't buy it.

Jeff finally breaks down and admits that he finds the woman attractive. Kathy is now sulking, feeling insecure, and asking him to give her all kinds of beauty advice to improve herself so that she can look sexier for him. Now he's really on the spot. She's opened the door, but dare he walk in? If he agrees with her that she should grow her hair longer and lose 10 pounds, he can kiss the entire evening goodbye. If he disagrees and says no, then he is missing out on the chance to motivate her to look sexier for him.

The bottom line is, men hate this type of setup because they lose no matter what! If you don't want to hear the honest answer, don't ask the question.

Men Have a Push-and-Pull Syndrome

John Gray refers to the push-and-pull syndrome as the rubber-band effect, whereby men will leave in order to come back. Most women who don't understand this syndrome personalize it and think that there is something wrong with them. When a man pulls away from a relationship, it is because he has become overwhelmed with his feelings and needs the time to regroup. It doesn't mean that he doesn't like the woman or that he doesn't want to be with her. It just means that he needs to regain his identity and deal with his own fears before he can continue on to the next level.

This pulling away can be the most critical time in any relationship. If a woman doesn't understand that a man is going through his push-and-pull syndrome, she can alienate him further by insisting they be together, which further stretches the rubber band until it breaks. Instead, she should allow the rubber band to snap back and return to normal on its own.

Bridging the Gap

Give a man his space, which he often needs after periods of emotional intimacy. Leave him alone, understand what's going on, and he will most often proceed as usual. It may even make your interaction stronger when he does come back.

Men Avoid Toxic Women

What kinds of women turn men off the most? According to a survey I conducted, here's the answer:

1. **Blabbermouths.** Men don't like women who talk all the time—especially about nothing. They find this both boring and grating on their nerves.

2. **Bigmouths.** Men don't like women who can't keep a secret and who share intimacies. A man doesn't want your sister to know that he sucks his thumb before he falls asleep—that's for your knowledge only!

3. **Loudmouths.** Men don't like loud, aggressive-shouting and belligerent-sounding, tough-mouthed women, or women with annoying guffawing laughter. They find such behavior embarrassing and a huge turnoff, especially if the woman does it in public.

4. **Ice mouths.** Men don't like women who don't say nice, complimentary, ego-boosting things to them. They don't like women who withhold verbal affection—or any affection for that matter!

5. **Priss mouths.** Men don't like "school-marmish," uptight women who freak out when they hear a curse word or who constantly admonish the man for his humor or behavior. They don't like being verbally punished or reprimanded or given a look if they do or say something that is typically "male."

6. **High drama-queen mouths.** Men can't take women who make a huge production out of the slightest thing. Although the high drama may be exciting at first, especially the fighting and then kissing and making up, it gets old and terribly exhausting rather quickly. Most men can't take the emotional roller-coaster rides of such a relationship.

In the next chapter, all of you men out there will learn some secrets about women that just might help you understand them a little better.

The Least You Need to Know

➤ Men aren't afraid of commitment, they're afraid of committing to the wrong person.

➤ Men fear rejection just like women do.

➤ You can never change a man against his will. In the long run, he'll resent you and go back to his old ways.

➤ Men lie, but often it's to protect other persons, not just themselves.

➤ There are certain types of behaviors that are extremely "toxic" to men.

Chapter 18

Top Secrets About Women

In This Chapter

➤ Speaking in tangents: how women discuss things in a nonlinear fashion

➤ Changing her mind to consider all options

➤ Appreciating the emotional man

➤ Being reassured increases a woman's confidence

➤ Women take flirting seriously

This chapter is designed to tell men everything they ever wanted to know about women but were afraid to ask. It sheds a different light upon women by getting rid of unjust stereotypes. Understanding what makes women tick will help men avoid pushing the wrong buttons. Let's take a look.

Women Think Nonlinearly

Men constantly complain about how difficult it is to follow women's conversations. The reason for that is, most women do not think in linear fashion, but instead follow tangents. Instead of telling a story that has a beginning, a middle, and an end, she may tell the story at the beginning but then get sidetracked by something interesting in the beginning, which leads her to another topic. She will eventually get around to finishing the story, but it may take a while.

For example, here is how a woman might tell a story about walking her dog:

> "Rover and I went for a walk at the park this morning. You know there were so many people in the park. The park is so much safer now than it was even three years ago. It's probably because they have all of the new security there. Anyway, we went for this walk, and you can't imagine what happened. Rover, who never likes any dog because he is so territorial and thinks he is king of the hill ... By the way, have you ever seen that cartoon *King of the Hill?* It's really clever. Anyway, he sees this other Lhasa Apso that looks as though it could be his twin except that it is a girl and has longer hair and the cutest little pink bow on her head holding the hair out of her eyes. Well, it was like a magnet. Rover pulled me as hard as he could. I went flying across the walkway—you know the one that's near the long bench where the pond is? Well, the two of them were wagging their tails and they were jumping all over each other. I've never seen Rover so happy in his life. When it came time to leave, he wouldn't go, and neither would the other dog, who is exactly the same age as Rover and is named Calista. Isn't that an adorable name, Calista? It's like the television actress, Calista Flockhart."

Look at how many tangents this woman took in her story. Instead of saying, "I took Rover for a walk in the park this morning, and I think he fell in love with another Lhasa named Calista," she talked about the security in the park, *King of the Hill,* the other dog's hairdo, and Calista Flockhart, the actress.

To a man, this makes no sense at all, but to another woman it makes perfect sense. The woman told the story beautifully—so beautifully that you retain that image of the cutest dogs not wanting to leave. You see the park, and the visual picture that was painted is perfect. You feel as though you were there.

Men should never get upset when a woman seems to be going on and on, as they perceive. She is not being ditzy or dumb or inane. Instead, she is being a very helpful and generous communicator.

Women Change Their Minds Easily

Some stereotypes arise because at the heart of it all, they are true in some way. Although women aren't necessarily more fickle than men, they do tend to discuss issues with others before they make any final decisions. This means that it may seem to some men, who tend to keep their inner workings private, that women change their minds often.

Greta and Heide were at a party when they met a wonderful young man named Michael. He was gracious to both of them and invited them to his beach house in Malibu for the weekend. At first, both women were excited about his generous offer and both agreed to the visit. As the evening progressed, they discussed between themselves the plan. They talked about what they had to do to get ready for the trip, such as the clothes they would bring, how much money they needed, who would take care of Greta's dog, and Heide's impending work deadline. Suddenly, after verbalizing it out loud, Greta didn't think that going sounded like such a good idea after all. She also realized that Michael liked Heide and that she might end up being a "third wheel" later on in the weekend. So Greta decided to stay home, work on her project, be with her dog, and let Heide enjoy her new potential romance.

Was Greta being fickle or just using her common sense and logic to make a more informed decision? Most men would answer "being fickle," but most women would disagree. Instead, they would think she was merely using good judgment.

Women Appreciate Men Who Cry

"The first time I heard my song on the radio, I cried. Men do cry. It's a very healthy habit." So wrote Puerto Rican singing star Ricky Martin in his autobiography, *Red Hot and on the Rise.* "My last concert was in Puerto Rico, my hometown. I am a man who cries, and I cried a lot."

I am certain that his openness and his tears have made Ricky Martin more appealing to his female (and even male) fans throughout the world. Now basketball great Dennis Rodman's secret is out: He too cries, or so claims a friend who says he witnessed such an event. As far as a woman is concerned, revealing his emotions and his vulnerability in such a way makes a man come across as a sensitive and compassionate person.

He Says, She Says

According to a recent survey in *More Magazine,* 60 percent of the fantasies women have about men tend to be romantic rather than erotic. That means women are aroused by a man who wines and dines them as well as makes passionate love to them. In essence, she dreams of a man who knows how to treat her as wonderfully in bed as out of bed.

Women Love to Shop

Perhaps it's because women were the "gatherers" and "nest makers" in traditional societies, but today's women also love to hunt down bargains and gather good deals. Indeed, women look at shopping in a completely different way than men do.

Women gather things to nurture and to make themselves as appealing as possible to the opposite sex. Most women consider shopping to be a challenging event, because finding the right thing to wear on the right occasion isn't always easy. Since women often have so many more options in dress than men do, one can see how women might look at this activity in this way.

Other women consider shopping to be a leisure activity because they can slowly peruse and analyze all of the beautiful colors and textures of the fabrics. They perceive shopping to be like going to a museum and getting to buy the works of art on display.

Women Feel Guilt About Anger

Women do get angry, but they tend to let out their anger in bursts, holding it in for as long as they can and then letting it out like an erupting volcano. A woman will soak up a lot more irritants than a man will before letting loose, for the simple reason that she has been conditioned since infancy that "nice girls don't get angry or curse a blue streak."

Even among women who have high-profile jobs that encourage displays of anger (such as trial attorneys), most find it very difficult to do so. I learned this firsthand when speaking to numerous women's legal associations across the country. Women don't feel comfortable expressing anger, even when it is appropriate to their jobs.

What I Mean Is ...

Women have a hard time expressing anger due to social conditioning. However, anger is a true basic emotion in which there is a penetrating stare; tension in the eyelid area; lowering, furrowing, and drawing together the eyebrows; tight, pursed lips; and a clenched jaw that is often jutted forward. When allowed to be expressed, vocal loudness occurs, breathing becomes more rapid, and harsh, staccato-like tones will emerge.

When a woman does blow off steam, she'll often apologize later for getting angry, even though it was justified and she may have felt good about it in the short run. Of course, this ends up diminishing her impact. If a woman's general modus operandi is to walk around angry or with a chip on her shoulder, she is labeled a "bitch," unlike a man who would be labeled "aggressive."

There are two female attorneys who frequently appear on television news shows. Whenever they are interviewed, they speak aggressively and vehemently about a topic. When they debate the issues, they do it with such verbal venom that many people who listen to them often comment that it is difficult to watch them. When women get angry, their voices tend to get shrill and loud, which further alienates their audience and prevents the opposition from clearly hearing what they have to say—their actual message. Most people don't like listening to or watching angry, screaming women. While it may make for good television at times, most people find a steady diet of this quite difficult to take. It's uncomfortable to watch.

Women Need Constant Reassurance

You can never give a woman enough compliments, especially if she knows they are true. Deep down, no matter how insecure she may be feeling, complimenting her and letting her know how wonderful she is adds to her confidence. Perhaps it is a throwback to the patterns that developed while she was a toddler, when people constantly told her how cute and adorable she was.

As an adult, of course, the woman doesn't hear these compliments so often, and this leaves her feeling insecure about her looks and her attractiveness. So, the bottom line here is that you can't reinforce a woman's attractiveness or her assets—her good points—enough!

Communication Breakdown!

Don't let yourself be fooled by the claims people make about "modern" women. Maybe you'll hear that in this day and age, women don't need the approval of others in order to bolster their own self-worth. But they do. Be aware of this need, and be generous in your praise and appreciation. Just make certain it is sincere. Also, remember that women bond through compliments. It makes them feel closer to one another and can make them feel close to you when you compliment them as well.

Women Are Really Little Girls

Just as all men are really just big little boys, women also are really just little girls who want to be fussed over and told how pretty they are. They love to laugh and cry and show a wide range of emotions. Fortunately, I've been told by many men in my practices that they find this unbridled verbal enthusiasm and childlike playfulness quite endearing in a woman, especially if it's not done all the time.

One client of mine is a very sophisticated woman who is not what you would call a ravishing beauty. But she might as well be, according to the many men smitten by her. She is very successful and very well-respected in her profession. On a personal and social level, men love her. They want to be around her, and she has a lot of trouble keeping her "dance card" free because so many men want to date her.

The comment she hears most often is "You are a combination of woman and little girl," which she takes as a great compliment. Other men have referred to her as having "girlish charm," which they find refreshing. She is extremely popular because men are enamored with the fact that she allows people to see both sides of her.

When a woman feels comfortable with a man, she will often reveal her own "girlish charm," which may be the essential ingredient for cementing a relationship between a man and a woman.

Women Are Ambitious

Women are just as ambitious as men are. Women have a great deal of tenacity and may know how to utilize a variety of approaches to achieve the results they want, whether it is being coquettish and using "girlish charms" which they turn on and off at opportune times. We've seen that anger and bullying aren't as effective in helping women reach their goals and, although women do manipulate situations to their advantage, they do it differently from the way men do it. Women, more so than men, tend to use words—via long explanations and verbal diatribes—and display a wider range of emotions, from shedding tears to expressing fears.

I'm not suggesting that women are Machiavellian, but women have the same goals and responsibilities and family obligations as men do these days, and they'll often do whatever it takes to succeed.

Women Start the Arguments

"She's always starting an argument. It's always something. Why can't we live in peace? Why do I always have to explain myself? Why do I always have to talk? Why does she get upset with everything I say?"

Do these questions sound familiar to you? These are the questions men often seem to be asking me when they are talking about their wives and girlfriends.

Bridging the Gap

Men: Open up! Talk, and steer clear of wisecracking comments and sarcasm. As so many of my couples clients have happily reported, it works like magic and prevents a lot of unnecessary arguments.

And I tell them, "Yes! You *have* to discuss how you're feeling." You need to talk about what you did or saw or are going to do or see. Women need to know. They get upset with you when they don't know and they feel they are shut out. You may think that everything is fine, but women certainly don't. They need to connect with you. Remember, young girls grow up learning to socialize and play in pairs, and now that you're in a relationship with a woman, you're the second half of that pair.

"Think about it," I say to my male clients. "Your lady doesn't get upset with everything you say. She just gets upset with what you say as it pertains to her. You can't say something mean or sarcastic to her and expect her to laugh. Women don't do that. It is not how they have been socialized. Although they may put up with it from time to time, they will eventually let it be known to you that they *don't like it!*"

So, when there is not an open, free-flowing channel of communication taking place, women get very upset. Sometimes they get upset right away; other times their anger festers until it finally ignites.

186

Women Take Flirtation Seriously

Another major cause of arguments between men and women is due to misunderstandings brought about by flirting. While men may look at flirting as an innocent exchange of banter or testing the waters to see if a woman is responsive to them, women view flirting in a more serious way. They tend to look at it as a sign of interest from a man. They see it as a prelude—a dance—in which the man is making the first move. If the woman isn't interested in the man, she may take his flirting lightheartedly and laugh off his advances. However, if she does like him and his flirting is insincere or just meaningless banter, it's a different story—she could end up being embarrassed and harboring a lot of hard feelings, even resentment and anger and a grudge against him for a long time to come. Nobody likes to be toyed with or manipulated. No woman likes to be made to feel as though they are the object of one's interest only to find out later they are of no interest to them at all.

This was certainly the case with Carmen, who met James at a party; he told her what a great smile she had. Throughout the rest of the evening, he continued to compliment her and she thought they had a lot of rapport between them. Carmen was sure that James was attracted to her and would ask her out. Throughout their conversation, he lightly touched her hand, and once even grabbed her watch to ask the time as he said, "It seems like an eternity being here with you." She took it seriously, because she felt the same way. After he sincerely looked into her eyes and said, "You know, I've never said this to anyone before, but do you believe in love at first sight? Because I'm falling in love with you."

She'd always hoped there was such a thing as love at first sight and was thrilled at the possibility that she might find out. After all, it might be standing right in front of her. She had no reason to believe that he wasn't being sincere. After spotting a friend heading for the ladies' room, Carmen excused herself to join her. James grabbed her hand and said "Don't be away from me for too long, *mi amor,*" and kissed the top of her hand. Carmen proceeded to the ladies' room to tell her friend all about this exciting flirtatious conversation.

Her friend Elizabeth was impressed, and they were headed out of the ladies' room to find James and introduce him to Elizabeth, but he was nowhere to be found—until she spotted him across the room standing close to a tall blond, holding her hand and kissing it. Now Carmen's heart was pounding, but no longer from excitement and attraction, but rather from anger—anger at him, and anger at herself—for falling for his meaningless lines.

A similar situation happened to another client of mine, who had a flirtation with a man in her office building for over a year. She was even considering asking him out for a cup of coffee so that they could get to know one another, because she knew that he liked her. One day she saw him with his wife and two kids in the coffee shop downstairs. This was a happily married man! She became very angry at him for

What I Mean Is ...

A **dawg** is a slang term for a man who is a cheater, a tease, or a "scammer" and doesn't mean what he says.

leading her on, which caused her to waste a lot of time fantasizing about him. She realized that he was a *dawg* and was totally turned off by him.

The bottom line is, for all you men out there: When you flirt with a woman, you'd better be interested in her and at least be available. When I was growing up, my late brother Manny Glass used to tell me something about dealing with men that made a lot of sense. He said, "Never start anything you can't finish." In essence, he was educating me in the ways of the world, and as a protective older brother, he wanted me to be conscious that my flirting could be seen as a way to lead men on. Men need to take heed from my brother and incorporate this advice into their way of thinking as well.

Women Are Better Drivers

Practically since the invention of the automobile, women have been labeled as bad drivers. Well, believe it or not, women are just as good as drivers as men. Women also score higher on driver's tests, and they receive fewer tickets and citations than their male counterparts, according to recent studies. So all those jokes about women drivers need to be nixed, because they are not funny and are false, especially in light of this new data.

The old Henny Youngman jokes may have worked in the 1940s, 1950s, and 1960s when there weren't that many women drivers, and there was speculation that women were not as capable and adroit as men. But times have changed. Today there are just as many female as male drivers, and the women are quite competent.

Women Have Better Memories

Ever notice how much detail a woman can remember about incidents that have long been forgotten by their men? This never ceases to shock a man, especially during an argument, when it is not uncommon for the woman to describe in detail things that happened years in the past. To hear her tell it, it's as though it happened yesterday. For example:

She: You even insulted me in front of Marsha by telling her about my cooking.

He: Your cooking? My God, that happened 10 years ago.

She: You told her the story of how I made the duck so perfect and went on and on to tell her how I garnished it. You told her that I made my very special sauce with chunks of orange in it and how I used orange marmalade. You told her how everyone was so excited to eat it—all 10 people who were our dinner guests—until they couldn't cut into it because it was still raw on the inside, and how some of the people screamed from disgust! How could you tell her that and embarrass me?

He: I didn't tell her that! I just said that duck is hard to cook and you need to leave it in the oven longer than you would a chicken.

She: Yes, you did. You even said that we had to order fried chicken from a fast-food place so people could eat. I know you told her that because I remember that she was laughing so hard she had to sit down on the couch. I remember, she had on a blue skirt with polka dots on it and a scarf of the same material.

I guess you get my point here. Women do remember! They remember what they ate, what you ate, what they wore, and what everyone else wore. And for the most part, they have excellent long-term memories, so most men are at a great disadvantage in this regard.

The Least You Need to Know

➤ Women often go off on tangents during conversations. It's their way of communicating a lot of information and including you in the experience.

➤ Women change their minds. It's not a sign of being fickle, but rather a sign that they keep reevaluating situations.

➤ It's important to reassure a woman frequently. In some ways, she is still a little girl and needs the praise a little girl needs.

➤ A woman takes flirting seriously. If you don't mean anything by your behavior, stop it so you can avoid misunderstandings and hurt feelings.

Part 6

Peaceful Co-Existence

Never mind the bedroom, what about the boardroom, you ask? Well, it seems as if getting along as equal partners and professionals in the workplace has never been more fraught with communication challenges than it is today.

In this part, you'll learn the best strategies for working together as professionals without falling victim to sexual harassment pitfalls and unhealthy competition.

We will also take a futuristic hop into the next century as we explore all the possibilities that will be available to men and women in the new millennium.

Chapter 19

What Men Want and Don't Want from Women

In This Chapter

➤ Letting him shine and feel like the "man" he is

➤ Keeping the peace

➤ Blending in through attire and behavior

➤ Keeping a sense of humor through it all

➤ Supporting him without smothering him or making him run

This chapter is based on interviews I have conducted over the years and my observations of my clients. It is also based on information that appears in the literature on gender differences. Let's discover what men really want from women.

Looks Count

As discussed in previous chapters, men are visual, and whatever turns them on visually is what they are attracted to. And men's tastes are as varied as men are, which means that losing 50 pounds or bleaching your hair blond will only attract the man who likes thinner, blonder women. There are some generalizations we can make: Most men usually aren't too fond of extremes, such as a woman being too skinny or too fat, but the rest depends on factors I discussed earlier, such as imprinting and cultural influences. What men look for in women's bodies may also vary from one region of the country to another.

As women, we drive ourselves nuts trying to please a man with our looks, but the truth is, unless you're trying to please a particular man, there's no sense in it. Also bear in mind that some men are completely focused on things you really can't change: He might like only women of color or very tall women. For men like this, if they don't find you physically attractive right away, chances are they never will. The only thing worth being, then, is the very best *you* can be.

Men Want to Be King

A man wants to be appreciated. He wants to feel as though he is the most important person in the world—*your* world. Even if he is not in control, a man still wants to feel as though he is. He wants the woman to listen to what he says and respect his thoughts, even if she chooses not to follow his advice. Men need to feel as though what they have to say and what they do is important.

Men Want Praise

It's important to reinforce a man verbally when he has done something that you like and appreciate. Men like loyalty and support in a woman. No man likes a woman who tells him what he is doing wrong. This is especially true if it's done on a constant basis. A man loves to be around a woman whom he feels he can make happy, so if she expresses her happiness at what he does, then he is in turn very happy making her happy. Whether in the boardroom or the bedroom, men want to be told that they are doing the right thing.

Men Want to Shine

While a woman may outshine a man in terms of her career achievements, finances, or lifestyle, she must never constantly overwhelm him with her triumphs, especially not on a personal level. As we've learned, most men have sensitive if not fragile egos. This is not just a myth—it's reality. Thus, a man needs to feel that if a woman likes him, then he must be something special, which is why it's so important for women to focus on men's achievements. Men also love it when women brag about them in front of others. They may claim that it embarrasses them and even tell women to stop doing it, but they really love it.

Take Stuart, for example. He'd just landed a really important client when Rita ran into two of his friends and excitedly told them about it. Not only did she tell them about Stuart's client, but she added that he was thinking about looking at some property in Aspen. She beamed about why she had so much respect for him and what a special and compassionate person he was, and told them about how he had started a charity to help children who needed special surgery but couldn't afford it. She radiated when she spoke of him.

His friends David and Paul were left shaking their heads in amazement, as one said to the other, "Wow, I didn't know all that about Stuart. I'm surprised." And they saw Stuart in a completely different light, thanks to his girlfriend. Several weeks passed, and Stuart ran into two friends at the dry cleaners. "Stuart, I hear you're doing great!" said his male friend, as he slapped him on the back. "Word is that your business is booming and you're working with all these famous people and you're buying a second home in Aspen." "Where did you hear that?" asked Stuart. "From Dave, who saw your girlfriend." The couple congratulated him again as they left with dry cleaning in hand. Stuart beamed. "Now I know why I love Rita so much," he thought.

A man loves to have a cheerleader who sings his praises and makes him look good to others.

A Lady at Table, a Mistress in Bed

No doubt you've heard the cliché: A man wants a lady outside the bedroom, but a mistress inside the bedroom. You have heard this expression time and time again, but it's true, and most men will tell you so. What this means is that most men don't want a woman groping them in public or being verbally vulgar or acting obnoxious—sexually or otherwise. But they want adventure in the bedroom. A recent *Redbook* survey of 5,000 men show that men want spontaneity, adventure, and variety in order to keep their sex lives stimulating.

He Says, She Says

Here are some comments taken from men who participated in a survey published in the August 1999 issue of *Redbook* magazine. Asked to describe what they want from a woman to keep their love lives exciting, they responded: "Meet me at the door nude and attack me." "Experiment more." "Have fun with sex." "Never have sex the same way twice." "Ask me to try something I've never done before."

Eat, Eat, Eat!

When a man takes a woman to a restaurant, he doesn't want her to not eat or insist she's on a diet. This is a huge turnoff for most men. Most men have hearty appetites and appreciate it if women keep up with them.

Of course, this can be difficult if he also wants you to be thin. Unless you have the kind of metabolism that allows you to eat like a horse without gaining a pound, or if you're an exercise fanatic and can work it off, you'll probably gain weight if you eat the way a man does. So it is essential to keep a balance and not overeat. But you still have to eat! If a man is spending money on a woman, taking her to a good restaurant, he doesn't want to see his money wasted. He wants her to be satisfied and enjoy her meal. Women who want to keep their weight down, and still please their man at a meal, should simply eat less when they aren't with their man, so they can eat more when they're around him.

No Punishment, Please

Have you ever said or heard of anyone saying: "I'll show him. He can sleep on the couch tonight. He's not going to get away with it this time."

When a woman uses her sexuality as a weapon by refusing to sleep with her man unless she gets her way, she is headed for a major disaster. Most women don't realize that by doing this they fail to get the man to do what they want, but instead make him resentful and even drive him to infidelity.

Men don't want to be punished, sexually or otherwise—it's just not an effective way to deal with them. Sure, men do stupid things, either intentionally or unintentionally, and they know when they've been wrong! But they don't want you to hammer it into them, especially when they already feel bad about it. They don't need you to make them feel worse.

Victor took Talia to the football game. Street parking was limited, and they were running late, so Victor just parked at the first open spot he could find. Talia suggested that they find another spot or pay to park in a lot, because she worried that the car would be towed. Well, guess what? Three hours later, the car did get towed. Instead of making him feel bad or saying "I told you so," she was compassionate. That meant a lot to Victor, who sang her praises to her friends and his.

Had she done the opposite and reprimanded him, he probably would have felt triply bad: bad that he had to deal with the time and money of getting the car back, bad that he had to inconvenience his date, and bad that she was giving him a hard time about it.

Things happen. Men are particularly sensitive about being in control and appearing as though they know what they're doing. That's why your reprimanding is an ego-destroying act to a man. If you want to keep the lines of communication open, just don't go there. Be empathetic and let it go. Remember about holding grudges: If you want to have a great relationship, don't hold a grudge with your man.

Get to the Point

Men are repulsed by small talk and drivel about the minutiae of a situation. They don't want to hear the details of your trip to the manicurist and what colors you ended up choosing on your fingernails and toenails. Believe it or not, conversations like this will make a man disrespect you, which is what happened with Paul and a woman he began seeing. He thought she was attractive and knew she had a reputable job and worked for a good company (so she wasn't dumb). But when she talked on and on about the most trivial parts of her existence, he got turned off and stopped calling her. When women get close to men, they think that they can tell men everything. Well, they certainly cannot.

As you'll discover in Chapter 22, "Women at Work," most professional men especially can't stand to be around women who don't get to the point. If rambling is something you've been conditioned to do since childhood, recondition yourself. Rambling is the best way to alienate yourself from men. They don't follow you, they have no idea where you are going with the story or why you chose to relate such a mundane incident, and they are bored by what you are saying. Get to the point. Tell the beginning, the middle, and the end … one, two, three.

Leave Feelings Aside

"Why does she always ask me what I'm feeling, or what I think about the relationship? If I wasn't feeling good about it, I wouldn't be here, would I?" That is a typical comment I've heard from all too many men. It's hard for them to talk about feelings, because they don't know exactly what women want them to say. They are confused. Since so many men aren't as in touch with their feelings (as we learned earlier in the book), they don't know how to communicate in the language of feelings—the language of, "I feel angry," or "You hurt my feelings," or "I'm sad," or "I feel like I want to cry …." Men feel as though their feet are on shifting sand—they don't want to say the wrong thing. Even though they may love their women, many men have an emotional wall built up from years of being on the defensive. This defensiveness oftentimes makes it extremely hard for them to express themselves openly and freely.

Lighten Up

A man can't take it when you constantly talk to him about your feelings and his feelings when you are down. He wants you to be able to laugh and—most of all—to laugh at yourself. Men don't want to be pressured into examining the heaviness of their relationships. They want to enjoy them and go with the flow.

Your man also does not appreciate mercurial behavior or excessive moodiness. He wants to be around a woman who is stable, who says what she means and means what she says, and reacts to events around her on a more consistent basis rather than in extremes.

He also doesn't want to play head games with you, whereby he has to guess why you're mad at him or in a bad mood. Men do not find this a challenge but rather a huge turnoff.

Leave Him Be

A man doesn't want you to embarrass him in any way. He doesn't want you to belittle him in front of others, especially if he's stretching the truth on purpose, or if he's made a mistake in the details of what he's said.

This distaste for embarrassment is why men *hate* scenes. He doesn't need you to "bust" him, and especially not in public. A man hates it when you start a huge argument with him in public, have a tantrum, cry, and carry on. Men reportedly cannot tolerate it when women cause a scene in a restaurant by being rude to or yelling at the waiter.

If a man makes a scene with someone, he may be proving his "manliness" or defending your honor, at least in his mind. But don't you do it. Don't fight his battles for him, especially in public. And if he's getting verbally overheated (not physically violent), don't get involved, and don't tell him not to get upset or to "cool it." He does *not* want to hear you reprimand him. Instead, he wants to hear your support and your encouragement. He doesn't want to hear you try to be the appeaser and the go-between. After all, you are not his mother!

Now, of course, there will be times when you do think he's acting like a jerk. But use your head when deciding how to handle situations like this. For example, he's complaining to the waiter about a bill. If you intercede directly, you will just make him more upset, and that won't benefit anyone. But if you let it ride, you can discuss the matter with him later at a more private and opportune time and let him know that you thought he went too far, if he did (while showing empathy for what he was trying to do). Be on his side and let him know that you know how he felt and that the waiter was a jerk. Tell him you hate seeing him getting so upset because you care so much about him and don't like to see him feeling bad. Whatever you do, don't harp on how poorly he acted. Instead, use positive reinforcement. Stick up for him. If he was really out of line, ask him in a calm tone if he considered looking at another solution. If he didn't, give your opinion, stating that you could see his point of view. State what you may have done, and then drop it! Let him react to what you said.

But don't reprimand him or go behind his back and apologize for him. That is for him to do, not you! Remember, it is his responsibility to handle his own battles. Keep remembering that you are not his keeper, his caretaker, or his mother!

Time Out

Men need time alone to regroup. As John Gray puts it, men need to go into their caves. They need that time to think and to process information. This is in contrast to women, who process information and regroup by verbalizing it, talking it out, getting a lot of feedback, and then making up their minds.

When men are alone in their caves, and spending their time alone, they don't want the women—or anyone else, for that matter—to enter their caves. If a woman tries to do so, the man often becomes annoyed, resentful, and grouchy.

Okay Anger

Perhaps the one emotion men feel comfortable with is anger. Greg came into my office to tell me that his girlfriend of three years just dumped him because he wasn't ready to commit to her. "How dare she!" he ranted. "How could she throw this relationship away after everything we've shared together? What a b - - - h! I'm glad I found out now what kind of woman she really is, because I wouldn't want to be with someone like her anyway." Greg's response is typical. Instead of crying or dealing with the sadness of the rejection, he instead gets angry and calls her the "B" word.

When men are frustrated or sad, they often substitute anger for these emotions. It may seem inappropriate and confusing to a woman, but it makes complete sense to a man. So if a man is getting angry instead of getting nervous or sad like you think he should, now you can understand why.

Blending In

Men in the corporate world dress for other men. They usually don't want to stand out. Unless they are rock stars or show-business celebrities, they want clothes that blend in, clothes that look like everyone else's. That's why, when you start dressing your man without keeping this in mind, you are unknowingly upsetting his sense of self—his sense of order and belonging to the group.

Men want clothes to be a sort of uniform that blends in, and every community has its own male uniform. On Wall Street, there is one type of uniform with variations on the "right" suits and ties. In the Midwest, there is another type of business-suit uniform. Even in Hollywood there is a business uniform. Unlike the business suits worn in other parts of the county, Hollywood's uniform consists of jeans, a blazer, and a cotton T-shirt, dress shirt, or band-necked shirt under the blazer. Shoes go to either extreme—Nikes or expensive Italian loafers. How men dress up or down in Hollywood depends on the shoes, shirt, and belt they wear. Wearing the same uniform makes Hollywood types comfortable around one another, just as wearing certain suits in certain colors and styles and textures makes other businessmen in other parts of the country feel comfortable with one another. Men in a particular region dress in essentially a similar manner. This is appropriate to the situation: It gives men confidence that they are talking and dealing with others who are like them.

He Says, She Says

According to a survey of 1,000 men conducted by the Roper Organization, most men say that they personally would rather be seen as "sensitive and caring" than "rugged and masculine." Two thirds of those questioned stated that they "ought to be more caring and nurturing as husbands and parents." However, when asked to pick traits they associate most with their sex, they rated "having a strong sex drive" and "being very interested in sports" much higher than "being a caring and sensitive husband" and "being able to show emotions."

You may think the pink paisley suspenders go with the pink and green and purple swirly patterned tie, and should be matched with a purple striped shirt with a white collar and white cuffs. He may not agree. Even if he wears the clothes you pick out for him, he may mistakenly think you know what you are doing (even though you are dressing him inappropriately), or he may just be trying not to hurt your feelings. In any case, it's essential that you ask his opinion and see what he's already wearing and what people around him are wearing so he can continue to fit in.

The Trust Quotient

Men will often egg you on to see how you react, or they'll ask you hypothetical or provocative questions to see your reactions.

Take Vivien and Raymond. Vivien met Raymond while she was away at college. Vivien had a very strong and lively personality and was a handful because she was so energetic. Raymond told her this on their very first date. Spontaneously, she said, "Well, if you think I'm energetic and lively, you should see my twin sister!" She didn't actually *have* a twin sister, but she said it as a joke. Since Raymond was so overwhelmed by her high-voltage personality, she thought, just imagine what he would say if there were two of her. It was just a toss-off comment.

He laughed and said "Oh my God—two of you. I can't imagine that!" So she made her point, and they were off to a blissful, fun-filled relationship. A month into the relationship, he asked about her twin sister. "Twin sister?" she said. "Yes, you mentioned you had a twin sister." "Oh," she laughed, "I was only kidding about that." Well, Raymond immediately got turned off and ended the relationship. He never called her again because she had lied to him. As innocent a lie as it was, it was still a lie *in his mind,* and so he lost all trust. So watch your exaggerations around men, even when they are spoken just for humor and aren't meant to mislead anyone.

To most men, there is no such thing as a little white lie. When they find out that you've told a lie (no matter how innocent), as I discussed with the age factor earlier in the book, men will always question whether they can ever really trust you.

Silence Is Golden

One of the reasons men won't open up is because women don't necessarily give them a chance to do so. Silence can be golden!

Bridging the Gap

Stick to the truth. Once you start lying, even out of playfulness, even if it is the tiniest, most innocent white lie, you can start a series of unintentional misunderstandings that leave a trail of mistrust in their wake.

Cookie, one of my clients, understood this. When she wanted her man to open up, she asked direct questions that required more than a "yes" or "no" answer. She used what I referred to earlier as an open-ended approach.

For example, when she wanted to know about what he thought of her brother and his new wife, she didn't say "What do you think of Tom and his new wife?" She instead phrased it in such a way that he had to answer and explain himself. She used the word "explain": "Please explain to me your view of the way Tom treats his new wife." She could have also phrased it "I am interested in your analysis of the relationship between Tom and his wife."

Now Tom hears her. She has basically told him what she would like him to do. She speaks to him in verbs such as "explain" and "tell." He heard her even better when she said "I am interested in your analysis of ..." A man doesn't usually hear you when you say the "f" word (feel). He stops listening to you because all he hears is "feel." A red light goes on in his head: "Oh, now, do I have to get into how I feel? I don't know how I feel." But he does know about his analysis, his observations, and how he can explain things. Now you are speaking his language.

A woman often has to wait for a man to express what's going on. The main thing is not to bug him about it. If you whine to him, "Why won't you open up?" or "What are you thinking?" you put a lot of pressure on him. Often, he is not thinking *anything.* Or he has nothing to say, or he just doesn't feel like talking.

If you ask a question, give him a chance to answer it. Sometimes that takes more time for a man than it would take for a woman, because maybe he never thought about it before and now has to think about what he's going to say.

Here are some phrases you can use to speak in a man's terms so he'll open up and hear you:

- ➤ Please tell me ...
- ➤ Tell me ...
- ➤ Explain your views ...
- ➤ How would you describe ...
- ➤ Characterize what you believe ...
- ➤ Think about what you would do ...
- ➤ Tell me what to do ...
- ➤ How would you handle ...
- ➤ Share with me ...
- ➤ Express to me your views on ...
- ➤ Tell me your views about ...
- ➤ What are your exact thoughts (or specific thoughts) on ...

Notice I have not included "How do you feel ...?" or "What is your opinion on ...?" I used strong words that will force him to listen to you. In essence, I am taking elements from the right side of his brain, the logical/analytical part, and then filling in the blank with some issue that is emotionally important that I need to discuss with him. Thus I'll get him to tap into and use the left portion of his brain, which deals with feelings and emotions. This way, he uses his entire brain to discuss the issues with me and to open up.

Confidence Is Key

Men love women with a strong sense of self, women who know who they are and have their feet firmly planted on the ground. Remember in the last chapter I talked about the importance of confidence and how sexy both men and women found it? Well, men especially find a woman's self-confidence an aphrodisiac.

When a woman walks into a room with her head held high, her shoulders back, tummy sucked in, chest out, and smile beaming, men love it. If you have the "he's lucky to have me" attitude, men will react in kind. I have seen it repeatedly, not only with my clients but with my friends. I once went to a dance with a friend who was, by her own admission, not blessed with a pretty face or a good body. Nobody knew about her professional successes, but they did know she was something special. She carried herself as though she was the most beautiful, sexiest woman in the room. And so men flocked to her because of the way she carried herself and how she presented herself.

I once had a client who was much more physically attractive than the woman whom her boyfriend ended up dropping her for. What did the other woman have that my client didn't have? She had herself. She liked herself and this man took her lead. My poor client was riddled with so many insecurities. She continuously put herself down until her suitor finally agreed with her. When women like themselves they radiate a self-confidence that men pick up on and find attractive.

It should be noted that men love women who are feminine and who are not trying to look, talk, or act like little men. They don't like tough-talking women, and don't want a woman who is so defensive or insecure that she's always trying to compete with the man. When a woman is sure of herself and of who she is and exudes confidence, she doesn't have to do those things. And men appreciate that.

Bridging the Gap

You've heard the glamorous RuPaul say, "Love yourself. If you can't love yourself, how in the world are you going to love anyone else?" That's not just a slogan. It's good advice for dealing with others and learning to attract friends and people of quality as potential partners.

Even though different men have different tastes, certain things tend to make a woman more attractive to a man, according to surveys. Here's a list of 10 things that turn a man off:

1. Being sloppy, ill-groomed, or slovenly
2. Being excessively overweight
3. Being excessively thin
4. Complaining all the time
5. Being obsessed about the foods she eats
6. Being argumentative and challenging to whatever is said
7. Being loud and boisterous
8. Having an offensive odor (body or breath)
9. Being untrustworthy (that includes telling his secrets)
10. Being insincere

Hold Back on the Doting

I had a client, Cindy, who was very, very sweet—perhaps too sweet. Even though she catered to every man she was with, she could never keep a man interested in her for the long haul. When Cindy was with a man, she would surprise him with presents, such as designer watches, shirts and belts, sports equipment, and computer equipment. She loved their reactions when she did this because, needless to say, they were quite flattered. She made lavish dinners for them, then cleaned up immaculately. She'd do laundry, then arranged their sock and underwear drawers, folding everything neatly. She did whatever they wanted to do. If the men wanted to see an action-adventure film, that's what she would do. If they wanted to go to a particular restaurant, that's what she did. If they called, she would drop everything to be with them.

Cindy did everything men wanted her to do and then some, without ever complaining. So she could never understand why in the world, if they were getting all of this good stuff, men all ended up dumping her.

It's because Cindy was too good and too much. A lot of men come to resent a woman for doing too much, unless the men are also reciprocating (or trying to). It may be that men don't feel they deserve this honor. They may feel a sort of guilt, or what *Kabbalists* call *bread of shame*. So instead of having to constantly feel the discomfort of guilt whenever they are around such a woman, men feel better (guilt-free) when they are not around her. So they end the relationship through attrition—they gradually set up greater distances between themselves and her. The woman, like Cindy, is always devastated, crying, "How could they do that to me, after all I did for them?"

What I Mean Is ...

Kabbalists are scholars who study ancient Hebrew teachings known as the **Kabbalah. Bread of shame** is a phrase appearing in these teachings and refers to the resentment and guilt someone feels when he or she doesn't reciprocate the giving of too much by another.

Although I am not a "rules" girl, I do agree with the authors of the book *The Rules*, Ellen Fein and Sherrie Schneider, that you shouldn't give too much (gifts, information) away, lest the man's interest in you wanes. John Gray, author of *Men Are from Mars, Women Are from Venus,* also preaches to women not to give a man too much and not to constantly do things for him.

Change Him Not!

Men cannot stand it when women are out to change them—their physical appearance, behavior, or attitudes. While they may go along with it at first, they will come to detest not being able to be who they feel they are. I have observed so many women alienate themselves from a potentially wonderful man just because they were trying to mold him into the image of their fantasy.

Jerry is a perennial flirt. He has flirted with women since he was three years old and got a lot of rewards for it. He flirted with his teachers all through school, which made him the teacher's pet. He flirted his way through college and was the envy of his fraternity, because he could have dated practically anyone he wanted to. He flirted his way to winning bets with his friends in bars that he could get a girl to go out with him. He flirted his way to becoming one of the top salesmen in his company—and yes, he flirted his way to finally getting *you*. Now you want him to take a lifetime of flirting—something that is as natural to him as breathing—and stop it.

You don't want him talking to anyone else but you. You want all of his time and attention. Well, he may indulge you for a while, but it's not natural to him. You're making him do something foreign to him that he is doing only to please you and to keep you happy. He will eventually break and return to his flirting ways. He's not cheating—he's flirting. You may think this will lead to cheating, but he doesn't. As you keep fighting with him about it and having hard feelings, don't be surprised if your prophecy comes true and he *does* end up with someone else—someone who isn't threatened by his flirting.

The key here is to give Jerry freedom and not bother him. Like the butterfly, Jerry can't be held too tightly or you'll destroy him. But when you give him freedom and let him fly, you can watch him do all the beautiful and natural things butterflies do—including flying back to you.

The Least You Need to Know

➤ A man wants you to be his biggest cheerleader and supporter.

➤ Men don't want to stand out in terms of appearance and clothing. Respect the way they dress for their particular jobs.

➤ Introspection and feelings are great, but a man likes when you can set aside moodiness and constant seriousness and enjoy life.

➤ Be supportive, but don't smother.

Chapter 20

What Women Want and Don't Want from Men

In This Chapter

➤ Being a gentleman to her

➤ Giving gifts

➤ Her need for commitment

➤ Accepting her friends

In the last chapter, we learned what some of the true secrets are about what men really want from the women they date. In this chapter, we will learn about women's true desires in a relationship and in their interactions with men.

Be a Gentleman

Believe it or not, a woman truly adores and respects and, in essence, loves a gentleman. It is a myth that women love men who treat them badly. It is an emotionally disturbed woman with terribly low self-esteem who is attracted to such a man and allows him to treat her with anything less than respect and admiration. An emotionally healthy woman dreams about a man who treats her well.

Men are not jerks or creeps. Men are indeed wonderful, and there are gentlemen out there. My late brother Manny M. Glass was a true gentleman in every sense of the word—just ask anyone who knew him. After he died, I found a card among his belongings, apparently given to him when he was a college student and pledged

Sigma Alpha Epsilon, a fraternity of which he was a lifelong member. Like all of his fraternity brothers, he had to memorize the words on the card (written by John Walter Wayland) and recite them. Twenty years later, he still carried the card with him and lived by each word.

The True Gentleman

The true gentleman is the man whose conduct proceeds from good will and an acute sense of propriety, and whose self control is equal to all emergencies; who does not make the poor man conscious of his poverty, the obscure man of his obscurity, or any man of his inferiority or deformity; who is himself humbled if necessity compels him to humble another; who does not flatter wealth, cringe before power, or boast of his own possessions or achievements; who speaks with frankness but always with sincerity and sympathy; whose deeds follow his word; who thinks of the rights and feelings of others, rather than his own; and who appears well in any company, a man with whom honor is sacred and virtue is safe.

If you are a man reading this, perhaps you too will keep a copy of it in your wallet, memorize the words, and live by them. If you are a woman reading this, perhaps you will keep a copy of it in your wallet to remind you of how a man should treat you. If you are a mother, perhaps you will share it with your sons. If you are a sister, perhaps you will share it with your brothers. If you are a wife or a girlfriend, perhaps you will share it with that very special man in your life. It truly defines what a real man is all about.

Studies show that women desire men who are unselfish and kind to them, which is much more important than how he looks or how successful he is. The way a man treats a woman is how she judges a man in the long run.

Stop Kidding Around

I've said it before in this book, and I'll say it again: If a woman lets you know that something isn't funny or that she doesn't appreciate you making certain personal comments to her, *stop it and stop it at once!* Otherwise you're headed for a major disaster. You're setting yourself up for the cold, silent treatment, sulking, or a full-blown argument. Women do not appreciate practical jokes, so don't play any on your woman unless you know that she is a good sport, enjoys being the brunt of a good joke, and doesn't mind laughing at herself. There are certainly women out there who will gladly appreciate this type of humor, but if you want to be on the safe side, rest assured that most women won't.

Help Them Eat Less

Women *detest* being told what they should and shouldn't eat. If a woman wants to gobble up everything in sight, it's her business, not yours. Don't treat her like a child who has to be told how and how much to eat. And don't think she necessarily eats in front of you the way she eats around others. Maybe she's eating like a maniac out of nervousness, because she is uncomfortable, trying to impress you, afraid of using bad table etiquette—there could be a million reasons!

On the other hand, a woman appreciates it when you honor her diet and don't treat it frivolously. Insisting that she take a spoonful of dessert when she says "no" is unacceptable. For someone on a diet, and especially for those who really have to battle overeating, it takes an act of extraordinary discipline not to take a bite, because, like an addict, dieters know one bite can lead to another.

This happened to someone I know, who had had various eating disorders since she was a teenager. She lost 20 pounds through strict discipline. In a weak moment, her boyfriend seduced her into taking just one bite of a dessert, even though she'd repeatedly said no. That was the beginning of the end of her diet, and she descended right back into the most obsessive and unhealthy eating habits.

Since there is such a high incidence of eating disorders in this country, there's a decent chance that the woman you are dating is struggling with this problem. So don't tempt her. Otherwise you will be sabotaging her hard-earned efforts at staying thin.

Communication Breakdown!

Men have to realize that seemingly simple encouragements to "go ahead and try some" can stimulate women to eat in unhealthy ways. Don't interfere—support a woman in her eating choices.

Treat Them Like Queens

Women want to be put on a pedestal—to be loved, admired, adored, and appreciated. They want to be catered to, showered with gifts, and wined and dined. A woman wants to be showered consistently with wonderful words of sincere praise. They want to be told how beautiful they are, how special they are, and how much you love them.

On the Internet I saw a great joke that clearly reflects everything a woman wants from a man and what it would take to impress her. A list of 11 things women want was included as part of the joke:

A man should ...

➤ Protect her.

➤ Hug her.

- ➤ Hold her.
- ➤ Spend money on her.
- ➤ Wine and dine her.
- ➤ Buy things for her.
- ➤ Listen to her.
- ➤ Care for her.
- ➤ Stand by her.
- ➤ Support her.
- ➤ Go to the ends of the earth for her.

This is *exactly* how a woman wants to be treated! (The punch line of the joke was that it only takes two things for a woman to impress a man: Show up naked, and bring beer!)

What amused me about the joke was that it captured—in a humorous way—how universal women's desires are. Women do want to feel as though they are important. They always want their Prince Charming, and they want him to act like a prince at all times. The joke makes most of us chuckle when we read it because it reflects so much truth in terms of catering to a woman's needs, and any man who takes heed and follows it is headed in the right direction.

Now that we've seen a list of what women want from men, here's a list of the top 10 guaranteed ways men can turn off a woman:

1. Not being able to manage his finances
2. Being highly critical and judgmental
3. Being unhygienic or slovenly
4. Doing socially unacceptable acts involving bodily functions in public
5. Being boring
6. Being obsessed with hobbies, sports, his mother, etc.
7. Not paying attention (especially to you)
8. Being rude, bullying, and controlling
9. Being uptight, rigid, and inflexible
10. Being cold and unaffectionate

Women Expect Presents

This desire is pretty gender-specific. For whatever reason, a woman absolutely does think less of a man who forgets her birthday, remembers her birthday but forgets to give her a gift, or buys her a completely inappropriate gift.

A man should know better than to buy a woman a blender, a toaster oven, a popcorn popper, a set of floor mats for her car, or a mop. A hastily purchased chartreuse scarf made of rayon won't cut it either, considering that she told you how much she hates green. The key to getting a woman a gift she wants is to listen to her over time. She will usually reveal what she likes and what her tastes are if you pay attention (which, unfortunately, most men don't do because they don't remember to be "interested and not interesting"). If men paid attention, it would enable them to become great listeners so they'd know what to get their women and how not to get into trouble on their birthdays and other holidays. It is so simple, and if most men did this, they would avoid a multitude of arguments and unnecessary aggravation.

He Says, She Says

Men: Remember, Valentine's Day is February 14. Have this date etched into your brain forever. For most women who have someone special in their lives, Valentine's Day is a major holiday. It is one of the most important days in their lives. So mark that date on your calendar. Forgetting Valentine's Day or buying a last-minute card—or worse yet, a cheap box of chocolates—can cause you to have a bad year and, believe it or not, can even cause you to lose your relationship. Also etch into your brain the birthday of that special woman in your life. Put it on your calendar and your day runner. *Do not forget it!* Do something about it. A card usually isn't enough!

The key to gift giving is to give gifts of quality. That doesn't mean they have to be from Armani, Tiffany's, or Chanel (although many women wouldn't mind that). It means your gifts should be top-of-the-line, which shows that you think of her as someone who deserves the best.

If, on the other hand, you get her a tacky gift, an obviously used gift, or a hand-me-down, it says to her on a subliminal level that you think she is tacky, cheap, and not deserving of anything better. But what about money, you ask? Well, what about it? When it comes to giving gifts to a woman, borrow from Peter to pay Paul. Save your change, borrow the morning paper, eat homemade sandwiches for a month instead of fancy restaurant lunches, forgo evenings out at the movies, ride the bus, carpool with a friend—anything to save a dime for that quality item. Believe me, it will be appreciated.

If you are super broke, write a love poem on beautiful paper or make something. If you took woodshop in high school, find a friend with a power tool, cut out a heart shape from a piece of wood, and carve both of your initials in it. But don't do a last-minute job. Take your time and make sure that it looks great and it's something unique that she will cherish. Then give it to her along with some flowers you pick from the garden. Women do savor these things. It touches them emotionally. It moves them that you took the time to think of them and went out of your way to make something for them. The key is to make your gift special, something you know she will love.

Impersonal gifts are distancing and hurt her feelings, whether she admits it or not. Do not buy her a gift because *you* can use it. It must be purchased with only her in mind. So no computer games, power tools, or golf clubs, unless she really loves these things herself. Unless she specifically requests one, it's best to stay away from toasters, vacuum cleaners, blenders, and other household appliances—it may look like you are just giving her more work to do.

Gift-giving is a serious matter as far as women are concerned. No matter what anyone tells you, the truth is, it's the gift that counts (and of course the thought that went into picking out the correct and appropriate one). Remembering to pay close attention to what you've just read can improve your relationship 100 percent.

Here are some gift ideas that most women appreciate:

➤ Quality jewelry of *her particular* taste and style.

➤ A certificate for a day of pampering (spa, facial, massages, hairstyling, manicure, pedicure).

➤ Quality accessories of her choosing.

➤ An elegant frame with a photo of the two of you in it.

➤ Sexy lingerie in her exact size (picked out by you personally).

➤ A computer with appropriate programs (but only if she will be the user, not you). If she is not that computer-literate, get her an instructor that goes with it, or better yet, you be her instructor.

➤ A romantic weekend getaway for just the two of you in a place where she has never been before.

Understanding Biological Time

There is a fabulous cartoon that makes most people crack up when they see it. It shows a very worried-looking woman with her hand over her forehead. The caption above her reads "Oh, no! I forgot to have children!" Of course, scientific advances have made it possible for women to give birth later in life than ever before in the history of man- or womankind. Even so, with motherhood being delayed later in life because of the demands of a woman's career, a woman's concern that her biological clock is ticking is often a valid one.

This is one of the main reasons why some women seem so desperate to get that ring on their finger and a man in their life! The bottom line, honest-to-goodness truth is that they *are* desperate—especially if they're over 32. The older their eggs get, the more difficulty women have conceiving, and the greater the likelihood they will have problems (such as birth defects) during and after giving birth. Even though it is possible to conceive later and later, that still does not eliminate the higher incidence of problems that is associated with birthing and age. This is why women are very sensitive to acting *now* and getting you to commit sooner rather than later. So help her out for goodness' sake! Don't add to her life's pressures by being a commitaphobic and not being able to make up your mind!

If you respect and admire her, if you get along most of the time and have fun together, and if you appear to be compatible—have a lot of common interests, share similar value systems, and have chemistry—what are you waiting for? Go for it! On the other hand, if you don't have all of this, you really are not a commitaphobic— you just don't want to commit to this particular woman. Move along your merry way so that she can find someone else with whom to share time on her biological clock! I'll discuss more about commitment a little later on in this chapter.

He Says, She Says

It is a reality that genetic disorders such as Down's syndrome increases to one in 20 after a woman reaches the age of 35. When she is 40, she has a one in five chance of having a child with Down's syndrome. In addition, there are other genetic abnormalities too numerous to name that occur more often as a woman's age increases as well as when a man's age increases.

Romance Is Queen

Women want to be wined, dined, and romanced. Look at the popularity of romance novels in this country! Millions of romance novels are sold every year to allow women to vicariously live out their fantasies of romance. They really do want romance, and they want it desperately! If you aren't the romantic type, buy one of these books and read it to see how women really think. Any of the Harlequin Romances you can pick up in the drugstore or grocery store will do.

What you may think is corny isn't corny to a woman who has been brainwashed (as we learned in Chapter 5, "The Role of Mother Nurture") with images of Cinderella and Snow White, women looking for their knights in shining armor. It is very endearing to a woman to be surprised with gifts, as you will discover after reading enough of these romantic novels.

A woman wants you to make her feel safe, make her feel that everything is working. That is why she is always asking you about what you think of her or what is going on in the relationship. That means she wants to know where you are going. Don't give her a reason to doubt you. Be honest, open, caring, understanding, and—most of all—sensitive. Let her in on your feelings.

Friends, Just Friends

The ideal relationship that most women (and most men, for that matter) strive for is to be friends as well as lovers. So when a woman tells a man that she "only" wants to be friends, what she is actually saying between the lines is the following: "I really like you, but I don't like you that much. I don't know how to tell you without hurting your feelings. You can forget about the reality of ever getting any closer to me physically. There is no chance of us ever being lovers."

This doesn't mean she doesn't have male friends whom she genuinely likes. It just means that there is a limit to the relationship and that she is not about to get physical with them.

Commit, Commit, Commit

Commitment means a lot more to a woman than it does to a man. You may have been living together for years, and you may believe that a marriage certificate is pointless, that "a little piece of paper" can't bind you together.

No matter. You can try to tell her over and over again how bound you are to one another and even show her by your wonderful actions. But a woman will still want that piece of paper that says you belong to one another. It makes her feel more secure that she is pledged to you. A formal commitment is a validation to a woman. It means a great deal to her. It means that she is desirable and worthy and that, if she wants to have children, they will have a "legitimate" father.

When a woman thinks "commitment," she sees a whole life ahead of her and the excitement of working together as a team to accomplish their collective dreams. This is what she was geared to do as a little girl while playing in pairs, and now you are her paired significant other.

Most men feel trapped when they hear the dreaded "m" word (marriage), because to them it often means the end of dating anyone else. It's *over*. When a man says he isn't ready to commit to a woman after they've been together a long time, know one another, and really love each other, it is a great insult to a woman. To her, it's the ultimate rejection—it means she isn't wanted, she isn't good enough for him to marry. It is devastating. It makes her upset, angry, and hurt. In fact, many women handle a man's lack of marriage commitment, especially after having a solid relationship for a long period of time, as a death. Women may go through a grieving process with all of the same stages they would go through when mourning an actual death.

This is why a woman will oftentimes tell a man who won't commit that she never wants to see him again: For her it is the ultimate rejection, to not be committed to, so she is simply closing the chapter—returning the rejection—and dealing with the death of the relationship.

Widening the Circle

A woman looks at her friends as a reflection and an extension of herself, so when you don't accept her friends, you are in essence saying that you don't accept her.

So many relationships have been destroyed over a woman's friends. A woman's friends usually have been in her life a lot longer than you, the man, so you need to respect that fact, respect her friends, and respect the relationship she has with them. You don't have to have personal relationships with each one of them (in fact, it may be better if you don't). But you do have to treat them nicely and politely and not be threatened by them. Try to be cordial and be a gentleman at all times.

If she has single friends, she often wants you to fix them up, so they will have someone in their lives and experience a happiness like the relationship she has with you. So oblige her, but make sure you don't fix her friends up with people who are inappropriate.

Many of her friends may not like you, and may even dislike you, or be jealous of you or threatened by you. Don't let that throw you. Her friends may be envious of the fact that the two of you are in love or angry that you have come between them. They may even be secretly attracted to you. Who knows and who really cares why her friends may not like you? The bottom line is, don't do things to alienate her friends or make them dislike you even more than they already may.

It is essential to try to win them with your charm and patience so they can see why she is in love with you. Women desperately want you to be nice to their friends—and to their families, as well. The woman can moan and groan all day long about her mother, but don't you follow suit. She doesn't want you to. She wants you to keep quiet and let her vent. Always remember this rule of thumb: Women love a gentleman, and a gentleman treats others' friends well.

Feeling Sexy

You must never tell a woman she is fat or refer to her weight under any circumstances. It is not just a hot button with a lot of women—it is a *scalding* button. It could even be the end of a relationship. If you monitor what she eats, or grab hold and knead her extra layer of fat when you are both lying naked together, it could be the end of your intimate relationship. Why? Because a woman wants to know that she is *always* sexually appealing to a man, whether she has a few pounds on her or not, whether she has a pimple on her face or not.

A woman will often put you through a test by trying to get you to say she has put on a few pounds. Never admit it. She is trying to trick you, to see how much you really care about her and what you really think about her. Believe it, a woman can jump from hearing you innocently say, "I've seen you lighter," to screaming that she never wants you to see her naked again. A woman wants a man she can really feel "naked" with at all times, someone who will accept all of her—including her body—unconditionally. What's more, a woman will respond much better to a man sexually when she is assured that he totally accepts her—fat cells and all, cellulite and all.

Women will also never forget what you said. Remember, they tend to hold grudges, so even if you apologize profusely for commenting on her imperfections, rest assured, you have lost points forever.

TLC for PMS

PMS—premenstrual syndrome—is a very real thing. It is something that most women cannot avoid. Around a week before a woman menstruates, she will often become more edgy, more sensitive, more tearful, and much more emotional than she is at other times of the month. This has to do with certain hormonal changes going on inside her body during that time. It is also the time when the body swells due to fluid retention. The fluid retention also occurs in the brain, which causes some of these reactions. While some pills and vitamins claim to treat PMS, for the most part it is still there. It is part of what makes women *women*. Therefore, when a man observes that a woman may be slightly on edge, he needs to be sympathetic, caring, and understanding. He needs to use kinder, gentler, and more loving tones to help assuage any tension.

Help Out!

No woman ever wants to feel like she is your maid or your slave or that she is working for you. Lazy, sloppy men who sit around the house creating a mess is what no woman wants. If you use a dish, she wants you to wash it immediately or stick it in the dishwasher.

It takes the same amount of energy and muscle function to put a dish in the dishwasher or wash it as it does to leave it in the sink. If you are a messy person, have a special place—like a hamper—where you can drop your clothes. If you spill stuff, clean it up. If you drop stuff, pick it up. Women want that from you. In doing so, you will be able to avoid a number of potential arguments and hurt feelings. So to avoid it, *immediately* take care of the messes you make.

Since she has specific chores, she wants you to have specific chores as well. If hers are going grocery shopping and walking and feeding the dog, yours could be washing the dishes and throwing out the trash or taking the clothes to the cleaners. She wants you to pitch in. You can no longer use your parents as a role model, especially if your mother was a housewife who stayed at home to care for the kids. That is very rare today, so you need to help out. If you are lucky enough to employ a maid to do these things, you still need to pick up after yourself and do serious chores to help around the house.

Courtesy, Please

I can't reinforce enough how much a woman wants a gentleman—and a gentleman is considerate and has manners. If you have the nerve to say you are going to call, then *call*. That's the right thing to do. Women hate when a man says he will call or be somewhere at a specific time and he doesn't or isn't. A woman takes this very personally, so she wants to hear from you, on time. Otherwise it makes her feel a bit insecure and uncomfortable.

While you may feel free to burp loudly and pass gas with your male friends, please have some consideration and do not do this around a woman; if it is unavoidable, be discreet. To them it is gross and disgusting. A woman also doesn't want to hear gross and disgusting commentary. She'll often roll her eyes and sigh as she grimaces after listening to one of your gross or lame jokes.

And while we're on the subject of manners and respect, a woman does *not* want to be interrupted. She wants at all costs to finish what she is saying. She finds this to be the ultimate sign of disrespect for her as a person, her intelligence, and her views. Women want to be heard—they want every word heard. If they didn't think it was important for you to hear, they wouldn't have said anything.

It all boils down to showing some respect and consideration. Women insist on it, and rightfully so!

The Least You Need to Know

➤ The idea that women go for jerks who mistreat them is false. Women truly appreciate gentlemen.

➤ Women value gifts when there is real thought given to the kind and quality of the present.

➤ For most women, commitment, engagement, and marriage *do* matter.

➤ You don't have to make a woman's friends your own, but you should find a way to accept and appreciate their role in her life.

Chapter 21

Men at Work

In This Chapter

➤ Sexual harassment

➤ Bad attitude

➤ Flirting in the workplace

➤ Giving criticism

This chapter will show us how men approach the work environment and what they need to do in order to be more successful in their interactions with women there. Reading this chapter can help a man avoid unnecessary problems, including possible legal ones, he might encounter as a result of not knowing how to communicate well with women. You will learn how what you may be doing may be extremely offensive to women, even if you don't intend it to be.

Avoiding Sexual Harassment Suits

Many men and women don't realize it, but they bring on their own sexual harassment woes. Learning to recognize some of the sex differences and how they can be misinterpreted by the opposite sex can definitely reduce your odds of becoming a victim of sexual harassment. For instance, some men may hear women's nervous giggling and certain vocal inflections as encouraging sexual advances. The mere fact that women continue to communicate in sexually stereotypical ways may be debilitating to their careers.

Falling Down the Corporate Ladder

Just as women may have advanced more slowly up the corporate ladder because they haven't understood the communication differences between men and women and used them to their advantage, men have fallen down the corporate ladder because they haven't understood women, how to talk to them, and how to deal with women customers, coworkers, superiors, and subordinates.

Communication Breakdown!

You might think you already know what sexual harassment is. But do you realize how many ways of communicating—the words you use, the tone of your voice, touch, and even simple gestures—can create discomfort for the other person and land you in trouble?

Jed was a rising young star in his company. He was ambitious, accomplished, and hard-working. When he was recruited from one of the finest universities in the country, everyone in the company assumed he would rise up that corporate ladder to a middle-management position in no time. But he didn't—there was something stopping him. It was *himself.* It was the way he looked at and dealt with the women in his company—from female secretaries to his peers and superiors. Jed had a cocky attitude that screamed "I'm superior to you," "You don't know what you're talking about," and "I'm a man, so I know better." This attitude held him back. Other people who were less qualified than he and had been with the company fewer months moved up, but Jed stayed put. After a year and a half of watching people surpass him, he angrily went into his boss's office to complain.

"Sit down, young man," the boss said. "I know you have a brilliant mind, and there's no question that you can do the job, and probably do it better than some people who are in higher positions than you. But that's not enough."

"What do you mean it's not enough?" Jed asked in a hostile tone.

"The way you treat female members of our company is atrocious. I've wanted to fire you several times, but hesitated because you are so talented. I've received so many complaints about you from so many of the women in the firm."

Jed was now speechless. "You are arrogant, you are condescending, you boss them around, and bark out orders—even when they are your superiors. You act as though you are in charge. You have made derogatory comments about the women to some of your male colleagues—that this firm hires only ugly women for management, but the secretaries are babes. In fact, one of the secretaries told me something you said to her that could have landed you in a court of law and put our company in jeopardy if she'd chosen to pursue the matter. You're lucky she's my niece and wouldn't think of suing us! You now have to change your behavior, or I'll have to let you go," said his boss firmly.

Jed felt sick to his stomach. He had no clue that he was causing so much havoc and creating such a hostile work environment for the female employees. He never thought about how he treated women (that was his first mistake). He never thought of himself as barking commands. He knew he was impatient and wanted things done immediately, but he couldn't imagine ordering anyone around. Sure, maybe he was a little on the harsh side when he asked for things, he thought.

But the thing that floored him the most was when he heard that he had said something that could have led to a lawsuit against him! "What could it be?" he thought. He was always nice to the secretaries, he thought. In fact, he always complimented them. He even whistled at Maria whenever she wore that flowered sweater and told her what a sexy mama she was. And he always gave Jennifer a neck rub in the coffee room.

Earth to Jed! Wake up! You are now in a new millennium, so stop acting like you have returned to the beginning of the last millennium. You can't treat women like that. You cannot say what you said to these women. And yes, you are lucky you still have a job and aren't spending your hard-earned dollars on a lawyer to defend you in a sexual harassment suit.

I wish I could say that Jed's case was rare, and that he was the only client who ever came to me so utterly oblivious to the realities of the modern workplace. Unfortunately, it happens all the time. There are still men out there with a Neanderthal point of view when it comes to women. Who knows why? I don't want to get Freudian or Jungian and blame it on a man's mother or anything else. It doesn't matter *why*. All that matters is that a man becomes consciously aware of what he's doing and *stop it* immediately.

Sexual Harassment: A Quiz

You may be sexually harassing someone and not even know it, so I have provided a list of questions that further define the legal meaning of sexual harassment. This questionnaire will allow you to determine if you have harassed someone. If you answer "yes" to any of the questions, you have! Obviously, if you are *still* doing any of these behaviors, stop immediately.

Answer the following questions "yes" or "no." Be honest with yourself about your own behavior.

Yes	No	
❑	❑	1. Have you made any unsolicited and unwelcome contact that has sexual overtones?
❑	❑	2. Have you made any written contact that has sexual overtones, such as sexually suggestive or obscene letters, notes, and invitations?

continues

continued

Yes	No	
❑	❑	3. Have you made any verbal contact, such as sexually suggestive or obscene comments, threats, slurs, epithets, jokes about gender-specific traits, or sexual propositions?
❑	❑	4. Have you made any physical contact such as intentionally touching, pinching, brushing against another's body, impeding or blocking movement, assault, or coercing sexual intercourse?
❑	❑	5. Have you made any visual contact, such as leering or staring at another's body, gesturing, or displaying sexually suggestive objects or pictures, cartoons, posters, or magazines?
❑	❑	6. Have you continued to express sexual or social interest after being informed directly that the interest is not welcome?
❑	❑	7. Have you used sexual behavior to control, influence, or affect the career, salary, or work environment of another employee?

Bringing Home the Bacon

While the workforce is about 40 percent women (depending upon which statistics you read), the numbers are growing by leaps and bounds. More women are entering responsible positions never thought possible a decade ago. The thought of a female presidential candidate was unthinkable (or not seriously considered) until now. Women are important in the work environment, and they are here to stay, like it or not! So you need to get with the program.

Women have their own struggles and issues to contend with; I'll discuss these in the next chapter. But men don't have to make things any more difficult for women than they already are. In defense of men, some, like Jed, have no clue that they are doing anything wrong. So, men, as you read on in this chapter, you will learn what *not* to do, so that you don't continue doing something wrong in your attempts at communicating with women on the job.

Lose the Attitude

Jed thought he had a great attitude. He thought he was positive. He was glad he had a job at that company and only wished he had an even better one. So what did his boss mean by telling him that he needed to change his attitude?

Often the tone of our voice can give the impression that we have a bad attitude, even if we don't. Many men speak in a rather curt, staccato tone that (misleadingly) makes them sound angry or on edge. Especially to a woman, a quick "yep" or "nope" or "let's see" or even "okay" sounds like you have no patience with her, or you are upset with her, or just upset in general.

Now couple that clipped staccato with minimal responses, add to it a monotone, and you have a man who sounds like he has a "bad attitude."

So how do you change it? For one thing, you need to take some speech or elocution and voice lessons and learn how to speak, or read some books or listen to tapes on the subject. There are a lot of good resources on the market, such as my best-seller *Talk to Win—6 Steps to a Successful Vocal Image*. My audiotapes in particular have helped a lot of people modify some of their poor speech patterns overnight. (In Appendix A you will find out where and how to get this special tape.)

Politeness Is Potent!

Mind your manners at work. This is not your home, so you cannot act as crude or obnoxious as you choose. You are a guest in someone's environment. If it happens to be "your" environment—if you are the boss—that is all the more reason to be gracious and polite. Your employees are your guests, so treat them accordingly.

After Jed had his eye-opening meeting with his boss, he thought a lot about what was said. But he still couldn't figure out how his secretary could get the impression that he was ordering her around. He thought he had always spoken to her civilly. Well, as I had to explain to Jed, making a command without attaching the words "please" in front of the request and "thank you" at the end is not civil-sounding.

True, men speak to one another as they have been conditioned to do—giving one another commands. But you can't speak like that to a woman, especially a woman with whom you work. If the woman is a subordinate, she'll feel as though you are treating her like a slave or an animal. If the woman is a colleague, she will think, "Wait a minute. We are equals. Do it yourself. I'm not doing *anything* for you." She may also resist any further effort to be of assistance to you and just allow you to fail on your own. If you speak

Bridging the Gap

Be on the lookout for subtle hostility in the workplace. People who dislike you can find subtle ways to fight and undermine you—like losing your mail, misfiling important documents, and in general not making an extra effort when you could use it. Don't rely on an absence of open conflict—actively cultivate good relations.

like that to a superior, you may find yourself reprimanded for a "bad attitude" as Jed did. Or worse, you may find yourself out of a job.

So when you're at work, take the three magic words ("please" and "thank you") with you each morning, and use them with women as much as you can throughout the day. You may be surprised at how much more you will accomplish. Now women are willing to help you and even willing to go out of their way for you.

Men and the Woman Boss

When a man has issues with a female boss, it is often because he feels competitive with her. A lot of men who aren't used to working with female bosses are insecure about it, and as a result of their insecurity may react with anger. Since the emotion men find easiest to tap into is anger, they may react angrily to a woman boss, especially if she uses a lot of male communication patterns (giving commands and being abrupt). Men, especially those in their 40s and 50s, aren't used to this attitude in women, so it often confuses them. Men in their 20s and 30s don't seem to have as much difficulty dealing with female authority figures. Perhaps it's because they have been raised by women of a more liberated generation.

If you're having problems with a boss who happens to be a woman, search your soul first to find out if your difficulty with her is simply that she is a woman. Even though so many men claim they are hip about women's issues, deep inside many still have a problem seeing females in authority positions over them. If you do, get over it! *Fast!*

He Says, She Says

In the workplace, the words "honey" and "sweetie" need only be used in the context of how you like your coffee or tea (sweet) and what you would like in it (honey). Otherwise, drop the words. They and other terms of endearment can get you in trouble. Of course, "yeah, baby!" said in an Austin Powers "shagadelic" way might not get you into trouble (it's so obviously silly), but the other words certainly can. Lose them when you enter the work environment, no matter how chummy you get with a woman.

Office Flirts Hurt

When you flirt in the office, you not only run the risk of hurting others' feelings or insulting their integrity; you can definitely hurt yourself in more ways than you can imagine. As we saw with Jed, it can keep you from rising up the ladder of success or make you fall off the ladder completely because of the lawsuits that will be filed against you.

While there is such a thing as "chemistry," and office romances *do* happen, frivolous flirting that you don't mean seriously is offensive. It's offensive to the flirtee and to anyone else who may witness it. If you flirt with someone with whom you work just to amuse yourself, you are treading on even thinner ice—he or she might take your flirtations seriously, leading to disrespect of you, distrust, hurt feelings, and even animosity.

Another reason to limit your flirting to strangers or to people outside the office is that flirting can often lead to an office affair. As you flirt, you are testing the waters. Everything is safe because you are "only kidding." But at the right time and the right moment, temptation may take over, and there you are, involved with an office co-worker you had no intention of ever getting involved with. Now it gets messy as you try to keep everyone else from knowing (even though they probably all already know). You catch glances and stolen kisses and then—*boom*—it's over! Now you have managed to put a damper on your working relationship forever.

There may also be a trickle-down effect, because you will never know whom she knows and how well she knows them. Will she talk to others about your affair? This can muddy the political waters. So follow my advice here and keep your tongue in your mouth.

By the way, there are, of course, exceptions to every rule. In an earlier chapter, we looked at the example of the perennial flirt and how his girlfriend tried to change him. Should he have turned off his flirting when he walked in the office door? Well, in his case, flirting was so much a part of his style, and he flirted with everyone equally, that there was never any danger that anyone would take it personally. No one thought it meant anything, because he engaged everyone that way.

Keep Your Hands to Yourself

Speaking of flirting, keep your hands to yourself at all times, even if the lint on her left shoulder is driving you bonkers. Just don't touch anyone. Also keep your lips off another person. Now that might seem obvious—after all, how often do you have the desire to touch or kiss anyone in the corporate and business worlds?

But there are other worlds, such as the Hollywood film and television worlds, where touching and kissing is not always unacceptable. In fact, it is part of the protocol— you're considered *strange* if you don't touch. In Hollywood language, not touching means that you're angry at someone.

Neck rubs after long hours on a set together, kissing on the lips, and other signs of affection are commonplace in show business. Security hugs are the most common, whereby the talent (who is emotionally naked and may be feeling insecure) gets a hug from someone nearby. It's better if it's from the director, producer, or colleague, because it says "You've done a great job." In essence, the person is getting some energy from the hugger, as well as some positive assurance. In a flesh business such as Hollywood, there is an entirely different set of rules. But for the rest of the world, follow the rules I mentioned earlier.

Stop with the Jokes Already!

Just as flirting can get you in boiling water these days, so can joking around. While this is how men bond with one another, as I discussed earlier in the book, it was easy for men to do this bonding when there were hardly any women around the workplace. But now that women are here to stay, men have to stop joking in the workplace. While humorous things do inevitably come up from time to time, to routinely greet your fellow workers with a daily joke is not okay.

Communication Breakdown!

A coworker who may not like you to begin with may find a slightly off-color joke to be just the vehicle to do you in. So to be safe, save your jokes for your family and friends, not anyone with whom you work. It's too risky!

You probably heard the news story of a man who repeated the gist of a *Seinfeld* episode to his colleagues at work. The *Seinfeld* character couldn't remember the name of a woman he met and liked—all he could remember was that her name rhymed with a part of the female anatomy. The man merely *repeated* the details of what was then the top-ranked and most talked-about comedy in the country. Nonetheless, he was fired and sued for millions of dollars. This seemingly innocent joke on his part cost him his career and a lot of money.

I think the legal response was a bit overblown, but the point is that there are people out there who are extremely offended by mentioning any part of the anatomy below the neck. You have to be careful these days.

Let Her Speak!

One of the biggest complaints I hear from women against their male colleagues is that they can't get a word in edgewise because the men are ignoring them and speaking over them. They don't address their questions, and they bulldoze over the women when they do try to speak. Pay attention to what the woman is saying. You cannot keep interrupting her and expect her not to have any hostile feelings toward you.

If you are an interrupter, here's how to train yourself not to be one. As I mentioned earlier in the book, before you want to interrupt her, sip in some air through your mouth for two seconds. Then hold that breath for three seconds as you bite down on the sides of your tongue. Now exhale the air you held in for five seconds. All the while, bite on your tongue so you really *listen* to what she is saying. If you still can't contain yourself, just bite the side of your tongue a little harder—the jab of pain will remind you to keep quiet and let her finish what she has to say.

He Says, She Says

According to a Gallup Poll I commissioned, interrupting is the number-one annoying communication habit of all time. Close to 90 percent of those polled could not stand to be interrupted by others. Since this is a more male-specific trait, it is important for men to be aware of when and how often they interrupt others.

Making Eye Contact

Talking to a woman requires a dialogue, not a monologue. So many women complain that men are condescending to them. That may be the farthest thing from his mind. But when he talks at a woman, ranting on and on, not giving her the opportunity to speak, and lecturing her, it's not too difficult to see how she might come to this conclusion. Now couple that behavior with not looking directly at her, and how could she not think of the man as an arrogant guy, disinterested in what she has to say, obnoxious, showing off, and a know-it-all snob?

As I discussed earlier, communication is a two-way street, give and take. You give, she takes; she gives, you take. It is not all *you* giving (information and opinions) and *her* taking. So be extremely conscious of that. What's more, she's not your student, so watch that lecturing tone. If you want to share knowledge with her, be sure to involve her using questions: "Did you know that?" "What do you think of ...?" Ask for her feedback about the information you just disseminated. She may agree or disagree—that's called discussion and dialogue.

So, you want to give the woman the right impression. This means not appearing as if you are uninterested or that you find what she says unimportant—so unimportant that you glance around the room rather than at her. How can you give this impression? Do the facial exercise I mentioned earlier in the book. To refresh your memory:

When she is speaking, or when she is listening while you are speaking, glance at her entire face for two seconds. Now for two seconds look at her forehead. Move your glance down and spend two seconds looking at her eyes, then her nose, then her mouth (two seconds each), and now go back and look at her entire face.

At first it may seem uncomfortable to maintain your face contact, but the more you practice, the more it will become second nature. It will also force you to look at the woman above the neck, which will keep you from being accused of sexually harassing her with inappropriate glances toward her body parts.

The Art of Constructive Criticism

While you certainly do have to mind your p's and q's when it comes to dealing with women, it should not inhibit you from speaking up when the woman is doing something wrong or when her work is not up to par. You do not have to read her the riot act, of course. A lot of men who have grown up on sports teams have been "encouraged" to do a better job by being ripped apart. That's what goes on in locker rooms. Many coaches will berate the team or shame them in order to get them to play better.

A woman will be devastated if you try to do this with her. It is like punching her in the stomach. Most women have never been exposed to such behavior, nor should they ever be. So when you use this "kick butt" approach it can leave terrible scars for years.

I remember when I was completing my post-doctorate degree, and a horrible bully would berate all of the females in the department. He would try to intimidate them into doing better or accomplishing more. He would yell at women and, as unbelievable as this may sound, literally throw their work on the floor when they didn't do something to his specifications. Although this man was hated by all (he was an equal-opportunity bully), it was the women who seemed to suffer the most. Each day another woman would come out of his office in tears. Today, of course, there is no way he would get away with such actions. Women know better!

If you have to tell a woman she is wrong or you have to offer criticism, do it in a gentlemanly fashion. That means no shouting or yelling. Use terms of politeness and try to phrase your criticism in a more positive way. Saying something like, "Perhaps it might be approached ..." or "Don't you think that it would be more effective if ...."

When offering your opinion, use more emotional-state verbs so that you are speaking her language. Say "I feel that ...," "I was hoping that ...," "I'm unhappy about ...," and "I'm not too thrilled about ..." This way, you are being more sensitive to her feelings.

Also, when criticizing a woman, try to start out with something she did right, not with something she did wrong. It will help to take the edge off. A woman is very sensitive when it comes to being criticized. What you say can diminish her morale or affect her self-esteem, thereby leaving lasting scars because your harsh words resonate years later. So be careful how you couch your criticism. Be sensitive to what you say and how you say it!

The Least You Need to Know

➤ Sexual harassment in the workplace is a serious matter. Educate yourself about how to behave acceptably.

➤ Men, be careful about the attitude you convey toward women. If you give the signal that you can't deal with women in authority, you're in big trouble.

➤ Keep flirtatious behavior out of the workplace.

➤ Make sure you criticize fairly and constructively. Otherwise, you won't get the result you want, which is improved performance from those around you.

Chapter 22

Women
at Work

In This Chapter

➤ Women's special contributions

➤ Being "one of the guys"

➤ Getting personal

➤ The crying game

The purpose of this chapter is to help women see how men perceive how they operate in the work environment. Women can take the information in this chapter and make their work lives even more advantageous. As we have discovered by now, men and women certainly do see things differently and express themselves differently. In their personal and intimate lives, it is easier for women to express their displeasure to their mates or loved ones and ask them to do something about their behavior. But it's not so simple when women are forced to work next to someone who's not a lover or even a friend. There is no place or time for heart-to-heart talks, no time to explain themselves. That's why this chapter can help you, as a woman, learn how to comport yourself and create the best advantage for yourself in the predominantly male workforce.

The Bottom Line: Money Matters

Women's earnings are below those of men. In 97 percent of the occupations for which data are available, women's median weekly earnings are less than men's earnings. It's unfortunate, but it's a grim reality. In many industries, women earn less because they don't reach the top of their field, and if they do reach the top, women's salaries are still less. That has to change. There must be equal pay for equal work, as our fore-mothers of the women's liberation movement called out in their marches across the nation. Now there are legal channels to make sure this is accomplished. Don't hesitate to use them if you've been discriminated against by receiving less pay.

Communication Breakdown!

Ease up on the competition. The old argument that the man has to earn more because he's the breadwinner doesn't fly anymore. There are too many single mothers bringing home the bread, and deadbeat dads *not* bringing it home, to even consider such an absurdity today.

Monkey See, Monkey Do!

I once gave a talk to a group of terribly angry women who worked for a financial investment group in New York City. There were a myriad of problems in their company, not to mention the fact that the male CEO and founder of the firm sexually harassed practically every woman who worked there. In addition, no woman had ever been promoted to top-level management, so there were no female role models or mentors to give other women guidance. On top of that, there was a high level of attrition among the women.

Their main concern was the disrespect they received from their male colleagues, even those who were younger than them and had less seniority in the firm. They hated the teasing and the jokes, the "I'm better than you are" competitive attitude. No wonder they were so hostile. Nobody gave them the respect they felt they deserved—not the boss, not any of the other officers or account managers, and not those young whippersnappers, who followed the example of the senior men.

What were they to do? Well, they could do nothing, short of filing sexual harassment charges against their boss, or yelling and fighting with their male colleagues and subordinates, or leaving. This was not a woman-friendly company, and this fact was reflected in the women's tense attitudes.

For this reason, it was important for these women to learn more about the ways men and women communicate differently. If they didn't want to sue the company, at least they could use what they learned to negotiate more effectively with others.

She's Not the "B" Word!

When a woman takes charge and knows what she wants and wants what she knows, she is not considered professionally aggressive or a person with fine business acumen. Instead she is referred to as the "B" word. A man can do the exact same thing, refusing to budge on prices or stating firmly the terms he wants for negotiation, and no one will think anything of it—or, more precisely, everyone will respect him for his political savvy. When a woman does it, however, it's an entirely different story. This double standard is unfair, and the label she receives is inaccurate.

Suppose a woman displays "male" communication patterns such as speaking in sentences that may be choppy and staccato, direct and to the point, with little or no emotion, and constantly interrupting in order to get her points in. By speaking this way, she'll alienate not only men but women as well.

This may tell us something. Perhaps it shows us that women can be effective in business without having to "become men" or use male communication skills. There are, of course, "women" things women do when they communicate which are not acceptable in the business world. In that case, they do need to emulate what men do. These include: getting to the point, not discussing personal information, not crying, speaking up so they can be heard, not holding grudges, saying what's on their minds, not smiling or agreeing when something isn't pleasant or agreeable to them, and sticking up for themselves.

When a woman takes the worst of male communication traits and adapts them as her own, *forget it!* She will become a major outcast. When women get into leadership positions, all too many of them think they need to take the worst behaviors of men and use them as their own.

In the following box is a profile of a woman who has the following "bad" male characteristics. (Remember: There are good ones, too, as we learned earlier in the book.) Would you want to work with her or for her, much less be around her? I doubt it.

Would You Want This Woman as Your Boss?

1. She doesn't return your smile, much less say hello (she's too preoccupied with work).
2. She brags about herself and boasts of her achievements.
3. She doesn't apologize, even when she's wrong.
4. She engages in a monologue or debate, talking at you, not to you.
5. She doesn't look at you when she speaks. She glances off to the side, giving the impression that she's suspicious of everything you have to say.
6. She speaks in a choppy, loud, staccato monotone devoid of inflection and emotion.
7. She tells dirty jokes and uses lots of four-letter words.
8. Whatever you say, she will try to top it.
9. She uses anger to manipulate and is harsh in what she says.
10. She's more than to the point: She's blunt, paying no attention to how what she said may affect your feelings.

Obviously, this type of boss would be a "toxic terror" on wheels no matter what sex she or he was. The fact that she was a woman who exhibited the worst of all "male" characteristics is not endearing to anyone. It does not endear her to her colleagues, male or female, but rather alienates her from them.

Bringing in Something Unique

Women do bring something special to the workplace. According to a study done by the U.S. Department of Labor, women bring a new sensitivity and a new level of humanity to the work force. It's not that men are inhuman, but that women are more maintenance-oriented, more concerned with how their fellow workers are doing.

Women bosses, who retain many of their feminine communication patterns, are concerned about people's families, relationships in the workplace, and how people get along with one another. Women in the workplace have much more dialogue and more of a win-win attitude, rather than an "I won, you lost" attitude or a desire to win at all costs. They're more humble than men and offer a lot more praise. Women say a lot more that makes people feel better about themselves and about what they are doing at work. These are the best traits of women that add a tremendous amount to the workplace and add to productivity.

Women also tend to often look at the bigger picture and take a broader view than their male colleagues do. They tend to look at both sides of an issue more readily than men. Women's flexibility and creativity are assets that few businesses who really want to succeed in today's market can do without.

So, women do not have to act like men or adopt male-oriented behaviors to be effective in the workplace. They just need to understand male behavior.

What I Mean Is ...

The **glass ceiling** is a phrase coined in the 1980s when women were rising up the corporate ladder to indicate that they could go no farther. It meant that they had reached a certain level in the corporate structure and could go no higher. Even though things looked equal on the surface, as though the sky was the limit and that women could advance as high as they wanted to go, there really was a limit as they were kept from advancing by the corporate structure and corporate leaders.

Breaking Through the Glass Ceiling

Time and again we've heard that women seem unable to break through the *glass ceiling,* no matter how hard they try.

Well, some women do break through the glass ceiling, and they break through because they've learned over the years that there are some things that they, as women, cannot do in a male-dominated environment if they want to succeed. They have learned who they are and are secure with what they can and cannot do in order to achieve optimum results. For example, these women know that they can't speak like little girls or use the cutesy approach or cry when things don't go their way or their feelings are hurt. While such tactics may work in the short run, they can't work for long.

He Says, She Says

Here is a list of things women *cannot* do if they want to get ahead with men and break through the glass ceiling. They *cannot* ...

➤ Act vulgar or gross, or tell risqué jokes.

➤ Cry.

➤ Pout or hold a grudge.

➤ Sound too cute, babyish, or flirty.

➤ Divulge personal information about their lives.

➤ Speak without thinking of the consequences.

➤ Ramble on and on without stopping.

➤ Take rejection personally.

She's *Not* One of the Guys

So you want to be one of the guys? You think men will accept you more, and life will be a lot easier when you work with them every day? Well, you can't, and they won't, and it isn't! Men won't accept you as one of the guys, and life won't be a lot easier. Besides, not having the same physical anatomy, brain anatomy, or the same way of thinking, you'll never be one of the guys anyway, nor should you ever attempt to be.

Let's say you decide to do some "male bonding" and become a jokester, telling jokes to all the men in your organization. You even tell them some off-color ones. You don't mind because you think, "Hey, after all, I'm just one of the guys. They'll all laugh, and everything will be fine."

Well, they may laugh, but everything won't be fine. Here is one example. Rhonda wanted to be "one of the guys" at work. She began to think of herself as one of the guys as she drank beer and partied with her male colleagues after work. She drank as much as they did, trying to keep up with them and matching one joke after another. Some of the jokes were vulgar, and she spilled them off her tongue without a blink. One day after work with the guys, while she was getting plastered, trying to keep up, there was a band in the bar, and one of her male colleagues asked her to dance.

While on the dance floor, he made some physically suggestive advances toward Rhonda and said some vulgar things to her regarding what he wanted to do to her. She suddenly realized she was not one of the guys. She was still a woman and was deeply offended and hurt at what her colleague said, not to mention shocked. She went into the bathroom, threw up, and cried. Rhonda got a dose of reality. She was not a guy and could not bond with them.

In her case, she couldn't even drink with them. They could have four beers and could hold it, because they were a lot bigger than she was. While they got just a buzz, she got drunk. While they talked vulgar trash about women in general, she could play along, and didn't bat an eye. But when it was directed toward her, it was a different story.

Seeing she was upset, the colleague who made the advance pulled her aside to tell her he thought she wouldn't mind, because he thought she was giving all the classic signals that she was "that kind of girl," that she wouldn't mind his advances. Of course, she did mind—she minded a lot. "How could you have even thought I was like that?" she sputtered. "Well, you talk about sex all the time, you joke about it, you laugh at our jokes. I thought you liked it and that's what you wanted." "*What!?*" she screamed, "I'm just one of the guys. I was just joking around." "Well, you're not one of the guys. You're a lady, but you don't act like one. I would never talk to a lady the way I talk around you, but you didn't seem to mind. You took it in stride."

Communication Breakdown!

If you're a woman, never attempt to "male bond." There's simply no such thing!

Rhonda was sick to her stomach. She finally got it! She was coming across like a "floozy" or a "loose woman" whom anyone could take liberties with. Now she realized the reason why she never got promoted. She wasn't taken seriously. She was seen as the jokester and now the "loose woman." She was embarrassed—so much so that she left the company to begin anew and not make the same mistake again.

Keep Your Personal Life Close and Personal

If a woman really wants to succeed in the business world, she has to act professional at *all* times. That means she must never ramble on about her family and personal business, personal activities, what she did, where she went, and how she and her husband and kids feel about everything. It's not important and nobody really cares. People are thrown together to earn a living and to contribute something of value to society. They really don't want to get into your personal business, mainly because they are too concerned about their own.

When you share your personal business, it may and usually does come back to haunt you. Sometimes you think you're telling a confidence to just a single confidant, but soon the whole office will know you're having an affair with the guy down the hall. It can get really ugly.

Work is no place to divulge your marital woes. Even if you come to work long-chinned and puffy-eyed, when someone asks you what's the matter, tell them you have allergies. (It's not a lie—you're allergic to them prying into your business.) Never tell anyone at work that you've been up all night crying because your husband came home at three in the morning, and he is having an affair with his office secretary and now wants to leave you for her. Your coworkers may be sympathetic at first and even give you that proverbial shoulder to cry on, but watch out! As the day progresses you'll become grist for the gossip mill, and your professional life will be tarnished forever. The people with whom you work aren't your therapists, and this isn't group therapy.

I have seen too many open-hearted, open-mouthed women share too many things with the wrong people at work (people they assumed were the right people), only to have it come back to haunt them. Men really think less of women who tattle on their husbands or divulge negative secrets. Men fear that you may do the same to them at work, divulging their peccadilloes. This is a major issue that alienates men and women in the workplace, so be aware, and keep your home life out of the job. If you have to make a personal call or deal with a personal issue, make sure that others (especially your male colleagues) are not around to hear it.

Take your cell phone and go outside for a break and talk; don't do it in the presence of prying ears. You lose respect when coworkers know too much (good *or* bad) about how you live your life.

You Don't Have to Answer

Women in particular have difficulty withholding information. Why? Because women are honest and don't like to lie. So when they are asked their age, they will lie and then feel bad about it. Or they will tell the truth and feel worse about it. The best way to handle age questions is to say "I'm ageless," smile, and then drop the subject.

Many women feel intimidated when they're asked a personal question and feel compelled to answer it. As a result they "spill the beans," often revealing something they're not supposed to or something that's not in the best interest of the company. You may divulge critical information unconsciously, automatically, just because you're asked. Well, it can no longer be automatic, because you can cause a lot of damage to your business and to the businesses of others when you say too much.

Bridging the Gap

When you're on the verge of answering a question that might divulge too much about yourself or your firm, ask yourself: "Is this in my best interests or my company's best interests?" As you attempt to answer the question, remember not just to *think before you speak* but also to *breathe before you speak*, so that you can decide what you will or will not reveal.

The best way to avoid spilling the beans is to get into the habit of thinking before you speak. Take a breath of air in through your mouth for two seconds; hold it for another two seconds, then slowly release the air for five seconds and think about the question you were just asked. If you need more time, repeat the question you were asked until you come up with an answer. If you still don't have an answer, say, "Let me think about that," or "Let me give that some thought." You don't have to be forced into answering anything. Never feel pressured or intimidated to answer anything you don't feel comfortable answering. You are in control of everything that comes out of your mouth. Nobody but you can stop your tongue from making the movements it must make to say any words. You have the power, so use it to control what you say to others.

A lot of what people ask you is none of their business, and you need to be discriminating about what you tell to whom, how much to tell, and why you're telling it in the first place. If you keep these things in mind, you will never get into trouble and lose respect or self-respect in the work environment.

Hold No Grudges

In an earlier chapter, I spoke about how women hold grudges. The example I gave was a woman and a man at a meeting, agreeing with each other, but disagreeing with another man over an issue. The woman takes the disagreement to heart, and so is upset later when she sees the two men acting like pals as they head out for a meal together. She was expecting her ally in the meeting to remain by her side and hostile to the other man. This was a sign of the difference between men and women: She personalized the disagreement, while the two men regarded it as simply one part of what happens in the workaday world.

What the woman didn't see was that business is business and fellowship is fellowship; like most women, she mixed the two together. When women hold grudges like this, it keeps them from breaking through the glass ceiling. So the message here is: Get over it, and get over it fast! The workplace is no place for holding grudges and hanging on to hurt feelings.

No Crying Games

A woman must *never* cry in front of her colleagues, male or female. And it doesn't matter what her reason for crying might be—for pity, to get her way, or because someone really hurt her ego and lowered the boom on her self-esteem. Whatever the reason, it makes others think less of the woman. Most men don't know what to do when a woman cries. And they feel doubly bad if they were the ones responsible for making someone cry. After that happens, the interaction is never the same. Men will usually feel embarrassed and try to avoid the woman; obviously, this can interfere with the work. Other times, men won't be able to speak openly and honestly, colleague to colleague, for fear they might upset her and make her cry again. They feel as though they are walking on eggshells when talking to her. Finally, if they feel she has "turned on the waterworks," crying simply for effect, they will resent her, distrust her, and think a lot less of her.

So, the bottom line is: Don't cry.

Communication Breakdown!

Never cry in front of coworkers. Bite your lip. Dig your fingernails into your hand. Do anything not to cry. If you must, run into the woman's bathroom (stall) and sob away. Or leave the premises or find a utility closet to hide in. But do it quietly. Don't let anyone see you cry, or it will definitely come back to haunt you.

Speak Up!

Speaking up means saying things so that you can be heard and saying what's on your mind. If there is something bothering you, don't be silent but deadly. Too many women act like volcanoes; they bottle up things that bother them and then—*kaboom*—let loose with a stream of verbal venom that is enough to have the toughest and strongest of men shaking in their boots. Their adrenaline is flowing like molten lava as they dredge up every negative item that was ever said or done during the past decade. This is totally inappropriate. It is horrible for your health, and it's horrible for your image. Men fear this trait in women, and they refer to women who do this as "crazy," "out of control," and "wild."

In order for this not to happen, speak up immediately when something is annoying you. Don't wait—it could be dangerous to your health and to your reputation.

Where's the Mouse?

Where's the mouse? And I'm not talking about the computer mouse—I'm talking about that little mouse voice that women use. This turns men off. It makes women sound weak and helpless. And, in fact, they are helpless: Women who talk this way get stepped on.

They aren't respected or perceived as being very smart. How could they be? These women sound like little girls, and little girls aren't very smart because, after all, they aren't grown up yet. Well, you *are* smart and grown up, and you're *not* a little girl. So stop sounding like one! I'm serious—not taking my advice in this area can hold you back forever. I have seen it with countless people in my practice.

Open your mouth when you speak. Push your stomach muscles out when you speak. In essence, bear down on these muscles. Watch your voice get stronger, and listen to how the pitch drops. Be sure to open your jaw a little wider and open up the back of your throat as though you are yawning. It's a simple thing to do, but it works! I know. I've spent years teaching women how to lower their voices, with great success. So you can do it, too. Improve your speaking voice and let people hear you, so they don't think you're a lightweight by your light voice. You can change your voice. If you need additional help, my *Talk to Win* books, tapes, and videos (see Appendix A in the back of this book) can be of assistance to you.

In the meantime try the stomach muscle-control exercise I presented and see if people don't treat you with more respect when you speak from your guts. I can assure you people will speak to you with a lot more respect.

Spit It Out Already!

When women speak to men in the business world, they often fail to get to the point quickly enough. It's annoying enough when a man is married to a woman who does this, but when he has to listen to a woman go on and on at work, where time is of the essence and so precious, it is even more irritating. Precious time can be lost, which translates into information and dollars and cents. People don't have the time to listen to the details. They don't have the time to stay on the phone and listen to you go on and on. They want it fast, and they want it now. They want the bare essentials.

So, get to the facts. Hit the bottom line immediately. Men don't want to hear every detail of your lunch meeting with Mr. Jones—they want to know if Mr. Jones wants the product or not. Once you tell them what they need to hear, you can then try to elaborate. That first sentence is called the "meat" of communication, so spit it out quickly when talking to a man. No ifs, ands, uhs, wells, ums, likes, or buts about it.

De-Personalizing Rejection

Dealing with rejection is not a woman's strong suit. Nine times out of 10, she takes it to heart and personalizes it. After all, it hurts to be cast out or refused something, for whatever reason. And it's virtually impossible not to take things personally, because self-esteem is involved here.

But if you're going to personalize what happened, allow yourself to be hurt for a limited time, and then get over it quickly. Life is way too short for you to harbor hurt feelings for a long period of time. It really isn't worth it. Anyone who has lost a relative or a friend unexpectedly knows exactly what I am talking about. Save feeling awful and dejected for something that is really significant.

That's just the way it is. Men are a little better at handling rejection, perhaps because they have had more experience getting rejected. For example, in sports, they get rejected from making teams. And many men in certain generations and cultures take the responsibility of making the first move, so they set themselves up for rejection more easily than women do. That doesn't mean that men are less sensitive than women are. Men still feel rejection, but they deal with it a lot quicker. Whether it is due to their conditioning or perhaps denial of their own feelings of hurt, they do have a tendency to move on to the next situation a lot quicker than women do, instead of dwelling on the hurt and pain of rejection.

You shouldn't keep kicking yourself or feeling horrible when things don't go your way. Lighten up and look at the bigger picture. Learn from your rejection. Rejection can also spur you on and motivate you to take a different direction that will be even better for you in the long run. Men are very much aware of this. Many men have ended up in completely different and better directions in their lives because of being rejected from something they initially pursued. They have often learned to look at rejection as a blessing in disguise. That's why they don't spend too much time wallowing in "Rejectionville." They just move on! So take heed and follow their lead as they move on!

The Least You Need to Know

➤ Women bring unique contributions to the workplace, such as creativity and flexibility.

➤ Women—you are not "one of the guys," and you never will be. By trying to act that way, you'll just confuse men and give them the wrong impression of you.

➤ Personal issues have no place in the workplace.

➤ *Never* let your colleagues see you cry. If you are doing it just for manipulation, people will come to distrust you. If the tears are genuine, people will feel awkward around you.

➤ Work on handling rejection. Don't let it devastate you. Instead, let it motivate you to keep going.

Chapter 23

Seeking
Similarities

In This Chapter

➤ Take it easy, take it slow

➤ Secrets, secrets

➤ Jealousy

➤ No cheering for interfering

Although we may come at the same issues from different points of view, men and women do have similarities, and we need to identify those similarities in order to share a peaceful co-existence. We are more alike than we think. In this chapter, we will see just how similar we are. Perhaps by seeing how similar we are, we'll be able to become a lot more sensitive to one another and treat one another with the respect, caring, and kindness we all so richly deserve. It is not just about mankind or womankind—it's about humankind.

We All Carry Baggage

As bad as men think they've had it with failed relationships with women, women, too, feel awful about their past histories with men. We've all been through the mill and learned from the school of hard knocks. We've all cried our tears and licked our wounds after experiencing rejection and failure. Recently divorced men and women are dangerous to get involved with because they are often so needy, looking for band-aid therapy, that quick fix to take away their agonizing loss. For either sex, jumping into another relationship without the therapy of some intense self-analysis can lead to the same disaster.

These days, multiple divorces are not uncommon. The reason is that people often marry others they are familiar with in personality type and in character. If that particular personality type is toxic to you, and you haven't yet discovered that, you will undoubtedly repeat the same pattern. As Sigmund Freud once said, "What we don't resolve, we repeat." So unless people resolve what it is they are drawn to because of that negative familiarity, there will often be third, fourth, and fifth marriages.

Nobody of either sex is baggage-free. Everyone has a past. And if they don't, they either aren't human or haven't lived. Being afraid to get involved with a woman or man who has a past is unrealistic. The trick is to see if our own pasts are harmonious and can we get along with one another.

Men and women both know what it feels like to feel lonely, to have that empty feeling gnawing at the pit of their stomachs. Because of this loneliness, men and women often feel a desperation to latch on to another person so that they don't have to live in the abyss of emptiness. It is too easy for a man or a woman who is just divorced to fall into the wrong arms and feel even lonelier. It is hard for men and women to meet one another. We all feel awkward and silly when we are forced into artificial environments such as singles dances or dating services. We both find it hard to be ourselves. We find it a real effort to push ourselves out there and meet new people. So when one of us actually does make the effort to approach the other, it is not to be taken for granted. We are both reaching out to close the gap of loneliness.

We All Want to Feel Like Number One

Each one of us wants to feel as though we are and always have been the number-one person in our man's or woman's life. Therefore, no one wants to hear the gory details of a past relationship and how terribly in love with the other person you were. We want to know that, until we came along, your life was not as great as it is now that we are in it.

Sometimes unknowingly we stimulate our mates to talk about their exes by asking them all kinds of questions. But that was another time and another place with another person. So don't dig unless you're prepared to find out things that you might not enjoy hearing. You want to feel as though you are number one and just the person he or she needs to add sunshine to his or her life. We both need to be loved, and we need to love back and to feel that we are the most loved.

No One Likes Secrets Revealed

Men and women do not like hearing things they told you, either in confidence or in an intimate moment, thrown back in their faces when they confided in you by telling you. Those things said in private moments are just that—private. If you hear those things repeated by the person you confided in, you feel naked, cheated, betrayed, and belittled. It works this way for both men and women. I have seen many relationships break up over couples not respecting each others' confidences. It erodes trust and, if done more than once, your partner won't feel that he or she can trust you, so your partner will withhold information from you, thereby destroying any possible hope for future honest and open closeness and intimacy.

If you once had a problem with the law, and you opened up to your mate that when you were in your 20s you got arrested for protesting or shoplifting, you don't want to hear about this embarrassing incident 20 years later. You don't want to hear about it even if your mate is "only kidding" or calling you his or her "little jailbird" or "little criminal." You don't want to hear it thrown in your face. Regardless of what sex you are, you don't want to meet your negative past in the present—especially from someone you're intimate with.

Nobody Likes a Gold Digger

Neither sex wants to feel as though they are loved conditionally because they are pretty, have a good body, have money, or have a nice house. Of course, these things are nice assets. And let's be honest—if faced with a choice of two identical people with the same personalities, you would have to be a fool not to choose the person who brings more other qualities to the table and has more to offer. Why not? It will enrich the quality of your life. On the other hand, you don't want to be in a situation where you are liked just because you are wealthy, have a great body, or are famous.

Nobody wants to feel used. Men and women both are suspicious of people who angle for money in a relationship. We've all seen women's magazines, books, and even courses that give advice on how to land a millionaire. It's one thing if women—and men, for that matter—have decided that the kind of life they want for themselves would be better served by having access to more money. But this can never be the driving force for a relationship, or the relationship is *doomed.*

It is degrading and hurtful to be liked only for your money. While statistics show that women prefer a man who has money, and men prefer women who are attractive, neither sex wants to be liked just because of those things. We want to be liked and loved for who we are, not for what we have and how we look.

Often when you manipulate, you're manipulated in return, as one client of mine has come to find out. She thought she could use a man to buy her nice gifts. He certainly did buy her a lot of gifts, but unbeknownst to her, with her own credit card. He would charge the gifts he bought her over the phone while using her card. He would always be out of money, ask for cash, and write her a huge check for 10 times more than he borrowed. Of course his check was bogus. This con, also known as a *scrub,* knew that this woman was out to use him, and she got used instead. Moral: Use and get used.

While you see it all the time, and yes, there are people who are satisfied by this arrangement—the man knows the woman is with him because of his money or status, and the woman knows he is with her because she is young and beautiful—these interactions rarely last. And if they do last, they are filled with a lot of inner resentment and emotional pain.

Everyone wants to be in a relationship that is give and take. Nobody wants to give more than the other person. Regardless of which partner (man or woman) is the total breadwinner, the other partner needs to contribute just as much to the relationship in other ways, like chores, home activities, or getting them involved in social activities. Both men and women want someone who gives them something back and doesn't take from them all the time. Nobody wants to feel taken advantage of, regardless of their sex.

Love Us Just the Way We Are

Neither women nor men want to be used as an arm piece, someone who looks good on their arm, or a "trophy," or liked or disliked for their looks. I have a client who tracked her husband's moods based on whether she was overweight or not. When she gained a few pounds, his bad mood would reflect it. She felt loved conditionally. I found the same thing with men, regarding money matters. When everything was going according to course and there was smooth sailing, women reacted a lot more lovingly than when their husbands were out of a job.

When Cleo married Eugene, she was thin and sexy. Throughout the years, the weight piled on after two kids and a few family tragedies. She noticed how Eugene grew more and more distant as her weight became more and more prevalent. He would bug her about it, and finally she lost the weight. He began to change, as though he was her amorous suitor of a decade past. The only problem was that she resented him and was now repulsed by his touch. "If he didn't like me fat, he doesn't deserve to have me now that I'm thin," she said.

The same thing happened to Mitch, who was 100 pounds overweight. The woman he tried to woo would treat him as though he didn't exist. When he took off the weight, he was actually gorgeous, and she was now all over him. Although he was flattered in a way, he was really seething inside. She even asked him out, and he went. She became aggressive, putting the moves on him, and he didn't resist. But what he did resist was her future calls. He told her to lose his number and that she was too superficial a person for him to even speak with, let alone date.

What You See Is What You Get!

Both men and women do not want to be changed. While we both idealize our perfect man, woman, and mate, neither sex wants to be changed.

Sometimes one party will try to get the other to change by embarrassing the other into it, making him or her feel guilty, or even withdrawing physical love if the person doesn't do what the other one wants. But we want to be accepted for who and what we are. We don't want our partners coming up with a laundry list of how we need to look, speak, act, smell, perform, talk, sleep, or eat.

Now, I'm not talking about asking people for small things, like asking your mate to wear your favorite cologne. I'm talking about attempts to change partners into completely other people. So many men want to re-design their women's bodies to look like a Barbie Doll or a famous sex symbol. They want their women to have huge breasts, little hips, and a tight behind. Well, guess what? That body type doesn't exist even in the sex symbol they're drooling over. She's all made, cut, and pasted, courtesy of plastic surgery.

I had a client who wanted such a woman and paid a lot of money to get her that way. She looked completely different from the girl he supposedly fell in love with. Now the formerly overweight, flat-chested brunette with an attractive face looked like a movie star, because he remodeled her from head to toe to fit his ideal fantasy of what a woman should be. Breast implants. Long, bleached-blond hair. Hips, thighs, and stomach liposuctioned, nose done, teeth capped, and gym-toned. She was *now* his dream girl.

At first she loved the attention and wanted to be as beautiful as possible to please her man, but then she came to resent it more and more, because nothing seemed to be good enough for him. He always wanted some kind of a change. Now he wanted her to change her New York accent. She felt she wasn't the "she" whom he married. And he wasn't the "he" whom she thought she married. She thought she had married a man who liked her for herself, not a Dr. Frankenstein who wanted to re-create her. Now that she was the ideal he created, she decided that she no longer wanted to be married to her re-creator, so she left him for one of the many men who liked this fantasy woman her husband had created.

When George, another client of mine, met Linda, he was fat, bald, wore polyester, and was a sloppy mess. He had thick glasses and an average job. Linda made it her project to fix him. He loved the attention, and she got him to dress very preppy, lose weight, have eye surgery so he no longer required glasses, and grow his hair longer in the back so that his hair looked fuller. As a result, he looked quite handsome. Through her connections, she also got him a new job, where he made more money. Now he was good enough for her—good enough to take to her parents to show him off, good enough to take to the club and to parties to meet her friends. At one of these parties, George met Linda's friends, one in particular whom he ended up with. He ended up gaining the weight back, going back to his polyester way of dressing,

Bridging the Gap

It's up to you, not your mate, to make yourself over if that's what you think is best. Beware if you sense someone is trying to take control of who and what you are.

cutting his hair, and leaving the higher paying job for a job similar to his old one. And guess what? His new woman loved him anyway. She loved him for *him*.

People of either sex resent being tampered with, unless they decide to tamper with themselves.

Slow Down!

All too often, a woman will meet a man she likes, and in her head, she already has the silverware pattern and the china picked out. She's visualizing herself in a wedding dress, and imagining the colors of her brides-maids' dresses. The more she likes a man, the mores she visualizes her future with him. This happens rather quickly for a number of reasons (biological clock, societal pressures, peer pressure, parental pressure). When she shares this information or lets it slip prematurely, most men freak out! They get scared when things are going along fine for several dates and then they hear her making plans as a couple: "We'll go here," "We'll go there." Men will either run away or clam up, and their behavior will change from one extreme to the next. They will get a little chillier.

Women, too, are put off by haste, but for a different reason. Instead of being fright-ened over having a long-lasting commitment, women are put off by men who rush into sex with them. Just as she is visualizing the marriage on the first date, he may be visualizing a great night of sex with her. And her reaction to the rushing is the same as a man's. The woman runs or clams up and turns off. So the moral of this lesson is that both sexes need time to establish a comfort level before jumping ahead in an attempt to make their fantasies become realities.

We're All Afraid of Commitment

We hear so much about the man being commitaphobic. Well, the reality is that women are just as commitment-shy as men. Women want to be with men who want them, just as men want to be with women who want them. The commitment issue is all about the loss of identity. Members of both genders are afraid to lose themselves in another person. Neither men nor women want to lose their freedom. Both genders want to make certain they are with the right person, and when men and women exhibit cold feet, most often it's because they have reservations about the other per-son and how he or she fits into the relationship.

A couple may have a beautiful relationship and be headed toward the altar, when at the last minute something happens to upset the apple cart. Maybe an old flame comes back into the picture, or one of the couple decides he or she needs that one last fling, or maybe they both pull away. Regardless of what sex you are, if you are on the receiving end of this, it can be agony. But the key to remember here is, it's not a man thing *or* a woman thing that makes this happen. It's a *people* thing—people are afraid to lose who they are and afraid of what the future will bring. This is why open and honest communication between couples is paramount, regardless of their sex. With good communication, this commitment phobia can often be overcome.

We All Want That Pedestal

Men and women both want to feel as though they are the greatest things on the planet to one another. I will never forget meeting a couple in their 80s who seemed like two little lovebirds. They were so cute to watch. All in love, hugging and kissing like 16-year-olds. They had learned the secret well: to treat one another as though they were the most important people on the planet. It is a failsafe method for keeping a relationship together.

If you positively reinforce someone, you can often turn the most difficult situation around. Encouragement, praise, and interest in the other person's total being on a consistent basis can make the other person treat you like a king or queen because it makes you so extraordinarily special. After all, how many other people are doing this for the man or woman you are with?

Communication Breakdown!

No one wants to feel manipulated or kept in the dark. Books that tell you to be a mystery, to be elusive, to keep your partner on edge, are very damaging, no matter if they are best-sellers or not. No man or woman wants to be toyed with, pushed, or pulled under any circumstances.

We All Hate Personal Competition

Although it is commonly thought that the male sex is the most competitive, this is untrue. Research shows that females are equally competitive. It just seems that men are more competitive because men are involved in sports to a greater extent than women are. But women will go to great lengths to win as well. This competition among women is more evident in the social milieus, where there will be competition for friends and boyfriends.

While some people thrive on competition because it gives them an adrenaline rush, you have to know with whom you are competing. When a man competes with a woman in the workplace, just as he would compete with another woman or another man, this may be a very good thing. It may be the factor that stimulates one to work harder and to be the best and come out ahead financially. However, there's no room whatsoever for competition when it comes to a personal relationship between a man and a woman. Neither sex likes it. It makes for hard feelings and tension, and nobody comes up a winner. Competing for the last word or for who gets what or does what first may be acceptable between brothers and sisters, but not between men and women who are engaging in an intimate relationship. In this competition, there are only losers—two of them. Couples need to be allies, not competitors.

Equal Aggression

Don't kid yourself if you think the male sex is the more aggressive. We are *both* aggressive, and when something is important to us, we both will become as bold as we have to be and go to the ends of the earth to accomplish our task. Overt hostile aggression, according to studies, is not looked upon favorably by either sex, because aggression brings forth fear, and people don't like to be afraid of one another.

Women do get angry, enraged to the point that they scream and yell and carry on like men do. It is a basic emotion that all human beings possess. While women may be a little more inhibited about letting out their anger, the truth of the matter is that they get just as angry and vocal as men do.

Green with Jealousy

Men feel jealousy as easily as women do. If a man sees his woman flirting unabashedly with another man, he is going to feel a twinge of jealousy. If a woman sees her man eyeing a beautiful woman at a party and spending the entire night cooing over her, ignoring the woman he is with, the woman will undoubtedly feel pangs of jealousy. It is human nature, and we need to respect that.

It is a cruel act for either sex to intentionally make the other one jealous, to test the limits of love, or to see how one really feels about the other. While entire books have been written for the sole purpose of teaching you how to purposely manipulate the opposite sex to get the other person to fall in love with you, this cruel game will always backfire on you.

It may work initially, when the person comes running back to you. But insecurity is not the basis for any relationship. These books perpetuate the goal of making someone else insecure and keeping that person off-balance. That is *not* what any solid relationship is based upon. A truly strong relationship is based upon respect and making the other person feel loved, secure, and confident that he or she has a safe place to go in the harsh cruel world—a place where a partner can receive caring, warmth, nurturing, and protection from an ally, not an emotional tormentor.

Men and Women Appreciate Good Grooming

Having respect for another person means maintaining certain standards of appearance. This means, at the very least, keeping yourself washed and well-groomed.

Indeed, paying attention to personal hygiene not only reflects the respect that you have for yourself, but it reflects how you respect others. Most people don't like living with a slob, regardless of whether they themselves are slobs. So if you are slovenly, clean up your act if you plan to connect with the opposite sex.

No Outside Interference

Nobody likes to know that there's a third person interfering in the relationship and determining its outcome. They don't like hearing references to it: "My mother thinks ...," "My sister thinks ...," "My brother thinks ...," "My psychic thinks ...."

Nobody wants to know that there is an astrologer, a family member, or even a shrink who is deciding the fate of your relationship. As a counselor, I must *always* keep in mind not to turn my value judgments and opinions into spoken judgments about whether the relationships of my clients will succeed or fail. Unless there is a history of physical abuse and violence, I don't do that.

And if I as a professional don't (and *shouldn't*) do this, neither should the amateur counselors in your life, the sisters, parents, and friends. Such people often try to intervene out of good intentions; but in the end, it's really not their relationship, and not their business. And if you let third parties take charge in your relationship, your partner will be threatened. He or she will feel that outside forces want control. This isn't just paranoia on your partner's part—your partner's right!

Of course, you will want to ask friends and relatives for advice from time to time. But don't give them control. And remember that no one is in the special position you and your partner are in to measure how the relationship is developing and what steps you need to take to keep it growing.

Cat Got Your Tongue?

It's often hard to speak up. Whether male or female, it's hard for us to express ourselves, to say what we mean, and to mean what we say. It's hard to tell someone something that might be uncomfortable and hurtful. As a rule, no one sets out to consciously hurt the feelings of a member of the opposite sex—it just happens by virtue of misunderstanding or inadequate words. Thus it is difficult for both parties to adequately express themselves. If this wasn't the case, men and women would surely be getting along a lot better with one another. But do your best to talk with your partner. Say what's on your mind in a caring, helping way, and you'll open up the lines of communication.

Very Human Cycles

There are times of the month when some women are simply more emotional than others. Discussed in practically every medical book on female health, premenstrual syndrome is the time of the month when women retain fluids in their bodies and brains, which causes a great deal of tension and irritability. There is also a hormonal cycle involved which causes monthly behavioral changes in women. Men, too, have these cycles. Although they, of course, don't menstruate, they do have changes in their biorhythms and energy levels.

The bottom line is we are all moody from time to time, depending upon what's going on in our lives, the particular stress levels we are under, and what our bodies are doing. Therefore we need to cut one another some slack when it comes to dealing with moody behavior and not take it so personally.

The good news is that in the average person, these blue moods don't last for a very long time and are cyclical. When you've been around your partner or colleague at work, you learn to pick up on the signals where the other person may be exhibiting low points in his or her moods. If you pay close enough attention, you spot that it often happens at the same time each month. Now that you have this knowledge, you can be a little more tolerant and understanding of others.

The Least You Need to Know

➤ Men and women both want to be treated with the utmost respect and accepted for who we are in a relationship. Both men and women dislike the other trying to change them.

➤ Men and women should never throw secrets back in the face of the other person. This will create distrust and anger.

➤ Men and women both feel jealousy. If you are trying to use jealousy to manipulate your partner, you are headed for disaster.

➤ Keep your relationship to yourself and your partner. Outside parties are just that—outside the relationship and not in a position to make demands about

Chapter 24

Men and Women in the Millennium

In This Chapter

➤ The importance of communication

➤ Openings in careers

➤ Cyber connections

➤ The partnership comes first

As we begin to live and enjoy life in the new century, a lot of things will change dramatically. We can no longer afford to hang on to old-fashioned thinking about the sexes. We can no longer afford to continue to perpetuate the sexual stereotypes of yesteryear. Men and women should work to develop a newfound respect and admiration for one another.

In this chapter, I will address gender-based communication issues with a futuristic eye. My observations are based upon trends I have seen, not only as a member of the human race, but as a psychologist and communication specialist. Read on and see if you, too, can appreciate what life will be like in the years to come.

Communication Now Is Key

Whether we are considering our business lives, our professional lives, or our lives in general, it is not enough just to open up and communicate, it's important to communicate with urgency!

One study that clearly demonstrates the urgency of timing was conducted at the University of Illinois. It was discovered that airline pilots made more errors when they didn't reveal and exchange information in a timely fashion. Thus, from this example, we learn that withholding information can not only threaten relationships but life and limb as well.

In business, we have repeatedly seen how timing is everything. A woman's tendency to confront problems immediately will be the best way we can communicate as we enter the new century. As technology grows at such a rapid rate, so should our abilities to express ourselves. If we conduct our personal lives with such communicative urgency, we will once and for all avoid the wasted time and energy of hanging on to hurt feelings brought about by not immediately solving problems and issues that bother us and gnaw at our psyches.

By not letting fester the poisonous feelings brought forth by keeping things in, we will be able to reduce, if not eliminate, our anger toward people we really love.

Equal Pay Is Here to Stay

Even though women don't make as much money as men do today, this is going to stop very soon. Women and men who believe in fairness and equality and who are motivated to do the right thing will no longer permit this to happen. Legislation will crop up on a local and national level to make sure this outrage doesn't continue.

Women will be encouraged to speak out in channels they have never before realized were available to them, should injustices and ancient thought patterns remain in their specific working milieus. As we begin to live and work in the new century, both men and women will respect one another's intellect and abilities, as we realize that sex differences have nothing to do with intelligence level, creativity level, or motivational level.

An Open Job Market

While it is true that because of anatomical issues and environmental concerns, women as a group may be better suited for certain jobs, men for others, this thinking must never hold back individuals of either sex from pursuing their dreams and living out their desires.

If sexual discrimination is more prevalent in a specific field where a particular sex is in the minority, we will find that society will become less and less tolerant of this behavior. And there will be greater means in our system to severely discourage this from happening.

If societal expectations in the job market are different for men and women, perhaps we can eliminate this early in life by providing young boys and girls with exposure to career options that have no sex bias attached to them. For example, we may have programs in which we encourage young girls to learn more about fields such as computing and engineering. Or we may expose men to more professions involving childcare.

In essence, we will make it socially acceptable very early in life for boys and girls—and subsequently, men and women—to do whatever they want to with their lives and their careers, with no penalty for choosing a career that in the past had a sex-biased stereotype attached to it.

We can no longer afford to tolerate any gender gaps in our lives that don't give us the freedom both socially and practically to live out our desires and pursue our dreams.

Sex Role Changes

Statistics have shown that more and more businesses are operating out of the home; this will make it so much easier for both men and women to have their cake and eat it, too, so to speak—to be with their families and to earn a living at the same time. There will no longer be a stigma attached to a man staying at home and raising the kids while the wife leaves the premises to work outside the home. Who knows?—it may even become the norm!

As a result of men being more exposed to little boys and girls in their formative years of development, there will be more support systems available to men in the area of child rearing and child development. Men will learn how to speak to children and how to raise them in a manner that brings about the highest of self-esteem as they mature into adulthood.

There will be more of a mutual equality in household chores and responsibilities and a joint effort on both sides to pitch in and help, no matter what the man and woman feel comfortable doing. Relegating jobs to "women's work" and "men's work" will be a silly notion of the past.

A Woman's Touch and a Man's Touch

As both men and women make their marks in society, they will bring to their positions their own gender-based approaches. Together, these perspectives will allow us to have a more holistic approach toward problem-solving, conflict resolution, and living a more positive existence.

Feminine thinking will begin more and more to affect how we view justice, health care, how we spend our free and leisure time, and how we deal with intimacy, love, romance, and child rearing, in addition to how we approach our lives on the job. Women have some unique and wonderful skills that have been overlooked for too long. For one thing, women approach business from a broader and less analytical perspective than their male colleagues, which means women tend not just to gather the data and analyze it in pieces, but also to "connect the dots."

In essence, women often see the broader picture more easily than men do. On the other hand, men bring such an important element to this problem-solving issue by looking at the components and carefully examining them on an individual basis. In essence, men are examining the trees in the forest, while the women "see the forest for the trees."

Now, when men and women bring their respective gifts to the table, the whole forest is looked at, as well as the individual trees. We are both right, and we are both respectful of one another's strengths and approaches.

When women's compassion, their ability to put themselves into the other's shoes, is combined with the men's bottom-line sensibility, a lot more harmony will be created in every area of life. The bottom line is that we will learn to respect, appreciate, and incorporate what one another brings to the table instead of fighting it, as we have done in generations past.

Exploring Neurological Nuances

In Part 1, "Sorting Out Our Differences," I discussed the differences in brain development in little boys and little girls. As new technology develops to study the brain, we will learn more and more about the neurological nuances that make men think and act like men, and women think and act like women.

We will learn things that will finally unlock not only the mysteries of sex differences in the brain function but the mysteries of the brain as a whole. Research like that recently done at Harvard's McLean Hospital's Brain Imaging Center in Boston will occur more and more as we gain more knowledge and have the technology to test that knowledge. The McLean study, which used a highly technical method of looking at brain function through the use of MRIs (magnetic resonance imaging), provided a highly detailed analysis of brain activity and found that men's and women's brains react differently to visual stimulation as measured by images of brain activity. Recent studies also show that there is a difference in aging between men's and women's brains, which may have significant medical implications.

Instead of lumping men and women together in terms of how they behave, we need to take a more detailed look at what happens within the brain to make us react and behave as we do. The findings of this study show differences in the location of the brain's responses, indicating additional neurobiological significance. In men, brain activity occurred primarily in the right hemisphere; in women, responses were equal in each hemisphere. It stands to reason that men and women would process information a lot differently and behave differently.

Life-Saving Differences

As science continues to improve on technology to measure how our bodies operate, we will continue to learn more about how women's and men's bodies are so different.

Men and women have different needs and require different medicines and foods in order to heal and function. For example, recent studies indicate that blood itself is different in men and women. Young women appear to have lower hemoglobin levels than men, and these levels have a tremendous effect upon issues such as what foods should be eaten, how much exercise is optimal, surgery effects, and what drugs are most effective in what dosages, depending on age and sex.

Recent studies also show that certain drugs might be more effective when men take them versus when women take them. We may eventually find out that certain foods are better utilized in the body by one sex than the other, and this can further allow us to achieve more optimum health.

Knowledge Equals Power of the Sexes

Knowledge equals power. The more you know, the less you get upset, and the more you understand a situation. You learn the nuances of what is really meant by what is said, and your interactions will become easier. This can help you in your interactions. Franklin Delano Roosevelt was right: You have nothing to fear but fear itself. We stand at the dawn of a new millennium. We are moving forward. Let's embrace the new possibilities, moving forward to having a better personal, social, intimate, and business life with the opposite sex.

Keeping Some Territory Sacred

While equal pay is a must and the equal opportunity to choose what you want to do for a profession is imperative, there are still "male environments," and no matter what a woman does and how many lawsuits society takes on against male bastions to force men to open the doors to females, there is an unspoken male domain where women will never be accepted, no matter what they do or how hard they try! The reality is that women may not want to be accepted once they are let in.

A well-known, all-male club in a very prominent city was told that they needed to get with the times and accept female members. Several prominent women, who were clients of mine, were chosen to be members. Most of the women who initially were so eager to break down the "male" walls couldn't wait to put them back up. These women quickly resigned when they realized that this was definitely a "male" club, complete with very "male" behavior in addition to rampant off-color jokes, cursing, sports talk, lots of fattening food, card playing, gambling, and an excessive amount of conversation pertaining to women and their anatomy. The men felt that those women who didn't like it there could leave—so most of the women did just that—they left. So, one has to question whether going through all the motions of allowing women to integrate into a predominantly male social environment is what women really want to do.

Are there some female environments where women would like to be separate? Are there environments where having men around would inhibit the flow of female energy and camaraderie, so to speak?

My belief is that we can in certain situations maintain our separateness, while maintaining our equality. When we learn to accept one another in business and socially, we may realize that there may be times where either of the sexes want to be alone, as Greta Garbo would say. Maybe there will be male and female organizations and social clubs to which we each may want to go for a respite as we live with one another.

Perhaps We'll Be More Tolerant

Perhaps after beating our heads against the wall, we will finally learn that nobody is perfect or has it all. Perhaps we will be more tolerant in our expectations and realize that what we see in people is essentially what we get. Of course, people may enrich our lives, and we may strive to change when we observe how people interact with others and strive to follow suit. Or perhaps we will learn about history, world affairs, or psychology by hearing others talk or by listening to others' points of view. But we will come to realize that we cannot change others and they cannot change us. Only we can change ourselves.

Are You Really Compatible?

I was once a guest host for a morning television show in Detroit, Michigan, where I interviewed a number of bridal consultants of various types. Most of them told me that without a doubt they could tell which couples would stay together and which ones would not based on the way they dealt with one another during the stressful planning of the wedding. They could tell by the tone of voice or how the couple responded to each other. And you know what? Most of them were absolutely correct.

Many ministers or therapists who see couples before marriage can tell if a couple has a good chance of staying together by how they talk to one another. Couples who are sarcastic, critical, and bossy don't make it. The ones who treat one another with respect, politeness, and affection are the ones who make it. Just because a couple comes in dewy-eyed and lovey-dovey, or even passionate, doesn't mean they will necessarily be a couple who will have an easy time of it.

Perhaps there will be a new type of premarital counselor and evaluator whom we can go to for an assessment of our behavior to see how compatible we will be with our future mates. Perhaps couples will be observed in nonthreatening social situations, unbeknownst to them (or known to them). They will be shown how they really act toward each other. If their behavior is not acceptable, perhaps this dose of "reality therapy" will be a wake-up call to the couple, alerting them to end the relationship or be completely aware of what unfortunate mess they may be stepping into by going ahead and marrying each other.

Perhaps these types of evaluations will be the answer to decreasing the high divorce rate and, once and for all, help us avoid getting involved with Mr. *or* Ms. Wrong and, instead, help us to finally marry Mr. or Ms. Right.

Here is a questionnaire I devised to help couples see just how compatible they are as they address the real issues couples must address in order to survive. These open-ended questions allow men and women the opportunity to not only explain their points of view, but also expound upon how they arrived at their positions, thereby enabling their partners to get an even more in-depth picture of why they feel the way they do. It allows them to really see things from their partners' points of view.

Dr. Lillian Glass' Relationship Compatibility Questionnaire

1. What would I need to have financial security, and how would I achieve it?
2. How do I feel about money? What is my spending philosophy?
3. What would I do if my partner cheated? Under what circumstances would I cheat?
4. What do I really want out of life? Do I realistically see achieving my life goals?
5. What kind of lifestyle do I want? How will I go about achieving it?
6. Who in my life is really important to me? How will it affect my relationship with my partner?
7. What are my politics? Why do I feel this way about certain issues?
8. What are my spiritual and religious beliefs? What led me to them?
9. What is essential in my sexual relationship? What can I live without?
10. What is my view on child rearing? How did I come to believe what I do?
11. What was (were) the most significant moment(s) in my life, and why?
12. Who made my life the most miserable? How did that person do it, and why do I think he or she did it?
13. Who made my life the most pleasurable? How did that person do it, and why do I think he or she did it?
14. What was the saddest time in my life, and why?
15. What was the happiest time in my life, and why?
16. What are my views about health? How did I arrive at them?
17. What are my views on weight and diets? How did I arrive at them?
18. How do I view death? How did I arrive at that view, and why do I embrace it?
19. What are my general views about the world and about people?
20. How do I feel about punishment and forgiveness?

Cyber Romance

The advent of cyberspace will continue to create an entirely different environment in which men and women communicate. We will learn how to develop more intimacy with one another through the written word and through getting to know one another via computer. Perhaps we will be as romantic with one another as we were back in the Victorian era, when men and women exposed how they truly felt about the other person through the written word. They let down their inhibitions and wrote from their hearts.

Today, and even more in the future, we will type from our hearts as we reveal our true selves. It will become more and more difficult to play games with one another, because we will really get to know who one another is as a person.

Because of cyberdating, although we may see a photograph, our real attraction to someone will be the result of getting to know who that person really is—that person's essence, feelings, values, politics—all before we even meet the person, let alone sleep with him or her.

Communication Breakdown!

One word of caution, even though cyberdating is here to stay, it is essential to follow rules of caution as you would in any dating situation and learn to read between the lines. Look for inconsistencies in what they tell you, and look for "red flags" that come up during the written communication. Do they put themselves down a lot? Do they use self-deprecating humor followed by "I'm only kidding"? Look for lies. Ask a lot of questions, and don't get too caught up in the literary flowery romanticism of their written words. Look a lot deeper "between the lines" as to what they are really telling you.

Kareena and Josh are married. They met on the Internet. They *really* met—their hearts and souls met before their eyes or their bodies met. They were already smitten as they spent hours and hours revealing who they really were on the Internet. Before they met, they made a vow that if they met and they weren't physically attracted to one another, it would be okay, because they would remain great friends. Well, luckily, they were attracted when they finally met, and they kept their vow to remain best friends. Months after they met, they married. It is six years later, and these two are still in bliss. After years and years of game playing and superficially getting to know others, the Internet stripped them of their defenses as they got emotionally naked and shared their souls. Now they share their lives.

Virtual Relationships

As I am writing this last section, I'm imagining what will happen as we march further on in time. Wouldn't it be something if we could try on relationships just as we try on clothing? Wouldn't it be great to see how two compatible people, based on their values, likes, dislikes, and who they really are as people, would act if they disagreed on this issue or that? What would they do if a problem came up? How would they react if faced with some serious dilemmas like financial issues, sexual issues, or issues involving children? We would see in virtual reality how they would most likely react to one another based upon their personality types, which would be predetermined via computer analysis.

Perhaps if a couple could actually live the problem in virtual reality, they could surpass these problems in real life or deal with them more effectively as they came up.

One could also examine hypothetical situations that may occur in the business realm through these virtual reality techniques. One could see how his or her boss might react under different situations and how he or she would feel emotionally when faced with confronting the boss. One could actually experience it and explore alternate options of dealing with problems at hand.

For those who are terrified about getting up in front of an audience and speaking, virtual speaking will allow them to actually experience their stage fright ahead of time and cope with their fears so that when they have to do the real speech, they will have already conquered the worst of their fears and learned how to deal with them head-on.

Virtual Therapy

Perhaps in the future people will be able to go into a virtual reality chamber and work out all their problems of the past. They will be able to go back to crucial times in their childhood, or at any time in their past, and relive their traumas. Only this time, they will be able to speak up and change the scenario so that they can really dissect what went on in their past. It will be as though they are a third person looking in on their past and now righting the wrongs.

He Says, She Says

In the future, I believe we will see more peer relationships in marriage. We have seen how traditional relationships don't work when men and women are mysteries to one another, when they idealize one another, and make each other into something they are not, placing expectations so high that nobody can live up to them. Marriages will take the form of deep friendships that are real and true and emotionally intimate.

Let's say someone had never resolved a conflict they had with a parent. In the virtual reality chamber, the person would be able to express whatever he or she had always wanted to say to the parent, but never did.

Free-Flowing Talk

In the new millennium, we will become much better communicators, in my estimation. Men and women will have no choice but to say what's on their minds. They won't have time to play games and do the "dance of confusion." They will be so aware, through reading books such as this one, that nobody likes game playing and that if they want to know something, they need to *ask*. Whether it is to learn more about the other person or to ask what the other person's intentions are in life (or what the other person's intentions are with *them*), men and women will unveil the ignorance and speak to one another as respectful and decent human beings.

Better Daddies

As men and women become more and more evolved, they will become much better parents than their parents were to them. They will become so much more aware of what is really important in life. Men currently have become great fathers, spending much more time with their children than men in past generations did. Men have become more emotional with their children than ever before, hugging them, nurturing them, and pampering them. In fact, there are more fathers participating in their children's preschools than ever before.

This cannot help but create a new generation of secure, less emotionally hungry children. Men's influences on their daughters will create a different breed of women, who may have the biology of female wiring with a great deal of masculine influence. Similarly, while little boys are wired masculinely, their feminine influence will allow them to become more aware. Thus there will be more of a balance between the sexes as far as emotional development is concerned. Little boys and little girls will grow up to be much more fulfilled, complete people than their parents.

Creating a Hybrid

Perhaps men and women as we know them today will become a distinct hybrid. Perhaps there will be a new group of adjectives to describe this new breed, as we learn to smooth over one another's differences and relate to one another as similar beings.

This seems like a reasonable premise, considering how much we have learned about one another in just the past 10 years and how far we have come in the past 50 years in terms of men's and women's roles. We are considering things today that we would never have considered two generations ago, let alone one generation ago. Consider women athletes, women body builders, and professional women's basketball teams. We would never have seen so many women in such good physical condition in our parents' generation. Women CEOs? Sure, if it was their own small business. But now there are women CEOs, CFOs, presidents of companies, congresswomen, senators, and even presidential candidates. And yes, we will probably live to see a woman president of the United States someday in the near future. This was not even a consideration 80 years ago, before women had the right to vote.

The Ideal Balanced Human

In 1969, there was a pop song called "In the Year 2525," written by Zager and Evans. The lyrics seemed so far away, so impossible, as the singer crooned, "In the year 2525/If man is still alive/If women can survive."

The song went on to describe what would happen in the future. The song had a great catchy tune most people couldn't get out of their heads as the song rose to the top of the music charts. Well, it's been three decades since this song appeared, and it's eerie how many of the lyrics have come to pass.

To date, wannabe parents certainly have literally followed these lyrics word for word whether they realized it or not, by "picking their sons and their daughters, too, from the bottom of a long glass tube" as in vitro fertilization has become an option for couples who have trouble conceiving. Each day we are finding out more and more about humankind and what makes us who we are. We are learning ways to improve the human condition biologically, through using chemicals and mechanical intervention to extend lives, and environmentally, through exploring—how we behave socially with one another in certain enviroments.

While we have made exponential strides in what we have learned about humans, masculine and feminine energy and sexuality will never leave us. Even though our biology is preprogrammed in many ways, as we discovered in Chapter 1, "Finding Common Ground in Gender Differences," how we perceive one another is changing and will continue to change.

As science and technology continue to reveal to us the minutiae in the DNA that makes us men and women, we will develop an even stronger identity of who we are as men and women and honor those differences as part of the life force in the universe. We will embrace the masculine energy and the female energy which make up the chemistry of men and women.

The beauty is that we will be open to learn about one another. As we learn to accept our differences, we will celebrate those differences as we go forward into the new century.

Becoming True Partners

As we move into the new century, more men and women will have fewer definite stereotypical sex roles. They will be viewing their relationships as partnerships with interchangeable roles. Women will no longer be the "gatherers," the makers of the meal, and the cleaners of the house. Men will no longer be the "hunters" or the breadwinners. Stereotypical roles will blend. If a man likes to cook because he finds it to be a creative and relaxing enterprise, as well as providing nourishment for him and his family, he will cook. If he hates seeing a mess around him, he will clean.

If a woman has more education or a better job, or makes more money, she will bring home the bacon. Sometimes as life has its ups and downs, he will make more money and sometimes she may make more money. The couple of the future won't be hung up on this. They will look at money-earning capacity for the good of the relationship and not put their attention on who brought more money home.

As long as men and women start seeing their roles as contributors for the good of the partnership, they won't have to act in defined roles. In essence, the whole (which is the partnership) is bigger and stronger than the parts (the man's role and the woman's role). New thinking about relationships, in which partnership is the sacred entity, will eliminate so many of the petty arguments and ego bruising of the past.

This type of thinking will promote loyalty and fidelity as men and women strive to make that partnership the focus of what is important in their lives. I sincerely hope we all live long enough to see such opportunities come to fruition.

The Least You Need to Know

➤ Improved communication between men and women will be one of the greatest changes of the new millennium.

➤ Increasingly, women will be interested in and trained for men's work, and vice versa. Old assumptions about "women's work" and "men's work" will fade.

➤ The rise of the Internet will let more and more people share their deepest thoughts and feelings in words, much as people did in earlier generations.

➤ As couples focus less on sex difference issues, such as who has the upper hand, who is winning, and so forth, they can focus on what really matters, which is how to benefit the partnership.

To Order *Dr. Lillian Glass'* Products

Fill out the following order form; include VISA, MasterCard, check, or money order; and send to:

Dr. Lillian Glass
Your Total Image Inc.
P.O. Box 792
New York, NY 10021

You can place a telephone order by calling 212-946-5729; e-mail: info@drlillianglass.com; or visit the Web site www.drlillianglass.com.

All prices include tax, shipping, and handling! Allow four to six weeks for delivery.

Emotional Feelings and Mending Hearts

Set of two CDs of original songs that reflect every emotion you have ever felt! Some songs give you courage while others help heal tender emotions. Some stimulate your love while others motivate you to climb the highest mountains.

Item	Price	Quantity	Total Amount
Set of two CDs	$45.99		

Attracting Terrific People: How to Find and Keep the People Who Bring Your Life Joy!

Never be lonely again! Find out how to attract and keep the people who are best for you and create relationships that allow you to have the most fulfilling life.

Item	Price	Quantity	Total Amount
Book (hardcover edition)	$32.99		
Audiotape	$25.95		

Toxic People—10 Ways of Dealing with People Who Make Your Life Miserable

Find out how to identify those 30 toxic terrors. Use the 10 specially designed techniques, which really work, in order to put these hurtful people in their place and make your life a lot happier!

Item	Price	Quantity	Total Amount
Book (hardcover edition)	$32.99		
Videotape	$59.99		
Audiotapes (set of two)	$25.99		

He Says, She Says: Closing the Communication Gap Between the Sexes

Although men and women are different, there *are* things we can do and say to avoid fights, hurt feelings, frustrations, and pent-up anger against the opposite sex. Whether it be in our daily lives, at work, or in the most intimate moments, now we know what to do and exactly what to say to the opposite sex—anytime, anyplace!

Item	Price	Quantity	Total Amount
Book (hardcover edition)	$32.99		
Videotape	$59.99		
Audiotapes (set of two)	$25.95		
He Says, She Says Greeting Cards			
Cards for men to send to women	$25.95		
Cards for women to send to men	$25.95		

Talk to Win: Six Steps to a Successful Vocal Image

You don't ever have to hate the sound of your voice or be afraid to speak publicly again. Now you can use the same speaking and voice techniques Dr. Glass used with her Hollywood celebrity clients.

Item	Price	Quantity	Total Amount
Audiotape	$17.99		
Videotape	$59.99		

World of Words: Vocabulary Improvement

Never feel insecure about not understanding what another person is saying to you. You will learn the basic roots of words that allow you to figure out what most words mean, even if you have never heard them before. It's easy, fun, and takes minutes to learn.

Item	Price	Quantity	Total Amount
Audiotape	$17.99		

How to Deprogram Your Valley Girl

No matter what generation you are from, this classic, cute, and funny book has a serious side as well. It explains in easy steps how to teach your teens or children how to talk right so they don't embarrass you or themselves.

Item	Price	Quantity	Total Amount
Softcover book	$14.95		

Personal E-Mail or Telephone Calls with Dr. Lillian Glass

To arrange for a personal e-mail or phone call appointment with Dr. Glass you must be 18 years old or over or have your parents' written or verbal permission.

All telephone and e-mail appointments will not exceed 30 minutes in length. Dr. Glass will call the client collect at the appropriate scheduled time, and all telephone costs will be assumed by the client.

Due to the demand for Dr. Glass' services and her schedule, no refunds will be given due to a missed appointment unless there is a 48-hour notification.

The fee for personal appointments is $250 U.S. and must be paid in advance via credit card in order to secure space. We accept VISA and MasterCard. Otherwise checks or money orders may be made out to Dr. Lillian Glass.

Item	Price	Quantity	Total Amount
Appointment	$250		

Fill out the remaining information completely—including the "Release and Waiver of Claims for Damages" located at the end of this form—and send to:

Dr. Lillian Glass
Your Total Image Inc.
P.O. Box 792
New York, NY 10021
212-946-5729

Date: _____

Name: _____

Address: _____

Apt. or Suite #: _____

City, State, Zip: _____

Phone (daytime) (___) ____-_____ (evening) (___) ____-_____

E-mail address: _____

Date of birth: _____

VISA or MasterCard number: _____

Expiration date: _____

Name of cardholder: _____

Address of cardholder: _____

City, State, Zip: _____

I heard about Dr. Glass through (check *all* that apply) ...

a. ___ Her books or audiotapes (if so, which ones):

___ *Talk to Win*   ___ *World of Words*
___ *Attracting Terrific People*   ___ *Confident Conversation*
___ *Say It Right*   ___ *He Says, She Says*
___ *Toxic People*   ___ *How to Deprogram Your*
___ *Speak for Success*   *Valley Girl*
___ *The Complete Idiot's Guide*
    to Verbal Self-Defense

b. ___ Radio interviews (which ones): _____

c. ___ TV appearances (which ones): _____

d. ___ Newspaper and magazine articles (which ones): _____

_____

e. ___ Internet (what sites): _____

f. ___ Referred by: _____

g. ___ Other: _____

268

Interests (check as many as apply):

___ Toxic person (people)
___ Verbal abuse
___ Shyness
___ Career crisis/career change
___ Public presentation skills
___ General communication skills

___ Relationships
___ Confidence-insecurity
___ Sexuality or intimacy
___ Loneliness/not enough
     friends
___ What to say in specific
     situations

___ Learning to better deal with:

___ Children	___ Parents	___ Boss	___ Friends
___ Lovers	___ Spouse	___ Teen	___ Family
___ Coworkers	___ Job rut	___ Esteem	___ Money issues
___ Mid-life crisis	___ Physical appearance issues		

Release and Waiver of Claims for Damages

I have contacted Dr. Lillian Glass on my own volition for the purpose of acquiring additional information specific to my needs as they relate to interpersonal issues which I may have in my life. I understand that the educational information which I will be receiving with regard to these personalized issues are only the opinion of Dr. Lillian Glass. I also understand that the information which I am receiving is based upon her books and tapes and other instructional materials. I release Dr. Glass and Your Total Image Inc. from any and all claims, whatsoever, that I might incur as the result of consultation, including claims for emotional, physical, or financial damages.

I understand that Dr. Glass' services and those of Your Total Image Inc. are for educational and entertainment purposes only. Should I experience, as an added benefit, any positive emotional, psychological, or motivational benefits, I understand that it was not Dr. Glass' and Your Total Image Inc.'s intention to serve as therapist, psychotherapist, psychologist, psychoanalyst, psychiatrist, speech pathologist, speech therapist, communication therapist, or member of the clergy, and she has never represented herself in this capacity to me. I also understand that no therapy—psychological therapy, speech therapy, voice therapy, or communication therapy—will be done at any time nor will there be formalized evaluations. There may be follow-up calls and e-mails for educational and entertainment purposes. Dr. Glass and Your Total Image Inc. will be released from being liable for any emotional, physical, or financial damages from which any claims may result from any subsequent e-mails and phone calls for entertainment and educational purposes as a result of these subsequent follow-up calls and e-mails. Should any legal actions occur, all of Dr. Glass' and Your Total Image Inc.'s attorney's fees and costs will be covered by me and I hereby release Dr. Lillian Glass and Your Total Image Inc. from any and all litigation.

_____ I accept agreement   _____ I decline agreement

References and Further Reading

Abbey, Antonia. "Sex differences in attributions for friendly behavior: Do males misperceive female friendliness?" *Journal of Personality and Social Psychology.* May 1982. 830–838.

ABC News-Science. "Gender Gaps on the Brain: Bigger Brains in Males Don't Mean Smarter Men." June 3, 1999.

Allen, Laura S., and Roger A. Gorski. "Sex Differences in the Bed Nucleus of the Stria Terminalis of the Human Brain." *The Journal of Comparative Neurology.* 1990. 302–367.

Associated Press. "Study Explores Male Sex Appeal." New York, June 23, 1999.

Baker, Mark. *What Men Really Think.* New York: Simon & Schuster, 1992.

Bailey, Patricia. "Television Cartoons Perpetuate Stereotypes." University of California, *Berkeley Clip Sheet.* August 6, 1995. 1.

Barbach, Lonnie. "Talking in Bed—Now That We Know What We Want, How Do We Say It?" *Ns.* January 1991. 64–65, 80.

Bazel, Robert. "Drug Reactions: Studies Show Hormones May Play a Role." NBC. *Dateline.* June 4, 1999.

Berkowitz, Bob. *What Men Won't Tell You But Women Need to Know.* New York: Avon, 1990.

Birdwhistell, Raymond. "Masculinity and Femininity as Display." *Kinesics and Context.* Philadelphia: University of Pennsylvania Press: 1970. 39–46.

Botting, Kate, and Douglas Botting. *Sex Appeal—The Art and Science of Sexual Attraction.* New York: St. Martin's Press, 1995.

Brend, Ruth. "Male Female Intonation Patterns, in American English," in *Language and Sex: Difference and Dominance,* ed. B. Thorne and N. Henley. Rowley, Massachusetts: Newbury House, 1975.

Cantor, Joanne R. "What's Funny to Whom?" *Journal of Communication* 26: 1976. 164–172.

Carter, Steven. *Getting to Commitment.* New York: M. Evans and Co., 1998.

Coleman, Ron. "A Comparison of the Two Voice Quality Characteristics to the Perception of Maleness and Femaleness in the Voice." *Journal of Speech and Hearing Research.* 1976. 19: 168–180.

Coleman, Ron. "Male and Female Voice Quality and Its Relationship to Vowel Formant Frequencies." *Journal of Speech and Hearing Research.* 1971. 14.

Collins, Glen. "Language and Sex Stereotypes." *This World.* April 26, 1981. 23.

DeWitt, Karen. "Girl Games on Computers, Where Shoot 'Em Up Simply Won't Do." *New York Times.* June 23, 1997.

Dornan, Leslie. "Doesn't Every Woman Have Her Own Ideas About What Makes a Man Great in Bed?" *New Woman.* March 1991. 48–50.

Dullea, Georgia. "Sex Differences in Speech." *New York Times.* March 19, 1984.

Eakins, Barbara Westbrook, and Gene Eakins. *Sex Differences in Communication.* Boston: Houghton Mifflin, 1998.

Edelsky, Carol. "Acquisition of an Aspect of Communication Competence: Learning What It Means to Talk Like a Lady." *Child Discourse,* ed. S. Ervin and C. Mitchell-Kernan. New York: Academic Press, 1997.

Edelsky, Carol. "Question Intonation in Sex Roles." *Language of Sociology.* August 8, 1979. 15–32.

Farrell, Warren. *Why Men Are the Way They Are.* New York: Berkeley, 1986.

Fein, Ellen, and Sherrie Schneider. *The Rules.* New York: Warner Books, 1995.

Feinman, Steven. "Why Is the Cross-Sex Role Behavior More Approved for Girls Than for Boys? A Status Characteristic Approach." *Sex Roles*. July 1981.

Frieze, Irene Hanson, and Sheila Ramsey. "Non-Verbal Maintenance of Traditional Sex Roles." *Journal of Social Issues*. 1976, 32, no. 3: 133–41.

Gerstman, Bradley, Christopher Pizzo, and Rich Seldes. *What Men Want*. New York: HarperCollins, 1998.

Gilligan, Carol. *In a Different Voice: Psychological Theory and Women's Development*. Cambridge, Massachusetts: Harvard University Press, 1982.

Glass, Lillian. *Attracting Terrific People—How to Find and Keep the People Who Bring You Joy*. New York: St. Martin's Press, 1998.

Glass, Lillian. *The Complete Idiot's Guide to Verbal Self-Defense*. New York: Alpha Books, 1999.

Glass, Lillian. *He Says, She Says—Closing the Communication Gap Between the Sexes*. New York: Putnam Publishing Co., 1992.

Glass, Lillian. *Say It Right: How to Talk in Any Social or Business Situation*. New York: Putnam Publishing Co., 1991.

Glass, Lillian. *Talk to Win—Six Steps to a Successful Vocal Image*. New York: Putnam Publishing Co., 1987.

Glass, Lillian. *Toxic People—10 Ways to Handle People Who Make Your Life Miserable*. New York: St. Martin's Press, 1998.

Gray, John. *Men Are from Mars, Women Are from Venus*. New York: HarperCollins, 1992.

Gruber, Kenneth, and Jacqueline Gaehelein. "Sex Differences in Listening Comprehension." *Sex Roles*. May 1979.

Harragan, Betty. *Games Your Mother Never Taught You*. New York: Warner Books, 1977.

Henley, Nancy M. *Body Politics: Power, Sex, and Nonverbal Communication*. Englewood Cliffs, New Jersey: Prentice-Hall, 1997.

Henley, Nancy M. "The Politics of Touch." *Radical Psychology*, ed. P. Brown. New York: Harper and Row, 1973.

Henley, Nancy M., and Barrie Thorne. "Womanspeak and Manspeak: Sex Differences in Sexism Communications, Verbal and Non-Verbal." *Beyond Sex Roles,* ed. A. Sargeant. St. Paul, Minnesota: West Publishing Co., 1977.

Hite, Sheri. *The Hite Report on Male Sexuality.* New York: Ballentine Books, 1982.

Hite, Sheri. *Women and Love: A Cultural Revolution in Progress.* New York: Knopf, 1987.

Jacklin, Carol Nagy, and Eleanor MacCoby. *Developmental Behavioral Pediatrics,* ed. M. D. Levine, W. B. Carey, A. T. Crocher, and R. T. Gross. Philadelphia: W. B. Saunders Co., 1998.

Jourard, Sidney M., and Jane E. Rubin. "Self Disclosure and Touching: A Study of Two Modes of Interpersonal Encounter and Their Inter-Relation." *Journal of Humanistic Psychology.* August 1968. 39–49.

Key, Mary Ritchie. "Linguistic Behavior of Male and Female." *Linguistics.* August 1972. 15–31.

Key, Mary Ritchie. *Male/Female Language.* Metuchen, New Jersey: Scarecrow Press, 1975.

Kornheiser, Tony. "Locker Room Confidential." *Esquire.* June 1989. 97–98.

Kramarae, Cheris. *Women and Men Speaking.* Rowley, Massachusetts: Newbury House, 1981.

Kramarae, Cheris. "Women's Speech: Separate but Unequal." *Language and Sex: Difference and Dominance,* ed. B. Thorne and N. Henley. Rowley, Massachusetts: Newbury House, 1975. 43–56.

Lakoff, Robin. *Language and Women's Place.* New York: Harper Colophon Books, 1975.

Leary, Mark, and William E. Snell. "The Relationship of Instrumentality and Expressiveness to Sexual Behavior in Males and Females." *Sex Roles.* July 18, 1988. 509–522.

Lewis, Michael. "Culture and Gender Roles. There Is No Unisex in the Nursery." *Psychology Today.* May 1972. 54–57.

Libby, William. "Eye Contact and Direction of Looking as a Stable Individual Difference." *Journal of Experimental Research in Personality.* 1970. 4.

Lynch, Joan A. "Gender Differences in Language." *American Speech Language Hearing Association.* April 1983. 37–42.

Maltz, Daniel, and Ruth A. Borker. *A Cultural Approach to Male Female Miscommunication in Language and Social Identity,* ed. J. Gumperz. Cambridge: Cambridge University Press, 1982. 196–216.

Martin, Carol Lynn. "Attitudes and Expectations About Children With Non-Traditional and Traditional Gender Roles." *Sex Roles.* 1990, 22, no. 3/4: 151–165.

McGhee, Paul E. *Humor in Its Origin and Development.* San Francisco: W. H. Freeman, 1979.

Medical News and Perspectives. "Venus Orbits Closer to Pain Than Mars, Rx for One Sex May Not Benefit the Other." July 8, 1998.

Mehrabian, Albert. *Nonverbal Communication.* Chicago, Aldine: Atherton Inc., 1972.

Milwid, Beth. *Working with Men: Women in the Workplace Talk About Sexuality, Success, and Their Male Co-Workers.* New York: Berkley, 1992.

Mitchell, Carol. "Some Differences in Males—Female Joke Telling." *Women's Folklore, Women's Culture,* ed. R. Jordan, and S. Kalcik. Philadelphia Press. 1985. 163–186.

Montagu, Ashley. *Touching: The Human Significance of the Skin.* New York: Harper and Row, 1972.

Naifeh, Steven, and Gregory White Smith. *Why Can't Men Open Up?* New York: Clarkson Potter Inc., 1984.

Newsday. "Ricky Martin Lets True Feelings Show." June 14, 1999.

Petrocelli, William, and Barbara Kate Repa. *Sexual Harassment on the Job.* Berkeley, California: Nolo Press, 1992.

Pietropinto, Anthony. *Not Tonight Dear: How to Reawaken Your Sexual Desire.* New York: Doubleday, 1991.

Pine, Devra. "From Tootsie to Dustin: The Sexes." *Health.* July 1983. 66.

Pollitt, Katha. "Georgie Porgie Is a Bully." *Time.* Fall 1990. 24.

Pomerleu, Andree, Daniel Bloduc, Louise Cossetle, and Gerard Malcuit. "Pink or Blue: Environmental Gender Stereotypes of the First Two Years of Life." *Sex Roles.* March 1990, 22, no. 5/6: 359–368.

Russell, Peter. *The Brain Book.* New York: Penguin, 1979.

Sachs, Jacqueline. "Cues to Identification of Sex in Children's Speech." *Language and Sex: Difference and Dominance.*

Sadker, Myra, David Sadker, and Joyce Kaser. *The Communication Gender Gap.* Washington D.C.: The Mid Atlantic Center for Sex Equality, The American University.

Schwartz, Pepper. *Love Between Equals.* New York: The Free Press, 1994.

Segal, Julius, and Zelda Segal. "Little Differences, Snips and Snails and Sugar and Spice: What Are Little Boys and Girls Made Of?" *Health.* July, 1983. 28–31.

Shapiro, Evelyn, and Barry M. Shapiro. *The Women Say, The Men Say.* New York: Dell Publishing Co., 1979.

Spencer, Dale. *Men Made Language.* London: A. Routledge and Kegan Paul Ltd., 1980.

Stechert, Kathryn B. *On Your Own Terms: A Woman's Guide to Working with Men.* New York: Vintage Books, 1986.

Swacker, Marjorie. "The Sex of the Speaker as Sociolinguistic Variable." *Language and Sex: Difference and Dominance,* ed. B. Thorne and Nancy Henley. Rowley, Massachusetts: Newbury House, 1975.

Tannen, Debra. *You Just Don't Understand: Women and Men in Conversation.* New York: William Morrow, 1990.

Ulliam, Joseph Allen. "Joking at Work." *Journal of Communication.* 1976, 26: 129–130.

U.S. Department of Labor—Women's Bureau. "Earning Differences Between Men and Women." *Facts on Working Women.* 1997.

University of Cincinnati. "'Please Hold' Not Always Music to Your Ears University of Cincinnati Researcher Finds." *Science Daily Magazine.* June 20, 1999.

Zimmerman, Donald H., and Candace West. "Sex Roles, Interruptions and Silences in Conversation." *Language and Sex: Difference and Dominance,* ed. B. Thorne and N. Henley. Rowley, Massachusetts: Newbury House, 1975.

Index

A

abuse, verbal, 115
acceptance (men), desire for, 247-248
acceptance (women)
  desire for, 247-248
  need for, 84
    compliments, 84-85
    resistance to change, 84
accomplishments (men)
  boasting about, 92
  recognizing importance of, 194-195
accusing men
  avoiding, 124
  victim talk, using, 123
actions vs. words (men), interpreting feelings, 99
affairs, reducing, 8
affection
  cuddling, 162-163
  touching, 162
    Touch Questionnaire, 167-168
aggression
  avoiding, 250
  nature vs. nurture debate, 59
ambition (women), 186
anger (men)
  biological effects, 113, 184
  causes, 113-116
  criticisms, 118
  effect on relationships, 111
  emotional effects, 114
  in place of other emotions, 173, 199
  thinking before speaking, 114-116
  verbal abuse, 115
anger (women)
  biological effects, 113, 184
  causes, 113-116

criticisms, 118
cultural expectations, 48-49
effect on relationships, 111
emotional effects, 114
guilty feelings about, 184
thinking before speaking, 114-116
verbal abuse, 115
apologies, 35
appearance (men)
  anxieties about, 146
  dating, importance of, 146
  nice appearance, desire for, 250-251
  obsessions, baldness, 147-148
  physical build, 153-154
  teenagers, 76
appearance (women)
  anxieties about, 146
  dating, 146
  "How do I look?" proper responses from men, 133-134
  as little girls, focus on, 53
  men's desires, 193-194
  men's ideas of attractive women, 147
    cultural influences, 146-147
    media influences, 146
    past relationships, 147
  nice appearance, desire for, 250-251
  physical build, 153-154
  teenagers, 76
appreciated, feeling, 194, 249
arguments (men), 34
  apologies, 35
  current problems, 34
  sex afterward, 163-164
arguments (women)
  apologies, 35
  hurt/frustration, 34

past wrongs, 34, 86-87
sex afterward, 163-164
starting, 186
asking questions (men)
  directions, 60
  open-ended questions, 105
  thinking before asking "What's wrong?" 122
  using "would"/"could," 88
asking questions (women)
  details, desire for, 125-126
  "Do you love me?" 130
    reassuring women, 131
  "How do I look?" 133-134
  open-ended questions
    helpful phrases, 202
    men's preference, 201
  vs. nagging, 89
assertive women, men's perceptions of, 232-233
assistance, asking for (men), difficulty, 21, 95-96
attention to detail (men), learning, 134-135
attention to detail (women), ability to remember, 16, 188-189
  nature vs. nurture debate, 61-63
  remembering past faults, 34, 86-87
  sharing as girls, 74
attitudes (men), changing, 222-223
attraction (men), 154-155
  assessing, 155
  body language, 159
  confidence, 156-157
  essential characteristics for women, 210
  top qualities, 155-156
  touching, 158
    first touches, 158-159
    handshakes, 158

attraction (women), 154-155
    body language, 159
    confidence, 156-157
    top qualities, 155-156
    touching, 158
        first touches, 158-159
        handshakes, 158
attractive men
    attracting the right people
        confidence, 148
        playing hard to get,
            149-150
        smiling, 149
        speaking style, 148
    essential characteristics,
        210
    physical build, 154
    women's ideas of, 147-148
        confidence, 156-157
attractive women
    attracting the right people
        confidence, 148
        playing hard to get,
            149-150
        smiling, 149
        speaking style, 148
    child-likeness, 185
    essential qualities, 203
    men's ideas of, 146-147
        cultural influences,
            146-147
        media influences, 146
        past relationships, 147
    physical build, 154

B

bad relationships, 119
    avoiding, 114
    dating, warning signs,
        151-152
    disrespect, 118-119
    healing, 119-120
    jealousy
        causes, 116-118
        professional help, 117
        reactions, 118
    leaving, 119
    questionnaire, 112
    self-esteem, 118-119
    toxic people, 113

*Toxic People—10 Ways of
    Dealing with People Who
    Make Your Life Miserable,*
    113
baggage, emotional, 243-244
baldness (men), obsession
    about, 147-148
bedtime-story stereotypes, 52
behaviorial expectations,
    nature vs. nurture debate,
    49-50
benefits of understanding
    opposite sex, 8
biological clock (women)
    birth defects in children,
        213
    men's recognition of,
        212-213
biological factors, 39
    brain structure, 40
        brain development
            (boys), 43-45
        brain development
            (girls), 44
        neurological differences,
            45-46
        pathways, 40-41
    differences in biology
        blood, 257
        learning more about,
            256, 263
        medications, effective-
            ness of, 257
    genetics, 41
    hormones, 42
    tone of voice, 62
birthdays, women's expecta-
    tions, 210-211
blaming others (men), nega-
    tive emotions, 82-83
blood, gender-related differ-
    ences, 257
boasting (men), importance
    of, 92
body language (men), 28
    communication skills,
        improving, 105
    eye contact, 18, 31
        attraction, 159
        importance of, 137-138
        improving communica-
            tion skills, 106

sexual harassment suits,
    avoiding, 227-228
facial expressions, 18,
    30-31
    amount of, 18, 48
    smiling, 18, 48, 149
fidgeting/shifting, 29
hand gestures, 30
listening, 29
myths, 18
nodding, misinterpreta-
    tion, 22
personal space, 29, 93-94
sitting positions, 29
standing positions, 30
teeth clenching, 31
body language (women), 28
    communication skills,
        improving, 105
    eye contact, 18, 31
        attraction, 159
        improving communica-
            tion skills, 106
    facial expressions, 18,
        30-31
        amount of, 18, 48
        smiling, 18, 48, 149
    listening, 29
    nodding
        misinterpretation, 22
        nature vs. nurture
            debate, 63
bonding, male bonding,
    97-98
books
    additional readings,
        271-276
    *The Complete Idiot's Guide
        to Verbal Self-Defense,* 49
    *He Says, She Says: Closing
        the Communication Gap
        Between the Sexes,* 14
    *Men Are from Mars, Women
        Are from Venus,* 126
    The Rules, 204
    Talk to Win, 148
    *Toxic People—10 Ways of
        Dealing with People Who
        Make Your Life Miserable,*
        113
    You Just Don't Understand,
        21

bosses, sexual harassment
suits, 224
boys
    aggression, nature vs.
    nurture debate, 59
    brain development, 43-45
    childrearing, differences in,
    24
    communication skills,
    nature of communica-
    tion, 70-71
    curse words, use of, 72-73
    music lyrics, 72
    disgusting/repulsive topics,
    71
    joking around, 71
    openness, lack of, 124-125
    teasing, 71
    teenagers, 75
        appearance, 76
        friendships, 76
        generation gap, 75
        important topics, 75
        talking to girls, 75
    vs. girls
        bedtime-story stereo-
        types, 52
        behaviorial expecta-
        tions, 49-50
        communication devel-
        opment, 68-70
        communication differ-
        ences, 69-70
        cultural expectations,
        48-49
        language skills, 7
        math skills, 6
        nursery-rhyme stereo-
        types, 50-52
        shyness myths, 8
        socialization differences,
        68
        teased as children, 7
        toys, 53
brain
    corpus callosum, 45
    neurological differences,
    learning more about, 256
    structure, 40
        brain development,
        43-45

neurological differences,
45-46
pathways, 40-41
bringing up topics, frequency,
23-24
business colleagues (men),
avoiding sexual harassment
suits, 219-220
    assessing behavior (quiz),
    221-222
    changing attitudes,
    222-223
    communication skills,
    220-221
    constructive criticism,
    228-229
    eye contact, 227-228
    female bosses, 224
    flirting, 225
    listening, 226-227
    off-color jokes, 226
    politeness, 223-224
    terms of endearment, 224
    touching, 225-226
business colleagues (women)
    answering personal ques-
    tions, 237-238
    being "one of the guys,"
    235-236
    crying, 239
    difficulties, 232
    direct statements, giving,
    138-139
    female bosses, 224
    getting ahead, guidelines,
    235
    glass ceilings, 234-235
    grudges, holding, 238
    listening to, 136
    making points, 240
    men's perceptions of,
    231-233
    rejection, 240-241
    speaking up, 239-240
    unique contributions, 234
    withholding private infor-
    mation, 236-237

C

calls
    keeping promises, 137, 217
    returning, 172
career-related differences
    men's perceptions of
    women, 231-233
    nature vs. nurture debate,
    61-62
    salaries
        gender-related differ-
        ences, 231-232
        twenty-first century pre-
        dictions, 254
    women
        answering personal
        questions, 237-238
        being "one of the guys,"
        235-236
        crying, 239
        difficulties, 232
        getting ahead, 235
        glass ceilings, 234-235
        grudges, holding, 238
        making points, 240
        rejection, 240-241
        speaking up, 239-240
        unique contributions,
        234
        withholding private
        information, 236-237
changing men, 127
    avoiding, 204-205
    dislike of, 175-176
changing mind (women),
182-183
child-likeness (women), 185
childrearing, differences
between boys and girls, 24
chores (men), helping out,
216-217
chromosomes, 41
closeness (women), need for,
88-89
clothes (men), 199-200
commands (men), communi-
cation styles, 95
commitment (men)
    commitment phobia, 98,
    248-249
        reasons, 171-172

importance to women,
214-215
rejection, fear of, 172-173
commitment (women)
fear of, 248-249
from men, 214-215
communication skills (men),
10
development of, 68-70
improving, 101-102
body language, 105
changing behavior, 102
common ground, find-
ing, 102-104
direct statements, avoid-
ing, 138-139
essentials, 105
expanding interests, 104
importance, 9-10, 102
interruptions, avoiding,
106, 135-136
listening, 104
looking at her face,
137-138
quips, avoiding, 139-140
tone of voice, 106-107
miscommunication/
misinterpretation, 10
sexual harassment suits,
avoiding, 220-221
assessing behavior
(quiz), 221-222
timing, importance of,
253-254
twenty-first century predictions, 262
communication skills
(women)
development of, 68-70
improving, 101-102
body language, 105
changing behavior, 102
common ground, find-
ing, 102-104
essentials, 105
expanding interests, 104
importance of, 102
interruptions, avoiding,
106
listening, 104
tone of voice, 106-107
miscommunication/
misinterpretation, 10

timing, importance of,
253-254
twenty-first century predictions, 262
communication styles (men),
92
commands, 95
narratives, 96
summary chart, 35-36
communication styles
(women)
as little girls, 54
summary chart, 35-36
talking with men, 96
compassion, 144
compatibility assessments
relationship compatibility
questionnaire, 259
twenty-first century predictions, 258
competition, personal competition, 249-250
*The Complete Idiot's Guide to
Verbal Self-Defense*, 49
compliments (from men)
encouraging, 97
honesty, 85
importance of, 84-85
need for, 185
compliments (from women),
97
concealing feelings, danger of,
254
concerns, 34, 77
teenagers, 75
top concerns, 17, 23
concise conversations, differences between sexes, 129
confidence
attracting the right people,
148
attractiveness, 148,
156-157
effects on relationships, 21
increasing, 157
myths, 21
in women, 202-203
conflict in the workplace, 223
confrontations
avoiding, 173
differences, 24-25
see also arguments (men);
arguments (women)

constructive criticism (men)
dislike of, 174
sexual harassment suits,
avoiding, 228-229
control (men)
avoiding when helping
women, 83, 87-88
importance of, 173
controlling men, *see* mothering men
conversational styles (men),
32
direct statements, 32-33
important topics, 34
interrupting others, 18-19
jokes, motives, 34
lecturing/monologues, 32
qualifiers, 32
tone of voice, 33
conversational styles
(women), 32
dialogues, 32
important topics, 34
indirect statements, 32-33
interrupting others, 18-19
tone of voice, 33
coping (men), 126
correcting men, dislike of, 94,
198
crude jokes (men), 176
avoiding, 139-140
dating, 208
during intimacy, 163
motives, 92-93
responding to, 93
sexual harassment suits,
226
crying (men), importance to
women, 183
crying (women)
arguments, 34
workplace, 239
cuddling, 162-163
cultural expectations
attractiveness, 146-147
nature vs. nurture debate,
48-49
curse words
boys' use of, 72-73
effects on partners,
114-116
girls' use of, 73

using in front of children, 72
verbal abuse, 115
cyberspace romances, 260

D

dating
  accepting women's friends, 215
  appearance, 193-194
  appreciating partners, 194, 209-210
  attracting the right people
    confidence, 148
    playing hard to get, 149-150
    smiling, 149
    speaking style, 148
  attraction, 154-155
    assessing, 155
    body language, 159
    confidence, 156-157
    top qualities, 155-156
    touching, 158-159
  biological clock, recognizing, 212-213
  changing men, avoiding, 204-205
  considerations, 144
  eating habits
    expectations of women, 195-196
    respecting, 209
  exaggerating, danger in, 150-151
  finding mates, 145-146
  friendship, importance of, 152, 214
  gentlemenly behavior, 207-208, 217
  getting to know others, 150
  gift-giving, 210-212
  giving too much, avoiding, 203-204
  household chores (men), helping out, 216-217
  interest in others, 151
  jokes, off-color, 208
  lying, danger in, 150-151
  mothering men, avoiding, 203-204

past relationships, leaving behind, 144-145
recognition, importance of, 194-195
rejection, fear of, 144-145
romance, women's desire for, 213-214
toxic relationships, warning signs, 151-152
trust, importance of, 200-201
turn-offs, 210
weight-related comments, 216
dawgs (slang term), 187
Defending the Caveman (play), 126
demanding, myths, 19
details (men)
  attention to, learning, 134-135
  avoiding, 197
details (women)
  ability to remember, 16, 61-63, 188-189
    nature vs. nurture debate, 61-63
    remembering past faults, 34, 86-87
  sharing as girls, 74
dialogues, conversational styles (women), 32
differences, reasons for, 4
direct statements (men)
  communication skills, 138-139
  conversational styles, 32-33
directions, asking, 60
disgusting/repulsive topics, 71
disrespect
  toxic relationships, 119
  of women, 89-90
dress (men), fitting in, 199-200
driving ability myths, 188

E

eating habits
  expectations of women, 195-196
  respecting, 209

emotions (men)
  basic emotions, 81
  compartmentalizing, 82
  discussing, 197
  emotional baggage, 243-244
  expressing
    actions vs. words, 99
    anger, 113-116, 173, 199
    apologies, 35
    arguments, avoiding, 186
    difficulty, 35, 91, 99
    jealousy, 116-118, 250
    learning to, 80-82, 134-135
    sadness, 91, 99, 183
  fear of rejection, 144-145
  negative emotions, 82-83
  when talking, 23
emotions (women), 35
  basic emotions, 81
  expressing
    anger, 113-116, 173, 199
    hurt/frustration, 34
    jealousy, 116-118, 250
  fear of rejection, 144-145
empathy (men)
  as competition, 97, 127-128
  helping women, 138
empathy (women)
  empathizing with men, 97
  sharing stories, 127-128
equal pay, twenty-first century predictions, 254
equality of the sexes, rise in ideology, 4-5
exaggerating, danger in, 150-151
expectations, finding mates, 145-146
extramarital affairs, reducing, 8
eye contact (men)
  amount of, 18
  attraction, 159
  body language, 31
  communication skills, improving, 106
  importance of, 137-138

sexual harassment suits,
avoiding, 227-228
vs. touching, 22-23
eye contact (women)
amount of, 18
attraction, 159
body language, 31
communication skills,
improving, 106
vs. touching, 22-23

F

facial expressions, 18, 30-31
amount of, 18, 48
smiling, 18, 48, 149
fantasies (women), 183
fast talking, 17
fear of rejection, 144-145
feelings (men)
basic emotions, 81
compartmentalizing, 82
discussing, 197
emotional baggage,
243-244
expressing
actions vs. words, 99
anger, 113-116, 173, 199
apologies, 35
arguments, avoiding,
186
difficulty, 35, 91, 99
jealousy, 116-118, 250
learning to, 80-82,
134-135
sadness, 183
fear of rejection, 144-145
negative emotions, 82-83
when talking, 23
feelings (women)
basic emotions, 81
expressing
anger, 113-116, 173, 199
hurt/frustration, 34
jealousy, 116-118, 250
fear of rejection, 144-145,
186
feminism, rise in ideology, 4-5
fidgeting/shifting (men), body
language, 29
fights (men), 34
apologies, 35

current problems, 34
sex afterward, 163-164
fights (women)
apologies, 35
hurt/frustration, 34
past wrongs, 34, 86
sex afterward, 163-164
starting, 186
flirting
men's attitude toward,
187-188
sexual harassment suits,
avoiding, 225
women's attitude toward,
187-188
forgiveness (men), holding
grudges, 85
forgiveness (women)
holding grudges, 85
remembering past faults,
86-87
foul language
boys' use of, 72-73
effects on partners,
114-116
girls' use of, 73
using in front of children,
72
verbal abuse, 115
friendships
accepting women's friends,
215
importance in dating, 152,
214
teenagers, 76

G

games, mind, 9
genetics, 41
see also biological factors
gentlemanly behavior
avoidance of, 176
characteristics of, 208
women's desire for,
207-208, 217
gestures (men), hand gestures,
30
getting to the point, differences between sexes, 129
gift-giving
expectations, 210-212
Valentine's Day, 211

girls
appearance, focus on, 53
brain development, 44
childrearing differences, 24
communication styles
characteristics, 54
tag endings, use of, 73
terms of endearment,
use of, 73
language skills, positive
reinforcement, 58
respecting, 72-73
talking
amount of, 73
revealing secrets, 74
sharing details, 74
teenagers, 75
appearance, 76
friendships, 76
generation gap, 75
important topics, 75
vs. boys
bedtime-story stereo-
types, 52
behavioral expectations,
49-50
communication devel-
opment, 68-70
communication differ-
ences, 69-70
cultural expectations,
48-49
curse words, use of, 73
language skills, 7
math skills, 6
nursery-rhyme stereo-
types, 50-51
shyness myths, 8
socialization differences,
68
teased as children, 7
toys, 53
giving too much (women),
203-204
glass ceilings, women in the
workplace, 234-235
greedy people, avoiding,
245-246
grudges (men), holding, 85
grudges (women)
holding, 85-87
remembering past faults,
86-87
workplace, 238

H

hand gestures (men), body language, 30
handshakes, attraction, 158
harassment (sexual) suits, avoiding, 9, 219-220
  assessing behavior (quiz), 221-222
  changing attitudes, 222-223
  communication skills, 220-221
  constructive criticism, 228-229
  eye contact, 227-228
  female bosses, 224
  flirting, 225
  listening, 226-227
  off-color jokes, 226
  politeness, 223-224
  terms of endearment, 224
  touching, 225-226
He Says, She Says: Closing the Communication Gap Between the Sexes, 14
help (men)
  asking for, 21, 95-96
  giving, 83, 87-88
holidays, Valentine's Day, 211
honesty (men)
  compliments (to women), 85
  difficulties, 251
honesty (women)
  difficulties, 251
  "What's wrong?" questions, 122
hormones
  basics, 42
  sex hormones, 7
household chores (men), helping out, 216-217
humor (men), 20
  as boys, 71
  importance of, 71, 197-198
  off-color jokes/quips, avoiding, 139-140, 176
    dating, 208
    during intimacy, 163
    motives, 92-93

    responding to, 93
    sexual harassment suits, 226
humor (woman), 20
  importance of, 71, 197-198
  jokes, 140

I

importance, feeling, 244
important topics (men), 17, 23, 77
  boasting about accomplishments, 92
  conversational styles, 34
  teenagers, 75
important topics (women), 17, 23, 77
  conversational styles, 34
  teenagers, 75
indecision (women), 182-183
independence (men), dealing with, 95-96
indirect statements (women), 32-33
initiative (women), men's appreciation of, 175
insults
  effects on partners, 114-116
  verbal abuse, 115
  see also quips/off-color jokes (men)
intercourse, *see* sex
interfering in others' lives (women)
  avoiding, 251
  men's perspectives, 127
interrupting others
  avoiding, 135-136
  myths, 18-19
intimacy, 161
  after arguments, 163-164
  cuddling, 162-163
  intimacy questionnaire, 165-166
  need for, 88-89
  refusing, 168
  sexual needs, 165
  talking, 20, 164-165

touching, 162
  touch questionnaire, 167-168
turn-ons, 162
intuition, myths, 16, 62-63

J–K

jealousy
  causes, 116-118
  professional help, 117
  reactions to, 118
  similarities, 250
jobs
  choosing, 61-62
  stereotypes, twenty-first century predictions, 254-255, 262-263
  see also business colleagues (men), avoiding sexual harassment suits; business colleagues (women); career-related differences
jokes (men), off-color jokes/quips, 176
  avoiding, 139-140
  dating, 208
  during intimacy, 163
  motives, 92-93
  responding to, 93
  sexual harassment suits, 226
jokes (women), 140
keeping promises (men), 137

L

Language and Women's Place, 16
language skills
  boys vs. girls, 7, 54
  characteristics of language, 54
  development of
    positive reinforcement, 58
    rate of, 57-58
  Language and Women's Place, 16
  see also communication skills (men); communication skills (women)

laughter (men), 197-198
leaving toxic relationships, 119
lectures/monologues (men), 32
listening (men)
  body language, 29
  communication skills
    importance of, 104
    improving, 135-136
  essentials of good listening, 9
  failure to listen, 9
  importance of, 9-10
  sexual harassment suits, avoiding, 226-227
  to men vs. women, myths, 16-17
listening (women)
  body language, 29
  communication, importance, 104
  empathizing with men, 97
  essentials of good listening, 9
  failure to listen, 9
  importance of, 9-10
  to men vs. women, myths, 16-17
lying (men)
  dangers of, 150-151
  reasons for, 176-177
lying (women)
  dangers of, 150-151
  effect on men, 200-201

M

makeup on women, men's preferences, 175
making points, 197, 240
male bonding, 97-98
manipulative people, 245-246, 249
marriage, twenty-first century predictions, 261
math skills, boys vs. girls, 6
media infuences, men's ideas of attractive women, 146
medication effectiveness, biological differences, 257

memory (women)
  details, 16, 61-63, 188-189
  past faults, 34, 86-87
Men Are from Mars, Women Are from Venus, 126
mind games, 9
miscommunication, 10
misinterpretation, 10
moodiness
  myths, 185
  similarities, 251-252
mothering men
  asking proper questions, 125-126
  avoiding, 94, 125, 198
  consequences, 203-204
  interpretation by men, 124-125
myths
  asking for help, 21
  body language, 18
  confidence, 21
  demanding vs. tentativeness, 19
  driving ability, 188
  humor, 20
  interrupting others, 18-19
  intuition, 16, 62-63
  listening to men vs. women, 16-17
  modern women, 185
  praising others, 18
  shyness, 8
  talking, 17

N

nagging (women) vs. asking questions, 89
narratives (men), communication styles, 96
nature vs. nurture debate
  aggression, 59
  bedtime-story stereotypes, 52
  behavioral expectations, 49-50
  biological factors, 39
    basic genetics, 41
    brain development, 43-45
    hormones, 42

    neurological differences, 45-46
    pathways (brain), 40-41
  careers, choosing, 61-62
  communication development, 68-70
  communication differences, 69-70
  cultural expectations, 48-49
  details, remembering (women), 60-63
  directions, asking (men), 60
  girls
    appearance, focus on, 53
    language characteristics, 54
  language development, 7
    positive reinforcement, 58
    rate of, 57-58
  math skills, 6
  nodding (women), 63
  nursery-rhyme stereotypes, 50-51
  playtime activities, 59
  role models, appropriate, 54-55
  socialization differences, 68
  teased as children, 7
  toys, 53, 60
negative emotions (men), blaming others, 82-83
negative self-talk, 21
neurological differences, learning more about, 256
nodding
  misinterpretion, 22
  nature vs. nurture debate, 63
noncommunication, verbal abuse, 115
"nothing" responses (women), interpreting, 122
nursery rhyme stereotypes, nature vs. nurture debate, 50-51
nurturing
  learned behavior, 43
  see also mothering men

nurture vs. nature debate, 6, 47
aggression, 59
bedtime-story stereotypes, 52
behavioral expectations, 49-50
biological factors, 39
basic genetics, 41
brain development, 43-45
hormones, 42
neurological differences, 45-46
pathways (brain), 40-41
careers, choosing, 61-62
communication development, 68-70
communication differences, 69-70
cultural expectations, 48-49
details, remembering (women), 60-63
directions, asking (men), 60
girls
appearance, focus on, 53
language characteristics, 54
language development, 7
positive reinforcement, 58
rate of, 57-58
math skills, 6
nodding (women), 63
nursery-rhyme stereotypes, 50-51
playtime activities, 59
role models, appropriate, 54-55
socialization differences, 68
teased as children, 7
toys, 53, 60

O–P

offering suggestions to men, 128
open-ended questions
asking questions, 105

helpful phrases, 202
men's preferences, 201
openness, lack of (boys), 124-125

parenting skills, twenty-first century predictions, 262
past relationships
anger, 116
baggage, 144-145
men's ideas of attractiveness, 147
see also dating
personal competition
avoiding, 249
empathy as competition (men), 97, 127-128
personal information, revealing
attitude toward, 129-130
privacy, respecting, 144-145
sharing details, 130
personal space (men)
appropriate response from women, 126-127
body language, 29
need for, 126, 198-199
male bonding, 97-98
taking up space, 93-94
phone calls
keeping promises to call, 137, 217
returning, 172
physical intimacy, 161
after arguments, 163-164
cuddling, 162-163
intimacy questionnaire, 165-166
jokes during, 163
men's expectations, 195
need for, 88-89
refusing, 168
sexual needs, 165
talking, 20, 164-165
touching, 162
touch questionnaire, 167-168
turn-ons, 162
withholding, 196
playing hard to get, 149-150
playtime activities, nature vs. nurture debate, 59
politeness (men), 223-224

poor self-esteem, toxic relationships, 118-119
positive reinforcement, language development, 58
praising others
men, 194
myths, 18
premarital counseling, twenty-first century predictions, 258-259
premenstrual syndrome (PMS), sympathy for, 216
privacy respecting, 244-245
problem-solving (men), 34
confronting, 24-25
helping women
controlling situations, 87-88
empathy, 138
guidelines, 83
instincts, 174-175
rubber-band effect, 126
problem-solving (women), 34
confronting, 24-25
professions
choosing, 61-62
stereotypes, twenty-first century predictions, 254-255, 262-263
see also business colleagues (men), avoiding sexual harassment suits; business colleagues (women); career-related differences
punishment, men's attitudes toward, 196
push-and-pull syndrome, 126, 178, 198-199
put "on the spot" (men), dislike of, 177

Q

qualifiers (men), conversational styles, 32
questions (men)
asking questions
directions, 60
open-ended questions, 105
"What's wrong?" 122-123
tag endings, 19, 73
using "would"/"could," 88

questions (women)
 answering questions,
  "What's wrong?" 122
 asking questions
  "Do you love me?" 130
  "How do I look?"
   133-134
  tag endings, 19, 73
 reassuring women, 131
  details, 125-126
  vs. nagging, 89
 open-ended questions
  helpful phrases, 202
  men's preference, 201
quips/off-color jokes (men),
 176
 avoiding, 139-140
 dating, 208
 during intimacy, 163
 motives, 92-93
 responding to, 93
 sexual harassment suits,
  226
quizzes/questionnaires
 intimacy questionnaire,
  165-166
 relationship compatibility
  questionnaire, 259
 sex talk quiz, 14-15
 sexual harassment, assessing behavior, 221-222
 touch questionnaire,
  167-168

R

reassurance (women), need
 for, 185
 compliments from men
  encouraging, 97
  honesty, 85
  importance of, 84-85
  need for, 185
recognition (men), impor-
 tance of, 194-195
rejection (men)
 dating, 144-145
 fear of, 172-173
rejection (women)
 dating, 144-145
 workplace, 240-241

relationship compatibility
 questionnaire, 259
relationships, toxic, 112
remembering details
 (women), ability to remember, 16, 61-63, 188-189
 nature vs. nurture debate,
  61-63
 remembering past faults,
  34, 86-87
repulsive/disgusting topics, 71
respect (men)
 boys' respect of girls, 72-73
 disrespectful habits, 89-90
 privacy, 144-145
role models, appropriate role
 models, 54-55
roles
 changes in, twenty-first
  century predictions, 255,
  263-264
 sex roles
  bedtime-story stereo-
   types, 52
  nursery-rhyme stereo-
   types, 50-51
  preconceived ideas
   about, 48
  role models, appropri-
   ate, 54-55
  toys, effect of, 53
romance, women's desire for,
 213-214
rubber-band effect (men),
 necessity of, 178, 198-199
The Rules, 204

S

salaries
 gender-related differences,
  231-232
 twenty-first century predictions, 254
sarcasm, communicating
 through, 10
saving face (men), impor-
 tance of, 174
scrubs, 246
secrets
 keeping, 244-245
 revealing, 74

self-confidence
 importance to men,
  202-203
 increasing, 157
 key to attraction, 156-157
self-esteem
 saving face (men), 174
 toxic relationships,
  118-119
self-talk, negative, 21
separateness, maintaining,
 257-258
sex, 161
 after arguments, 163-164
 cuddling, 162-163
 intimacy questionnaire,
  165-166
 jokes during, 163
 men's expectations, 195
 need for, 88-89
 refusing, 168
 sexual needs, 165
 talking, 20, 164-165
 touching, 162
  touch questionnaire,
   167-168
 turn-ons, 162
 withholding, 196
"Sex Differences in Listening
 Comprehension" (study), 16
sex hormones, effects on
 brain functions, 7
sex roles
 bedtime-story stereotypes,
  52
 changes in, twenty-first
  century predictions, 255,
  263-264
 nursery-rhyme stereotypes,
  50-51
 preconceived ideas about,
  48
 role models, 54-55
 toys, effect of, 53
sex talk quiz, 14-15
sexual harassment suits,
 avoiding, 9, 219-220
 assessing behavior (quiz),
  221-222
 changing attitudes,
  222-223
 communication skills,
  220-221

constructive criticism, 228-229
eye contact, 227-228
female bosses, 224
flirting, 225
listening, 226-227
off-color jokes, 226
politeness, 223-224
terms of endearment, 224
touching, 225-226
shifting/fidgeting (men), body language, 29
shopping (women), importance of, 183-184
shyness myths, 8
silence (men), 201
similarities between the sexes
acceptance, desire for, 247-248
aggression, 250
appreciated, feeling, 249
being taken advantage of, 245-246
commitment fear, 248-249
emotional baggage, 243-244
feeling important, 244
greedy people, avoiding, 245-246
honesty, difficulty, 251
interference from others, avoiding, 251
jealousy, 250
manipulative people, avoiding, 245-246, 249
moodiness, 251-252
nice appearance, desire for, 250-251
personal competition, avoiding, 249-250
privacy, respecting, 244-245
slow-moving relationships, desire for, 248
unconditional love, desire for, 246
sitting positions (men), body language, 29
slow-moving relationships, 248
smiling
amount of, 18, 48, 149

attracting the right people, 149
importance of, 150
social issues, twenty-first century predictions, 255-256
socialization skills, development of, 68
solving problems (men), 34
confronting, 24-25
helping women
controlling situations, 87-88
empathy, 138
guidelines, 83
instincts, 174-175
rubber-band effect, 126
solving problems (women), 34
confronting, 24-25
speaking up (women), 239-240
standing positions (men), body language, 30
stereotypes
bedtime stories, 52
cartoons, 52
forgetting, 144-145
job-related stereotypes, twenty-first century predictions, 254-255, 262-263
nursery rhymes, 50-51
toys, effect of, 53

T

tag endings (to statements), 19, 73
Talk to Win, 148
talking (men)
boasting about accomplishments, 92
bringing up topics, 23-24
during intimacy, 20, 164-165
important issues, 17, 23, 77
myths, 17
narratives, 96
sexual needs, 165
thinking before talking, 114-116

talking (women)
bringing up topics, 23-24
during intimacy, 20, 164-165
important issues, 17, 23, 77
myths, 17
sexual needs, 165
talking with men, 96
tangents, avoiding, 181-182
teasing, 7, 71, 163
see also quips/off-color jokes
teenagers, 75-76
teeth clenching (men), body language, 31
tentativeness, myths, 19
terms of endearment
during sex, 20
girls, use of, 73
sexual harassment suits, avoiding, 224
thinking patterns (women), understanding, 181-182
timing, communicating, 253-254
tolerance, twenty-first century predictions, 258
tone of voice
attracting the right people, 148
biological factors, 62
communication skills, 106-107
conversational styles, 33
men vs. women, 23
Talk to Win, 148
touch questionnaire, 167-168
touching (men)
affection, 162
attraction, 158-159
cuddling, dislike of, 162-163
sexual harassment suits, avoiding, 225-226
touch questionnaire, 167-168
touching (women)
affection, 162
attraction, 158-159

touch questionnaire, 167-168
vs. eye contact, 22-23
Toxic People—10 Ways of Dealing with People Who Make Your Life Miserable, 113
toxic relationships, 119
avoiding, 114
dating, warning signs, 151-152
disrespect, 118-119
healing, 119-120
jealousy
causes, 116-118
professional help, 117
reactions, 118
leaving, 119
questionnaire, 112
self-esteem, poor, 118-119
toxic people, 113
see also anger (men); anger (women)
toys, effect of, 53, 60
trust (men), importance of, 200-201
turn-offs
dating, 210
mothering men, 203-204
types of women, 178-179
turn-ons, 162
twenty-first century predictions
biological differences, learning more about, 256, 263
communication skills, 262
compatibility assessments, improvements in, 258-259
cyberspace romances, 260
equal pay, 254
job-related stereotypes, decrease in, 254-255, 262-263
maintaining separateness, 257-258
marriage, 261
neurological differences, learning more about, 256
parenting skills, 262
role changes, 255, 263-264
social issues, 255-256
tolerance, increase in, 258

virtual relationships, 260-261
virtual therapy, 261-262

U–V

unconditional love, desire for, 246
unrealistic expectations, dating, 145

Valentine's Day, gift-giving, 211
verbal abuse, 115
victim talk (women), 123
virtual relationships, 260-261
virtual therapy, 261-262
voice, tone of voice
attracting the right people, 148
biological factors, 62
communication skills, 106-107
conversational styles, 33
men vs. women, 23
Talk to Win, 148

W–X–Y–Z

wages
gender-related differences, 231-232
twenty-first century predictions, 254
weight (women), comments from men, 216
"What's wrong?" 122-123
workplace
answering personal questions, 237-238
being "one of the guys," 235-236
conflict, 223
crying, 239
difficulties for women, 232
getting ahead, guidelines (women), 235
glass ceilings, 234-235
grudges, holding, 238
making points, 240

men's perceptions of women, 231-233
rejection, 240-241
salaries
gender-related differences, 231-232
twenty-first century predictions, 254
sexual harassment suits, avoiding, 219-221
assessing behavior (quiz), 221-222
changing attitudes, 222-223
constructive criticism, 228-229
eye contact, 227-228
female bosses, 224
flirting, 225
listening, 226-227
off-color jokes, 226
politeness, 223-224
terms of endearment, 224
touching, 225-226
speaking up, 239-240
unique contributions, 234
withholding private information, 236-237

You Just Don't Understand, 21